The Best American
Food Writing 2019

GUEST EDITORS OF
THE BEST AMERICAN FOOD WRITING

2018   RUTH REICHL
2019   SAMIN NOSRAT

The Best American Food Writing™ 2019

Edited and with an Introduction
by SAMIN NOSRAT

Silvia Killingsworth, Series Editor

Mariner Books

HOUGHTON MIFFLIN HARCOURT

BOSTON • NEW YORK   2019

hmhbooks.com

ISSN 2578-7667 (print) ISSN 2578-7675 (ebook)
ISBN 978-1-328-66225-5 (print) ISBN 978-1-328-66309-2 (ebook)

Printed in the United States of America
DOC 10 9 8 7 6 5 4 3 2 1

Contents

Foreword

Generally speaking, the Food Establishment—which is not to be confused with the Chef Establishment, the Food-Industry Establishment, the Gourmet Establishment, or the Wine Establishment —consists of those people who write about food or restaurants on a regular basis, either in books, magazines, or certain newspapers, and thus have the power to start trends and, in some cases, begin and end careers . . .

The typical member of the Food Establishment lives in Greenwich Village, buys his vegetables at Balducci's, his bread at the Zito bakery, and his cheese at Bloomingdale's. He dines at the Coach House. He is given to telling you, apropos of nothing, how many soufflés he has been known to make in a short period of time.

—Nora Ephron, "The Food Establishment," September 1968

ONE OF THE most important things to consider about food writing, besides its entertainment value and journalistic virtue, is who is doing it. The subject of Nora Ephron's half-century-old essay—the first in her collection *Wallflower at the Orgy*—could essentially be summed up as "Who We Talk About When We Talk About Food." I kept returning to it while collecting stories for this year's anthology, for two reasons: 1) I wondered whom we might consider the Food Establishment today, and 2) I wanted to push back against the notion that a handful of people in anointed positions are the only ones who should be considered food writers.

Though Ephron may not come out and say it, she paints a pretty clear picture: the members of the Food Establishment are not the only ones with things to say and write about food, merely those who've been provided a podium and a megaphone (usually in the form of a book contract). And though she dutifully reports their identifying characteristics, Ephron is also very clearly ridiculing them. The Food Establishment then was mostly male, and lived not just in New York City but in a specific small, hip neighborhood. They shopped and ate at the same handful of hallowed and expensive locations and were perfectly obnoxious about their own talents in the kitchen. Does this sound like a group you'd like to be a part of? Thanks, but I'll pass.

Ephron, of course, was a foodie in her own right, and this is a supremely self-aware piece of food writing. Though the essay was written half a century ago (imagine buying your cheese at Bloomingdale's today!), it remains as relevant as ever. Today the Food Establishment may be less male and more geographically diverse, but it certainly has its blind spots, and Ephron's writing reminded me to look for them. The problem with the Food Establishment is not necessarily that it exists; it probably always will in some sense, because of the way media and industries and human nature all work. The more urgent thing is that it continues to expand and that we remember to look outside its confines.

In Ephron's piece there are only two wings: the revolutionaries (home cooks) and the traditionalists (haute cuisine purists). Today there must be at least eighteen factions, maybe only six of them officially recognized. We of course still have national food critics, but we now also have food bloggers, viral recipe creators, and a whole television series about what to eat while high on marijuana. There are diarists and dieters and modernists and minimalists. There are those who still believe that New York is the center of the culinary world, but there are many more who know better.

Indeed, everywhere you look there are people with strong opinions about food—just try logging into Twitter. Is Neapolitan pizza over? Is raspberry sauce an acceptable condiment for mozzarella sticks? Who is to be listened to, and why? Everyone has some kind of relationship with food, and everyone has preferences. It's the underpinning of the Latin maxim *De gustibus non est disputandum*—there's no arguing in matters of taste. Except of course that there is! Some days it seems that's almost *all* there is. I once started a short-lived online publication based on this contrarian logic. It was called *De Gustibus,* its tagline was "let's disputamus," and I invited friends and strangers to contribute.

I kicked things off with a screed about India pale ales. They were having a moment (it was 2015), but it was unclear whether people were drinking them because they were "good" or they were "good" because people were drinking them. I had a thesis—not everyone likes a hoppy beer—and it struck a chord. The piece went viral. The point was not that I was right or wrong, famous or obscure, but that I had something to say and an interesting way to say it. (I must admit, I don't actually hate IPAs, but I did find them overexposed at the time. I took a valid position for the sake of argument.)

Some of the other contributions to *De Gustibus* took similar opinionated tacks: the "proper" topping to get on a bagel (whitefish salad), the only good drink (cheap iced tea), where vermouth belongs (in the refrigerator, for goodness' sake!). They were the exact kinds of individual matters of taste the maxim said could not be argued. I insisted that I didn't need to agree to the premise of the pitch to publish the article. In some ways I constructed an experimental op-ed page for food. What I learned from this exercise was that everyone has a story, and if presented well, it's usually worth hearing out.

But of course food writing isn't all about preferences and taste and whether a restaurant is any good. It's also about journalism —probing the larger world for truths, asking where our food comes from, who cultivates it, and who prepares it—as well as cultural criticism, like examining racial stereotypes and celebrating fearlessness. And then there's pure storytelling: histories of hunger and chronicles of joy or pain. A catalog of all the complex thoughts a young woman can have at the sight of an egg. Food writing is just another way of looking at the world, and there is no one true form of it, despite what the scolds may say.

As for the question of who would be in the Food Establishment today, I think it depends on whom you ask. Each of us has our own Mount Olympus of food personalities, and maybe by polling everyone we'd arrive at some sense of who is most famous and popular. But name recognition is context-dependent. If you eat out in New York City, your Food Establishment might include chefs and restaurateurs who push boundaries, like David Chang and Angela Dimayuga. If you're a vegetarian, maybe it's Brooks Headley, whose delicious burgers and imaginative cookbook are shattering the notion that animal-abstainers have no fun. For others it may be the writers whose books you have the most of, like Mark Bittman, Ruth Reichl, and Michael Pollan. I would probably include J. Kenji López-Alt, the painstakingly scientific kitchen wizard, and the entire Cooking section of the *New York Times,* whose recipes I Google just as frequently as Kenji's. My friend and colleague Hannah Goldfield is the only person whose food descriptions I actually seek out, and Tejal Rao can wax rhapsodic about everything from Kit Kats to blood sausage.

As one of the arbiters of what appears in this book, I must necessarily include myself. But the real star of this show is the incomparable Samin Nosrat, surely an honest-to-goodness member of the Food Establishment as determined by popular vote. Part Harold McGee and part Julia Child, her best-selling cookbook, *Salt Fat Acid Heat,* has changed the way thousands of people think about food and cooking. The attendant Netflix series has introduced the world to her irresistible charm—I hope for everyone's sake that she continues to appear onscreen, where her joy is infectious.

In the forthcoming pages I hope you find a worthwhile mix of a bit of everything, from 19,000 words on a billionaire's farming empire to a few hundred on elderflower kombucha. I have done my best to supply Ms. Nosrat with as wide a selection as possible from which to pick this year's bests. I cannot thank her enough for taking on the much tougher job of winnowing down the selections into a select group of twenty-five. I'm as pleasantly surprised as she that we've ended up with such a diverse and wide-ranging roster of both publications and writers. I'm grateful to the food magazines, journals, general-interest outlets, and daily newspapers included here, all of which make space for great writing about food. Without them this anthology would not be possible. I'd like to thank all the writers (for a list of honorable mentions, see p. 255) for filling my year with such great reading, and my editor, Naomi Gibbs, for the opportunity to participate in such a worthy collection.

But as I've been saying, there is more to life than what all the people who win James Beard Awards think. One way to counteract that is to give different people James Beard Awards! But another is to make a point to look for valuable work in unlikely places from all kinds of people. This is a challenge I will continue to issue—to myself as well as to any North American editors reading this:

keep doing better. There is definitely great writing out there in the world that isn't included here, because of the limitations of either space or sheer human capacity. To that end, I implore you to send me your submissions for next year's edition before December 31, 2019. You can email me at silvia.killingsworth@gmail.com.

SILVIA KILLINGSWORTH

Introduction

AT SOME POINT in 2018, I realized, with no small amount of horror, that J. Kenji López-Alt and I are the only nonwhite authors whose work has been accepted into the canon of general cookbooks. *The Joy of Cooking, How to Cook Everything, Mastering the Art of French Cooking,* and every other general cookbook that comes to mind were written by white authors. A question I've long had inside me but was never quite able to articulate finally formed in my head: If good cooking is universal, then why is only a tiny sliver of the population granted the opportunity to write about it authoritatively?

A year and a half after my book, *Salt, Fat, Acid, Heat,* was published, after it had been on the *New York Times* bestseller list for eight weeks, after I'd been presented with the James Beard Award for best general cookbook, after the book was in its tenth printing and a global documentary series based on it was announced, I received an invitation to sit on a panel about general cookbook writing. The other two proposed panelists were (perfectly wonderful) white female colleagues of mine, the authors of books I love and value deeply.

While the invitation was full of flattery and many kind words, it didn't include an honorarium or an offer to pay for my travel or accommodations. Since I already planned to be in the area for another event, and since I welcomed the chance to sit on the panel with my beloved colleagues, I wrote back to the organizers to thank them for the invitation and say that I'd be happy to participate as long as they invited another writer of color to join as a panelist or a moderator. To relieve them of the burden of having to seek out potential panelists and moderators of color, I included lists of both for their consideration.

Two days later I received an email suggesting that I sit on an entirely different panel—a much more diverse one!—all about ethnic cooking. Maybe that was more appealing to me?

At first glance it seemed like an entirely reasonable offer, so I was confused by the fireball of anger I felt in my stomach. I got up from my desk and took a walk around the block before responding. I wrote that as someone who has experienced coded and noncoded misogyny and racism throughout my career, and indeed life, I'm making it a point to use my platform to effect change. I asked them to consider diversifying multiple panels instead of putting all the people of color on a single panel, thereby turning our races and ethnicities, rather than our work, into a topic of conversation.

In truth I'm not interested in discussing race for the sake of race. On the other hand, I am interested in combating the prevailing notion that only white people can write successful general books about cooking while people of color have the authority to write only about our ancestral cuisines. And I've learned that one way I can do that is to make inclusion and equity a condition for my participation in projects and events.

I was still burning when, days after that exchange, I received the invitation to edit this collection. I've grown too wary to expect more from a system that has no incentive to change its ways—I'd rather build a new one. So I answered quickly, with an enthusiastic yes, thrilled by the opportunity to build upon the progressive foundation laid last year by this series' inaugural editor, the legendary Ruth Reichl.

Months later, when I sat down to read through series editor Silvia Killingsworth's thoughtful selections, I considered using this opportunity to make a bold statement by exclusively choosing works by people whom the food world has historically undervalued and marginalized: people of color, queer folks, and women. The thought of letting conviction guide my choices was initially thrilling. Then it dawned on me that following such logic, I couldn't include Mark Arax's "A Kingdom from Dust," which was the single most powerful story I read in 2018 and the only one I knew I had to include from the moment I took the assignment. If this reasoning meant excluding one worthy piece, then surely it would lead to other blind spots too.

I thought about how, if the tables were turned, I'd want my own work to be considered for its merit and not my identity. I owed it to others to do the same for them. So I deprioritized ideology and instead decided to read everything blind. I printed out all the stories and asked a friend to redact the names of authors and publications with a marker. Then I spent two months reading and rereading until I'd narrowed the original group of one hundred pieces to about forty. At that point I knew I'd have to start breaking my own heart, because I loved all forty dearly.

I wasn't sure how to go on winnowing down my selections, so I thought I'd put names to each of the pieces to check how inclusive I was being. To my surprise and delight, the list I'd chosen blindly skewed toward women, people of color, and queer people. Credit for this goes to Ms. Killingsworth, who demonstrated impeccable taste with her initial selections. By handing me a truly diverse list, she carried a huge part of the load and relieved me of the burden of having to make identity a criterion for inclusion in the collection. Not only did she send works by writers from all backgrounds, but she also scanned the broader writing landscape, including stories from publications far beyond the scope of traditional food media. Ms. Killingsworth granted me the luxury of choosing pieces for no other reason than that I felt they were truly distinctive and distinguished.

Together with Ms. Killingsworth, I've come up with a collection I believe represents the best of food writing in America in 2018. But what does that mean, exactly? As I read and considered pieces for selection, I welcomed the opportunity to reexamine the terms *best, American,* and *food writing.*

At this point in my career, I've grown pretty cynical about "best of" lists in general and ones concerned with food in particular —it's all so subjective, so personal. Neither of my two industries —culinary and media—boasts an exemplary record of rewarding people who stray from an all-too-narrow definition of excellence. Without much trouble I can recall several egregious instances of narrow-sightedness and exclusion that have perpetuated the idea that whiteness, maleness, and a focus on Western-derived technique are somehow critical to success in these industries. Three come immediately to mind: *Time* magazine's unforgettable 2013 "Gods of Food" feature, which skewed overwhelmingly white and male; San Pellegrino's "World's Best Female Chef" award, which is handed out alongside "World's Best Chef" and whose mere existence suggests that female chefs are somehow disqualified from consideration in the latter category; and *Chef's Table,* one of the most influential food television series in the Western world, choosing to feature female and nonwhite chefs in fewer than a quarter of its episodes. And the list goes on.

How can we declare that a work is the best in its field if entire swaths of contenders aren't even considered? And also, what does *best* even mean? For what is the best part of a landscape? Is it the most dramatic peak to which the eye is immediately drawn? Is it the way the sunlight reflects off the calm surface of the glassy sea? The parting of the clouds? Is it the tiny bird or the soft gray moss? I'd argue that what makes a landscape breathtaking, sublime, is all its parts—even, or perhaps especially, the parts we might not always notice immediately. The awesome must be balanced by the subtle. The bright needs the contrast of the dark. Only a broad perspective can capture the entirety of a landscape, and so with this collection, I've aimed to present a panoramic survey of the year's best work.

I've always believed that good food writing is simply good writing: compelling, intelligent, at times lyrical, and driven by narrative and voice. Good food writing evokes the senses. It makes us consider divergent viewpoints. It makes us hungry and motivates us to go out into the world in search of new experiences. It charms and anger us, breaks our hearts, and gives us hope. And perhaps most importantly, it creates empathy within us.

Across the collection, pieces do all of this and more. Helen Rosner stunned me with her ability to process Anthony Bourdain's death quickly enough to reflect with both criticism and sensitivity on his journey as a human, a celebrity, and a feminist in her piece, "Anthony Bourdain and the Power of Telling the Truth." I never knew the history of veganism, which Khushbu Shah wrote about in "The Vegan Race Wars: How the Mainstream Ignores Vegans of Color," but in the year and a half since I first read the piece, I've referred to it countless times in conversation. By broadening my understanding, it earned its place here. Sam Anderson's meditation on language, flavor, and metaphor in "Flavors of Space-Time" perfectly describes the challenge anyone who writes about food must face—how to use words to describe a wordless sense: taste.

And of course there is Mr. Arax's "A Kingdom from Dust," the obvious result of many, many years of steadfast reporting on a famously media-shy subject, Stewart Resnick. I first heard of the billionaire "farmers" Mr. Resnick and his wife, Lynda, about ten years ago, when I learned that they, as private citizens, control and use—by various rights and contracts—more water than any other person in my drought-ridden home state of California. I've been anxiously waiting for a report on the Resnicks since then. Mr. Arax delivered a story with a grander scope and more damning detail than I could've dared to wish for. As with Ms. Shah's piece, I've referred to it repeatedly since it was first published, beseeching everyone I know to take the time to read it. And now I beseech you, dear reader, by including it here.

All the pieces in this collection have moved me in one way or another. They shifted, and continue to shift, my perspective, and I believe that they will do the same for you. My hope is that you'll walk away from the collection with an expanded idea of what the "best" can look like.

And in an era when the very definition of *American* is under constant debate, I think it's worth examining that part of this honorific a little more closely too. In a country where everyone but Native Americans and the descendants of enslaved peoples is an immigrant, anti-immigrant rhetoric certainly feels more pointed than ever. And since the vitriolic words and actions tend to be directed at people who are not of European descent, it feels like every day the definition of *American* contracts, becoming more and more a synonym for *white*.

With this collection I made it a priority to counteract that contraction by choosing stories that broaden our cultural understanding. Tim Carman's story, "In the Twin Cities, Asian Chefs Feel the Sting of Andrew Zimmern's Insults. They Say His Apology Isn't Enough.," is a phenomenal example of careful, balanced reporting about a complicated subject. By spending time with both Mr. Zimmern and a handful of chefs left offended in the wake of his comments denigrating Chinese American food and proclaiming that he's "saving the souls" of everyone from "having to dine at these horse—— restaurants," Mr. Carman was able to convey an Asian American story rife with emotion by letting everyone speak for themselves.

In her paean to peanuts, "Hot Wet Goobers," Shane Mitchell gives us a transcontinental history of the legume while showing us how it's dug its way into various identities of the American South.

With pieces like this one, Ms. Mitchell has firmly established herself as one of the great food writers in this country for her ability to sensitively roam the rich yet tricky culinary terrain of the South without avoiding or whitewashing the shameful parts of its history.

Michael Twitty gives us another look at the African roots of southern cooking in his essay "I Had Never Eaten in Ghana Before. But My Ancestors Had." "In Ghana," Mr. Twitty writes, "it's clear I have inherited a remarkably rich culinary tradition ... Yet everywhere we look are reminders of home ... There is barbecued meat on every corner, roasted ears of corn and sweet potatoes, bits of fried chicken cooked fresh on the spot, and black-eyed-pea fritters. Deep-fried smelt and *akple* look like fish and grits."

In "The Gay Man Who Brought Tapas to America," Mayukh Sen shines light on Felipe Rojas-Lombardi. The all-but-forgotten Peruvian immigrant was the founding chef of Dean & Deluca before going on to open a tapas bar in Chelsea in 1982, arguably blazing the trail for every small plate of food we now see on restaurant menus across the country.

Many more of the selections, including those by Melissa Chadburn, Soleil Ho, Charlee Dyroff, Priya Fielding-Singh, and Marilyn Noble, lend depth and dimension to the ways that food is integral to the stories we tell about ourselves as Americans, in all the myriad ways that they may manifest.

People often assume that *food writing* is just another term for restaurant criticism. But as a food writer myself, I couldn't be less interested in writing about restaurants. And while I don't often find myself compelled to read reviews of them either, I've loved reading Hannah Goldfield's work in *The New Yorker,* where she brings a refreshing sense of humor, duty, and joy to her post as the magazine's restaurant critic. As the sole piece of criticism in the collection, "Black History at Harlem Hops" is tightly written yet full of context and charm, as Ms. Goldfield's work tends to be. The lack of other critical works perhaps reflects my general disinclination toward the form (I never said these choices weren't totally subjective!), though I look forward to reading the critical contributions of Ms. Ho, Tejal Rao, and Patricia Escárega, three women of color named to critic posts at major newspapers in 2018.

Of course food writing can take any number of other forms. In "The Life of a Restaurant Inspector: Rising Grades, Fainting Owners," Priya Krishna makes her job as a journalist look easy. But as someone who has both worked in restaurant kitchens and reported for the *New York Times,* I know precisely how difficult it can be to get proximate enough to a subject as guarded as a municipal inspector to coax from him the narrative detail needed to satisfy an editor. That is to say, Ms. Krishna accomplished something nearly impossible and certainly very frustrating, and yet her story reads as effortless and even playful, despite being about the generally unglamorous topic of restaurant inspection. If this isn't proof of a skillful writer, then I don't know what is!

This collection comprises a full panoply of formats and styles, proving just how omnipresent food is in our lives, and that a great writer can use it to tell any sort of story. Yemisi Aribisala's essay-cum-meditation on eggs, "The Girls Who Fainted at the Sight of an Egg," weaves together food and sex and bodies into a luminous tapestry of flavor, shame, and memory. And then there is the brilliantly, tirelessly reported "Sliced and Diced: Here's How Cornell Scientist Brian Wansink Turned Shoddy Data into Viral Studies About How We Eat," which answered many questions I didn't even know I had. After Stephanie M. Lee's landmark investigation was published, Cornell University found Dr. Wansink guilty of academic misconduct, and he resigned—an incredible result for an incredible work of journalism.

The final lens through which I surveyed these works was time. Last year was filled with myriad challenges, disappointments, and successes. I wanted to make sure that both up close and from a distance, this collection accurately represented our year in food, in America, and on this precious planet.

In 2018 the food world, and indeed the world at large, suffered the loss of two of our greats. It was agonizing enough to lose Anthony Bourdain, our most beloved guide and teacher. But when our pioneering, poetical critic Jonathan Gold passed away a few short months later, it felt like a cruel joke. Benjamin Aldes Wurgaft's reflection on the profound influence of Mr. Gold's writing on his life as an Angeleno, and as a human, felt like an appropriate way to honor the critic.

The year also brought devastation in the form of wildfires—the most destructive in California history. The fires ravaged the largest and most profitable wine and agriculture industries in the country and certainly foreshadow worse blazes to come. Along with the autumn fires and other natural disasters came the publication of another alarming, unsparing report from the Intergovernmental Panel on Climate Change, imploring policymakers and citizens alike to heed its calls to limit global climate change to 1.5° C. In "Food Fight," Kathryn Schulz skillfully examines the intersection of cooking, politics, and the precariousness of our natural world.

At long last, 2018 saw the election of Native Americans to Congress. Historically underrepresented in politics, Native Americans have also long been victims of underrepresentation and appropriation in the culinary world. Ms. Noble's piece examines a particularly shameful instance of such appropriation—the Epic Provisions bison bar. And by contrast, Ms. Dyroff's "In Kotzebue, Alaska, Hunters Are Bringing Traditional Foods—and a Sense of Comfort—to Their Local Elders" allows us to hope that Native customs are indeed living on in the forms of food traditions, caribou, and seal oil.

With so many stories that reflect the bitter circumstances of our world, the collection would have been incomplete without a little something sweet. In addition to infusing "Big in Japan" with her signature curiosity, intelligence, and wit, Ms. Rao, my *New York Times Magazine* colleague, impressed me by managing to sneak the words *chocolatory* and *premiumization* by our hard-lining copyeditors. And with his attempt to correlate the Finnish love of *salmiakki*, or salty licorice, and the country's leading position on the 2018 World Happiness Report, Mark Binelli made me laugh out loud a dozen times. His piece was so convincing that I even felt moved enough to try some salty licorice myself—well, almost.

My hope is that the pieces that make up this collection will bring you joy and challenge your preconceived notions. They'll make you think, feel, and, inevitably, want to eat. As the twentieth-century poet and activist Muriel Ruckeyser said, the universe is made of stories, not atoms. In order to know our universe better, then, we need to hear as many different sorts of stories, from as many varied voices, as possible. In that spirit, I present to you twenty-five powerful, compelling, beautiful, charming, heartbreaking bits of that universe. Happy reading!

(For the record, the event organizers did diversify the general cooking panel, and I did join it.)

SAMIN NOSRAT

The Best American
Food Writing 2019

Flavors of Space-Time

FROM *The New York Times Magazine*

"Elderflower kombucha is like the bottled flavor of Scandinavian summers."
    —from *The Noma Guide to Fermentation,* by René Redzepi and David Zilber

IT'S HARD TO talk about flavor. Tasting something is such a direct neural jolt; words will always seem clumsy and vague. *Spicy* does not begin to express the riot of electrical fires sparking through your skull after you eat a Thai chile. *Sour* hardly touches the way a fresh lemon grips your whole consciousness and squeezes until it weeps.

So we turn to metaphor. Elderflower kombucha is a bottled Scandinavian summer: mild, light, yellow, easy. Coconut water is a Caribbean afternoon. Chianti, as any sommelier will tell you, is the blood of a mortally wounded Vespa. Sprite is a liquid hashtag. Imagine the agony of a ghost who is too nice to haunt anyone properly, and yet he tries and tries and tries for all of eternity. If you captured his flop sweat in a jar and put it under a heat lamp, it would turn—unfortunately—into the fermented dairy drink kefir.

Coca-Cola is all the gallons of lighter fluid harvested from discarded Bics in the aftermath of a Bruce Springsteen concert. Mezcal is a rusty canteen dipped into the burbling stream of consciousness of a Gila monster. Mountain Dew is the bottled tears of a guitar solo by Blink-183, a Blink-182 cover band.

We all have particular flavors of space-time that touch us especially deeply. To me, a warm gummy bear is the congealed essence of a 1980s school bus ride. You lean your forehead against the cool window and watch the countryside rolling by—the orchard rows, the cows—and although there might be some brief distraction (a crane flying overhead that looks for a second like a pterodactyl; Luis, in the seat behind you, doing the trick where he inverts his eyelids), mostly it is just field after field, the vineyards and the flocks of black birds, the irrigation spray feathering in long arcs over the moving landscape's bright, monotonous sweetness.

A Kingdom from Dust

FROM *California Sunday Magazine*

I. The Land Baron

On a summer day in the San Joaquin Valley, 101 in the shade, I merge onto Highway 99 past downtown Fresno and steer through the vibrations of heat. I'm headed to the valley's deep south, to a little farmworker town in a far corner of Kern County called Lost Hills. This is where the biggest irrigated farmer in the world—the one whose mad plantings of almonds and pistachios have triggered California's nut rush—keeps on growing, no matter drought or flood. He doesn't live in Lost Hills. He lives in Beverly Hills. How has he managed to outwit nature for so long?

The GPS tells me to take Interstate 5, the fastest route through the belly of the state, but I'm partial to Highway 99, the old road that brought the Okies and Mexicans to the fields and deposited a twang on my Armenian tongue. The highway runs two lanes here, three lanes there, through miles of agriculture broken every twenty minutes by fast food, gas station, and cheap motel. Tracts of houses, California's last affordable dream, civilize three or four exits, and then it's back to the open road splattered with the guts and feathers of chickens that jumped ship on the slaughterhouse drive. Pink and white oleanders divide the highway, and every third vehicle that whooshes by is a big rig. More often than not, it is hauling away some piece of the valley's bounty. The harvest begins in January with one type of mandarin and ends in December with another type of mandarin and in between spills forth everything in your supermarket produce and dairy aisles except for bananas, mangoes, and kiwis, though the farmers here are working on the tropical too.

I stick to the left lane and try to stay ahead of the pack. The big-rig drivers are cranky two ways, and the farmworkers in their last-leg vans are half asleep. Ninety-nine is the deadliest highway in America. Deadly in the rush of harvest, deadly in the quiet of fog, deadly in the blur of Saturday nights when the fieldwork is done and the beer-drinking becomes a second humiliation. Twenty miles outside Fresno, I cross the Kings, the river that irrigates more farmland than any other river here. The Kings is bone-dry, as usual. To find its flow, I'd have to go looking in a thousand irrigation ditches in the fields beyond.

There's a mountain range to my left and a mountain range to my right and in between a plain flatter than Kansas where crop and sky meet. One of the most dramatic alterations of the earth's surface in human history took place here. The hillocks that existed back in Yokut Indian days were flattened by a hunk of metal called the Fresno Scraper. Every river busting out of the Sierra was bent sideways, if not backward, by a bulwark of ditches, levees, canals, and dams. The farmer corralled the snowmelt and erased the valley, its desert and marsh. He leveled its hog wallows, denuded its salt brush, and killed the last of its mustang, antelope, and tule elk. He emptied the sky of tens of millions of geese and drained the 800 square miles of Tulare Lake dry.

He did this first in the name of wheat and then beef, milk, raisins, cotton, and nuts. Once he finished grabbing the flow of the five rivers that ran across the plain, he used his turbine pumps to seize the water beneath the ground. As he bled the aquifer dry, he called on the government to bring him an even mightier river from afar. Down the great aqueduct, by freight of politics and gravity, came the excess waters of the Sacramento River. The farmer moved the rain. The more water he got, the more crops he planted, and the more crops he planted, the more water he needed to plant more crops, and on and on. One million acres of the valley floor, greater than the size of Rhode Island, are now covered in almond trees.

I pity the outsider trying to make sense of it. My grandfather, a survivor of the Armenian genocide, traveled 7,000 miles by ship and train in 1920 to find out if his uncle's exhortation—"The grapes here are the size of jade eggs"—was true. My father, born in a vineyard outside Fresno, was a raisin grower before he became a bar owner. I grew up in the suburbs where our playgrounds were named after the pioneers of fruit and canals of irrigation shot through our neighborhoods to the farms we did not know. For half my life I never stopped to wonder, how much was magic? How much was plunder?

I'm going to Kern County, just shy of the mountains, to figure out how the biggest farmers in America, led by the biggest of them all, are not only keeping alive their orchards and vineyards during drought but adding more almonds (79,000 acres), more pistachios (73,000 acres), more grapes (35,000 acres), and more mandarins (13,000 acres). Even as the supplies of federal and state water have dropped to near zero, agriculture in Kern keeps chugging along, growing more intensive. The new plantings aren't cotton, alfalfa, or carrots—the crops a farmer can decide not to seed when water becomes scarce. These are trees and vines raised in nurseries and put into the ground at a cost of $10,000 an acre to satisfy the world's growing appetite for nuts and fruits.

Agriculture in the south valley has extended far beyond the provisions of its one river, the Kern. The farmers there are raising almost 1 million acres of crops, and fewer than half these acres are irrigated with flows from the Kern. The river is nothing if not fickle. One year it delivers 900,000 acre-feet of snowmelt. The next year it delivers 300,000 acre-feet. To grow, Big Ag needed a bigger and more dependable supply. So beginning in the 1940s, Kern farmers went out and grabbed a share of not one distant river but two: the San Joaquin to the north and the Sacramento to the north of that. The imported flow arrives by way of the Central Valley Project and State Water Project, the one-of-a-kind hydraulic system built by the feds and state to remedy God's uneven design of California. The water sent to Kern County—1.4 million acre-feet a year—has doubled the cropland. But not even the two projects working in perfect tandem can defy drought. When nature bites down hard and the government flow gets reduced to a trickle, growers in Kern turn on their pumps and reach deeper into the earth.

The aquifer, a sea of water beneath the clay that dates back centuries, isn't bottomless. It can be squeezed only so much. As the growers punch more holes into the ground looking for a vanishing resource, the earth is sinking. The choices for the Kern farmer now come down to two. He can reach deep into his pocket and buy

high-priced water from an irrigation district with surplus supplies.
Or he can devise a scheme to steal water from a neighbor up the
road. I now hear whispers of water belonging to farmers two counties away being pumped out of the ground and hijacked in the
dead of night to irrigate the nuts of Lost Hills.

I roll past Tulare, where every February they hold the biggest
tractor show in the world, even bigger than the one in Paris. Past
Delano and the first vineyards that Cesar Chavez marched against.
Past McFarland and the high school runners who won five state
championships in a row in the 1990s. Past Oildale and the box-
car where Merle Haggard grew up. Past Bakersfield and the high
school football stadium where Frank Gifford and Les Richter, two
future NFL Hall of Famers, squared off in the Valley Champion-
ship in 1947 in the driving rain. And then it hits me when I reach
the road to Weedpatch, where my grandfather's story in America—
a poet on his hands and knees picking potatoes—began. I've gone
too far. The wide-open middle of California did its lullaby on me
again.

I turn back around and find Route 46, the road that killed James
Dean. I steer past Wasco to the dust-blowing orchards that flank
Lost Hills, the densest planting of almonds, pistachios, and pomegranates on earth. This is the domain of Stewart Resnick, the rich-
est farmer in the country and maybe the most peculiar one too.
His story is the one I've been carting around in my notebook for
the past few decades, sure I was ready to write it after five years or
ten years, only to learn of another twist that would lead me down
another road.

Like the wheat barons of the 1870s who lived on San Francisco's
Nob Hill, Resnick isn't of this place. He's never driven a tractor
or opened an irrigation valve. He's never put a dusty boot on the
neck of a shovel and dug down into the soil. He wouldn't know
one of his Valencia orange groves from one of his Washington na-
vel orange groves. The land to him isn't real. It's an economy of
scale on a scale no one's ever tried here. He grew up in New Jersey,
where his father ran a bar. He came to California in the 1950s to
remake himself. Welcome to the club. He remade himself into a
graduate of the UCLA law school, a cleaner of Los Angeles buildings, a vendor of security alarms, a seller of flowers in a pot, a
minter of Elvis plates and Princess Diana dolls, a bottler of Fiji

Island water, a farmer of San Joaquin Valley dirt. He purchased his first 640-acre section in the late 1970s and kept adding more sections of almonds, pistachios, pomegranates, and citrus until he stretched the lines of agriculture like no Californian before him.

At age eighty-one, he's gotten so big he doesn't know how big. Last time he checked, he told me he owned 180,000 acres of California. That's 281 square miles. He is irrigating 121,000 of those acres. This doesn't count the 21,000 acres of grapefruits and limes he's growing in Texas and Mexico. He uses more water than any other person in the West. His 15 million trees in the San Joaquin Valley consume more than 400,000 acre-feet of water a year. The city of Los Angeles, by comparison, consumes 587,000 acre-feet.

Resnick's billions rely on his ability to master water, sun, soil, and even bees. When he first planted seedless mandarins in the valley seventeen years ago, the bees from the citrus orchards around him were flying into his groves, pollinating his flowers, and putting seeds into the flesh of his fruit. He told his neighbors to alter the flight of the bees or he'd sue them for trespassing. The farmers responded that the path of a bee wasn't something they could supervise, and they threatened to sue him back. The dispute over the "no-fly zone" was finally resolved by the invention of a netting that Resnick sheathes around his mandarins each spring. The plastic unfurls across the grove like a giant roll of Saran Wrap. No bee can penetrate the shield, and his mandarins remain seedless.

The control Resnick exercises inside his $4.5 billion privately held company does relinquish to one person: his wife, Lynda, vice chairman and co-owner, the "Pomegranate Queen," as she calls herself. She is the brander of the empire, the final word on their Super Bowl ads, the creator of product marketing. There's Cheat Death for their antioxidant-rich pomegranate juice and Get Crackin' for their pistachios and Untouched by Man for their Fiji water. A husband and wife sharing the reins is rare for corporate America, rarer still for industrial agriculture. He commands his realm and she commands hers, and he takes care to mind the line. "If he sticks even a toe onto her turf," says a former business partner, "she gives him a look that sends him right back."

Together the Resnicks have wedded the valley's hidebound farming culture with L.A.'s celebrity culture. They don't do agribusiness. Rather, they say, they're "harvesting health and happiness around the world through our iconic consumer brands." Their crops aren't crops but heart-healthy snacks and life-extending elixirs. Stewart refers to the occasional trek between Lost Hills and Beverly Hills—roughly 140 miles—as a "carpetbagger's distance." It seems even longer, he says, if you add in the psychological distance of being an East Coast Jew in a California farm belt where Jews are few and far between. Lynda is making the trip on the company jet more often these days. She's done giving big gifts to Los Angeles museums and mental health hospitals that name buildings after her and Stewart. The south valley—its people and poverty, its obesity and diabetes—is her newest mission.

In Lost Hills they call her "Lady Lynda." She shows up in high fashion and stands in the dust and tells them about another charter school or affordable-housing project she is bringing to them. They have no way to grasp the $50 million to $80 million a year that the Resnicks say they are spending on philanthropy. This is a magnitude of intervention that no other agricultural company in California has ever attempted. The giving goes to college scholarships and tutors. It goes to doctors and nurses, trainers and dietitians, who track the weight of workers, prod them to exercise, and wean them off soda and tortillas. As she announces the newest gift, the men and women in the back of the crowd smile and applaud politely and try not to show their faces to the publicity crew she has brought with her to film the event. Many are here without documents, after all.

Seventy-five years ago, writer Carey McWilliams, in *Factories in the Field*, lambasted the "ribboned Dukes" and "belted Barons" of California agriculture. If he were on the scene today, he'd have to add "sashed Queens" to the list. Measuring the reach of the Resnicks, it's tempting to lean on the hyperventilated language of the 1930s: Empire. Kingdom. Fiefdom. Feudal. Today most everything in this desolate reach of Kern County, save for the oil wells, belongs to Paramount Farming, which belongs to the Resnicks. But Paramount isn't Paramount anymore. By the decree of Lynda, who once contemplated a bowl of those juicy little seedless mandarins and on the spot named them Cuties, this is now the land of Wonderful.

It's the summer of 2016, eight weeks before the big pick, and I'm zigzagging across the almonds and pistachios, square mile after square mile of immaculate orchards lined with micro-irrigation systems and heavy with nuts. Of all the wonders of Wonderful, this is the one I find most mystifying. The State Water Project that allowed western Kern County to grow into a farming behemoth has given no water or very little water over the past three years amid the worst drought in California history. If this were any other part of Kern, the farmers would be reaching into the earth to make up the difference. But western Kern has no groundwater to draw from. The aquifer either doesn't exist or is so befouled by salts that the water is poison.

As a consequence, the farmland here, nearly 100,000 acres planted in permanent crops, is completely reliant on the government's supply of mountain water. This is gambler's ground unlike any other in California, and as I drive from hill to dale, examining each orchard, my head spins. *How can this be? No rain in five years. State water dwindling year after year. No water in the ground to make up for the missing government supply. So why hasn't this place gone to tumbleweeds? How can another record crop be sitting pretty on these trees?*

I do all the calculations from the numbers I am able to gather, and I cannot figure out how these nuts are getting enough water. There is a local water bank, a kind of underground lake, that the Resnicks control. In the years of plentiful rains and heavy snowmelt, the bank fills up with more than 1 million acre-feet of stored water. But most of this water has been spent by the Resnicks and other account holders in years two, three, and four of the drought. Whatever remains is not nearly enough to make up for the shortfall of imported water from the state.

Then I get lucky. I come upon a Wonderful field man in a four-by-four truck who listens to my bewilderment and takes pity. As he drives off, he throws a clue out the window. Turn onto Twisselman Road off I-5 and continue west until it intersects with the California Aqueduct. There, he tells me, in the shadow of the state's great concrete vein moving snowmelt north to south, I will find a private, off-the-books pipeline that Stewart Resnick has built to keep his trees from dying. The water is being taken from unsuspecting farmers in an irrigation district in Tulare County more than 40 miles away.

No stranger enters this zone unless it's to get rid of a body or dump waste from cooking meth or drown a hot car. Its vastness makes you feel safe and in jeopardy at the same time. I head straight into the glare of the sun shooting over the Coast Range. Through the haze I can see the knoll of the aqueduct come closer. Ever since

I was a kid, I have felt its pull—a gravitational presence on the land and in my own story. On a fog-drip night in January 1972, two men walked into my father's empty bar with gloves on and shot him to death. They dumped their stolen car into the canal's black waters and got away with murder for the next thirty-two years. In a valley of dead rivers, each one killed on behalf of agriculture, the aqueduct was the one river still alive. Its artificiality had achieved a permanence; its permanence had created my California.

I pull over into the dirt of a pomegranate orchard, the ancient fruit that the Resnicks have turned into POM Wonderful, the sweet purple juice inside a swell-upon-swell bottle. The shiny red orbs, three months shy of harvest, pop out from the bright green leaves like bulbs on a Christmas tree. I study the terrain. This must be the spot the Wonderful field man was describing. Sure enough, cozied up next to the bank of the aqueduct, I see a glint. I get out of the car and walk down an embankment. There before me, two aluminum pipes, side by side, 12 inches in diameter each, slither in the sun.

Where gravity needs a boost, the pipes run atop wooden crates used to pack boxes of fruit. Where the pipes butt up against Twisselman Road, a more clever bit of engineering is required. Here a crew has dug a culvert beneath the road and hiked the pipeline under the asphalt that divides one field from another. Here private water jumps from Tulare County to Kern County, but government jurisdictions don't count. On one side of the road and the other, for miles in both directions, the dirt belongs to Wonderful. I stand over the pipes and give them a hard slap. They slap back with the cold vibration of water. Where's it coming from? Who's it going to?

II. The Empire Builders

Water is what led me to Stewart Resnick in the winter of 2003. Back then the *Los Angeles Times* had a bureau in the middle of California. The bureau happened to be my house in northwest Fresno. I had finished the last chapter of *The King of California*, a book I wrote with a good friend about J. G. Boswell, who owned more land and controlled more water than any other person in the West for most of the twentieth century. He and his forebears from Georgia had dried up Tulare Lake, the biggest body of freshwater this

side of the Mississippi, and planted 100,000 acres of cotton outside the town of Corcoran. As it happened, just down the road,
on the other side of the lake bottom, Resnick had captured his
own body of water, the Kern Water Bank, and planted millions of
nut trees on desert scrub. No journalist had written a word about
his rise as an agricultural giant, how he had turned public water
into private water by grabbing control of California's largest water
bank, a project jump-started with $74 million in taxpayer money.
The deed had been done in a series of hidden meetings in Mon-
terey. Resnick wanted no part in my story. Each time I called, his
secretary hung up the phone.

I waited five years before placing another call to his headquarters. It was the early spring of 2008, and this time his secretary
didn't hang up on me. I had in mind a magazine profile on Stewart, the Nut King. "Why not send him an email?" the secretary suggested. A few weeks later, I found myself riding up the elevator of a
high-rise on the Westside of Los Angeles.

He sat behind a desk without clutter and stood up to shake my
hand. He was a small, trim man, no more than 5-foot-5, in his early
seventies, with thinning silver hair and brown eyes rimmed in pink.
The speech of his parents and grandparents, the Yiddish-inflected
New York with its humors and cut-to-the-quick impatiences, had
not left his own speech in the half-century since he'd come to California. He was dressed in the latest slim-fit style. Arrayed before
him were small bowls of almonds, pistachios, and easy-to-peel mandarins, a plate of ground white turkey meat cooked in olive oil, and
a glass of pomegranate juice. Everything but the turkey had come
from his orchards. He'd been diagnosed with early prostate cancer
and had no doubt that the juice was keeping him well. "My health,
knock on wood, is good. It gives me the luxury to keep on working.
Frankly, I'm having too much fun to think about retiring."

Even if he were inclined to wind down, he had no successor in
mind. None of his three children had the slightest interest in taking
over the company. Still, he was starting to think about his legacy,
and that's why he finally agreed to meet with me. "I've never given
an interview to a newspaper or magazine before. I've told them all
no. When you're making the kind of money we're making, what's
the upside? I'd rather be unknown than known." He had recently
read *The King of California,* and that got him thinking. "I'm not going to live forever, even with the massive amounts of pomegranate

juice I'm drinking. It might be nice if my kids and grandkids could turn to a book someday and read about what we've built."

He and Lynda were changing the way food was grown in California and sold to the world. If they were farmers, they were farmers who hung out with Tom Hanks, Steve Martin, David Geffen, Warren Beatty, and Joan Didion. They donated $15 million to found UCLA's Stewart and Lynda Resnick Neuropsychiatric Hospital and more than $25 million to the Los Angeles County Museum of Art to build a pavilion in their name. Unlike many other billionaires, they could poke fun at themselves. During the holiday season, they sent out four thousand gift boxes to their "nearest and dearest friends" filled with their fruits and nuts, along with a card of the two of them dressed in skin-colored body stockings, posing as Adam and Eve. "If only Eve had offered Adam a pomegranate instead of an apple," Lynda wrote, "every day could have been a holiday."

The Resnick story certainly deserved a book, but did he really want me to be the one to write it? Boswell had tried to tear apart a copy of *The King of California* when his secretary asked if he might autograph it.

"Why not we start with an extended interview or two?" I offered.

"Let's meet again in two weeks," he said.

The front gates of the 25,000-square-foot Beaux Arts mansion on Sunset Boulevard magically opened without a guard giving a nod. I exited my car and approached the entrance with its 14-foot columns and wrought-iron balustrades. Perched up there, a queen might peek out and utter, "Let them eat cake," Lynda once said. When the mansion was built, in 1927, it was known as the Sunset House. I was prepared to knock on the door, but a housekeeper, flanked by two blow-dried dogs, greeted me on the front steps and led me inside. I tried not to stare at the gold that was everywhere: heavy-legged gold furniture, paintings in thick gold frames, gold-leaf carpet, and gold-fringed drapes. From the vaulted ceilings with gold-leaf moldings hung two blown-glass chandeliers. The curtains were made of a fabric woven in Venice and substantial enough that they might finish off a person who happened to be looking out the window in the throes of an earthquake.

There was a majordomo of the house, a butler, a chef, a sous-chef, three housekeepers, a limo driver, and a trio of assistants who worked in the basement, juggling Lynda's calendar and the buying, wrapping, and shipping of gifts she handed out to her Rolodex of "highfalutin people." Stewart had made it clear that Lynda would not be joining us. She had her own book—about her genius as a marketer—going. He had spent the morning on his exercise bike reading *Fortune*. Fresh from a shower, a red Kabbalah string tied around his wrist and a multihued pair of socks covering his feet, he welcomed me. If he had his druthers, he said, he'd still be living in a little ranch house in Culver City. "None of this is my idea. This is my wife. This is Lynda."

Where do you begin with a man of great riches if not the distant places you might have in common? And so I began with slaughter and madness and then moved on to bartenders for fathers.

His grandfather Resnick had fled the Ukraine in the wake of another killing of Jews by Cossacks. The bells in the churches pealed, and out came the villagers with their scythes and axes, believing they had found the reason for their poverty. It was the early 1900s, and his grandfather and grandmother decided to secure passage to America. His father was three years old at the time. They settled in Brooklyn among Jews who had fled their own pogroms, and his grandfather went into the needle-and-embroidery trade. His father met his mother, the cantor's daughter, and they married. When the Depression struck, his parents migrated to Middlebush, New Jersey, where they bought a few trucks and peddled coffee and pots and pans. Stewart was the second of their four children, the only boy. "I sort of remember growing up on a farm," he said. "But we weren't there long." They moved to Highland Park, home to Johnson & Johnson and close enough to Rutgers University to hear the fans screaming at Neilson Field. Manhattan was thirty minutes in one direction, the Jersey Shore thirty minutes in the other. The borough measured no more than 2 square miles. It wouldn't even make a couple of sections of his almonds.

His father bought a neighborhood bar and ran it with the same iron fist with which he ran the house. He was short, bull-like, and didn't take crap from anyone. "He was about my size, but he was very tough. He was a big drinker, a big liver who loved the fast life. His bar was a place for guys, Damon Runyon–type guys."

Resnick's pals were all Jewish kids from upper-class families, so it wasn't easy being the poorest one, the one whose father was a gambler and capable at any moment of losing the few comforts they had. Once he came home from school and discovered the family car gone. His father had lost it in a bet. "He was tough on the outside. But inside he had these weaknesses. Compulsive gambler and alcoholic. Then he'd lose his temper and get the strap out."

Like many billionaires, Resnick didn't have a decent explanation for his fortune. Because he hadn't done it with Daddy's money or what he considered a superior brain, he attributed his wealth to luck and to a simple lesson he had learned early in life. He was thirteen and standing inside the Rutgers Pharmacy on the first day of his first job. The boss showed him a storeroom filled with chemicals tossed here and there and told him to bring order to the mess. He didn't know where to begin. He studied the situation. The stacks of bottles gave him no answer. The boss came back in, saw his do-nothing, and said only three words: "Just get started." He began to move, and the job went quickly after that. Digging in was its own wisdom, he discovered. Order finds itself through action. *Just get started* became one of his guiding principles.

At Highland Park High, he excelled in math and struggled in English. Upon graduation he only needed to look across the Raritan River to find his college. The idea was to enroll at Rutgers and study to become a doctor. A year into his studies, an uncle called from California. He had moved out to Long Beach, bought some property, and built one of those new strip malls. The money was too easy. His dad had sold the bar and was adrift. Why not California? Once his parents decided to go, he decided to go too. He left in 1956. "I never liked New Jersey, but I never knew why. California showed me why."

The making of a billionaire over the next half-century was a series of dots that connected in the California sunshine. It was linear, logical, fluid, and quite nearly destined.

He got into UCLA and joined a Jewish fraternity. One of his frat brothers was a wealthy kid whose father ran a janitorial business. He had an industrial machine, hardly used, that scrubbed and waxed floors. Resnick dipped into his savings from his job at a mental hospital and went in half on the machine. "After school and on weekends we'd clean and wax floors. It took time for the wax to dry. So in that time we started cleaning windows too." They named the business Clean Time Building Maintenance.

His frat brother got bored, as rich boys do, and Resnick bought out his half-interest for $300. He started cleaning pizza parlors and drugstores. Business got so brisk that he bought two trucks and hired crews. By the time he graduated from UCLA in 1960 and entered its law school, he was bringing home $40,000 a year —the equivalent of $320,000 today. "When I got out of law school, I probably had one hundred people I was employing."

At the buildings he was cleaning, he noticed that no one was watching the front and back doors. With that insight, he sold the company for $2.5 million and went into the security guard business. It then dawned on him that guards were good, but they had to be paid an hourly wage. Burglar alarms, on the other hand, offered round-the-clock vigilance without coffee breaks. He went out and bought an alarm company. That company led to another company, and he soon owned half the commercial alarm accounts in Los Angeles.

His first wife, the mother of his two sons and daughter, told him she was quite happy living in their $30,000 condo in Culver City. Month after month she made ends meet on a $1,600 budget. "She was a very frugal lady. She wanted me to put our $5 million in an account, draw interest, and we could live happily on the fifty grand a year."

She didn't understand his drive. He was going to Vegas, hanging out with his own Damon Runyon characters, and making plans to get even bigger. He packed his bags and left his wife and kids. It wasn't a midlife crisis, he told me. He did little, if any, catting around. Then one day he was trying to find a marketing person and got a call from Lynda Sinay, who worked in advertising. She was in her late twenties, almost a decade younger than Stewart, and the mother of two children. She had recently divorced and wasn't about to settle for a life in Culver City. She was the daughter of Jack Harris, a film distributor, who moved the family to Los Angeles when Lynda was fifteen to produce movies. One of his films, *The Blob,* became a cult classic, and they lived in a house on the Westside with two Rolls-Royces in the garage.

By age nineteen Lynda had dropped out of college, married a magazine ad man, and opened her own advertising agency. She wasn't content to pursue the usual list of wealthy businessmen as clients. She was aiming to surround herself with famous actors and artists and public intellectuals. She divorced her husband in 1968 and began dating Anthony Russo, who worked at the RAND think tank in Santa Monica with military analyst Daniel Ellsberg. From a safe, Ellsberg had lifted the Pentagon Papers, the secret history of how successive presidents lied to the public to cover up the failings of the Vietnam War. Russo and Ellsberg needed a place to photocopy the seven thousand pages, and Lynda volunteered the Xerox machine at her ad agency on Melrose Avenue. The three of them spent two weeks of all-nighters making copies. When a copy found its way to the *New York Times*, Lynda was pursued by federal prosecutors until they concluded she was more dilettante than radical.

The courtship of Stewart and Lynda went fast. They both knew what they wanted. They married in 1972, and he sold the alarm company for $100 million. He wanted to stay in the customer service business and heard from his doctor that Teleflora, the giant flower-delivery company, could be bought for a buyer's price. It was Lynda who came up with the idea of "flowers-in-a-gift." Roses are short-lived, she reasoned, but the teapot or watering can that the flowers arrive in is a keepsake. The concept changed the industry. She won a gold Effie, advertising's Oscar.

In the late 1970s he went looking for a hedge against inflation. His accountant suggested he buy apartments. He could collect the rents while he slept. But he wasn't looking for the monotony of steady. He was in the mood to gamble. On vacation in the South of France, he heard about a farming company called Paramount that needed a buyer for some of its orchards in Kern County. "They were selling twenty-five hundred acres of oranges and lemons and a packing house for a third of their appraised value," Resnick said. "It was simply a place to park some money and have another opportunity." He drove to Delano, the farm town where Chavez and his union had made so much trouble and history. By the time he drove back, he was a citrus grower. "I think I paid nine million dollars. Lookit, I'm from Beverly Hills. I didn't know good land from bad land. But I had some good people helping me."

He and Lynda decided in 1984 to buy the Franklin Mint, the maker of commemorative coins and other kitsch, for $167.5 million. They knew little about the company except it was selling its keepsakes for five times the amount Teleflora was. Shoving aside the coins, they introduced a Scarlett O'Hara doll that by itself generated $35 million in sales. They were pushing plates, costume jewelry, perfume, and model cars. They issued a commemorative medal of Tiger Woods winning the 1997 Masters that offended the golfer. He called it fake junk, sued, and won. Lynda spent $150,000 at an auction to buy the beaded gown and matching bolero jacket, "the Elvis Dress," that Princess Diana had worn on a visit to Hong Kong. The designers at the Mint made a porcelain doll with a tiny replica outfit so precise that Lynda made them count the beads to make sure they matched the 22,000 on the real dress. It was a hit. Annual sales at the Mint jumped to nearly $1 billion.

Bankers and their fair-weather financing exasperated Resnick. He hired Bert Steir, a Bostonian with a Bronze Star from the Second World War and a degree from Harvard, to come west and work his deals. The oil companies and insurance companies were looking to unload their farms in Kern County, Steir learned, chunks of earth that measured 20,000 and 40,000 acres. Mobil and Texaco and Prudential Life were willing to practically give the ground and trees away. This is how Resnick became a pistachio, almond, and pomegranate grower. Sitting in his mansion in 2008, he already counted more than 100,000 acres of orchards across five counties. His trees were drinking from the Central Valley Project and the State Water Project, from rivers and irrigation canals and the water bank. "My life is about California. I didn't grow up here, but if it wasn't for California, its openness and opportunities, I wouldn't be sitting where I'm sitting."

No other farmer, not even Gallo, had cornered a market the way Resnick had cornered the growing, buying, processing, and selling of pistachios. He had his hands on 65 percent of the nation's crop. One of the first things he did with his monopoly was kill the California Pistachio Commission, the industry's marketing group, by yanking his funding. He and Lynda wanted to run their own ads for their own brand. The independent growers and processors, no surprise, regarded him as a bully eager to employ teams of lawyers and tens of millions of dollars to force his agenda. A member of the commission, on the eve of its demise, told me, "Stewart wants to be a benevolent dictator. But if he thinks you're defying him, he'll start with 'Nobody realizes the good I've done for agriculture.' Then he moves on to 'Do you know who I am? Do you know what I am? I'm a billionaire.' He's got an awful temper he's trying to control through Kabbalah. That little red string is supposed to remind him to count to ten. But his ego—there's no controlling that."

Resnick had heard it all before. He was the bad guy in agriculture for no bigger offense than that he was big. "Look, these farmers go back two, three, and four generations. Me, I'm a carpetbagger from Beverly Hills. But you ask the growers we process, and they'll tell you that year in and year out, no one offers a better price. No one pushes their product harder." It was this persistence and, above all, good timing that explained his bigness. "I'd have to say that fully half of my success has been luck. Now in farming, we're in a unique position. The crops we grow can only be grown in a few places in the world. Still, none of it would have happened without luck."

What he and Lynda had done with the wretched pomegranate was another matter. They planted the first 640 acres, half the pomegranates in the country at the time, knowing there was zero market. Instead of trying to sell the fruit as a piece of fruit, they squeezed its seeds into POM Wonderful. If anyone doubted the health benefits of the juice, they spent more than $30 million in research to prove that it fought heart disease and prostate woes. Antioxidants that delivered 32 grams of sugar in each serving didn't come cheap: $11 a bottle. Lynda sent the first batches of POM, week after week, as gifts to David Bowie, Rupert Murdoch, and Disney head Michael Eisner. On Oscar night she handed out free samples to the stars at the *Vanity Fair* party. "Of course, I know everyone in the world," she told one reporter. "Every mogul, every movie star. You have no idea the people on my VIP list who drink it. But that doesn't make people buy a second bottle. They do that because they love it."

A POM craze followed. Stewart and Lynda planted 15,000 more acres and bought a juice plant. "Who would have thought that people would be asking their bartender to fix them a Pomtini?" he said. All of it was Lynda's doing, of course. There she stood in the foreground of the photo that accompanied a *New Yorker* profile titled "Pomegranate Princess." She was wearing a black pantsuit with open-toed silver pumps and a single piece of jewelry around her neck. In the distant background, under the gaze of a 10-foot-tall marble goddess, sat Stewart in a gold-skirted chair, head down. "She wanted to tell the story of the pomegranate," he told me with a touch of sarcasm. "For a long time she got no credit. Now she's getting lots of credit."

I returned for two more sessions, and then he and Lynda took off to their $15 million vacation house in Aspen, where they were warring with the locals over a housing project for community workers that was blocking their view. By the time they returned to Beverly Hills, he had lost interest in a book about his life, at least one that I might write. I kept my notes and tapes and waited for another day.

III. The Farmworkers

Lost Hills sits on an upslope. This is the closest to hills it comes. Main Street is Highway 46, which slices through the middle of town. At the east end, where the highway meets Interstate 5, the traveler gets a choice. Day's Inn or Motel 6. Carl's Jr., Subway, McDonald's, Wendy's, Love's, or Arby's. None of the sales taxes go to City Hall because Lost Hills isn't a city. It's known as a census-designated place, which is another way of saying that Kern County has every reason to neglect it. Highway 46 shoots past Resnick almonds and takes you straight into town, population 1,938. The tumbleweeds on open ground give you a peek into what Lost Hills looked like before the aqueduct made a river here.

The July sun is a scorcher, and I fuss with the dial on the AC long enough to blow past the town's one stoplight and the aqueduct too. I'm in another land, an expanse of hard, ugly, cratered-out earth the color of sand. Hundreds of giant praying mantises standing on platforms of concrete are pulling oil from a Chevron field. This is the west end of Lost Hills, the extraction end. The wind kicks up dirt from the reap of oil and almonds, and the dust cloud carries back into town, raining down on the elementary school first.

I park the car and walk in the direction of a scattering of buildings slapped together with stucco and corrugated tin. A meat store, an auto repair, a pool hall, and an arcade pass for a commercial strip. No one is out and about. They're either working in the heat or hiding from the heat. Three dogs, part pit bull, the menacing part, have given up on the shade and lie on the open road. Their tongues loll to their knees. I walk into the supermarket El Toro Loco, and the clerk directs me to the back office, where a tobacco-chewing Yemeni named Anthony Hussein is sitting beneath a photograph of an uncle in his U.S. Army uniform. The uncle died at age twenty-two fighting in Afghanistan. "Talk to me," Hussein says, draining a can of Rockstar. "What do you need to know, sir?"

"What's it been like here during the drought?"

"Drought, no drought, makes no difference. The aqueduct was built with tax money, yes? The aqueduct brings the water, yes? So everybody should have it, right? But this is water for Mr. Resnick. Not the people. When it doesn't come, he finds a way to make it come." He spits tobacco juice into the empty can of Rockstar.

"The checks the workers bring in here from Mr. Resnick are the same checks they bring in for years. I cash them the same. Nothing changes. Big fish eat the small fish here. Anything else I can help you with?"

He seems in a hurry. He guides me back into the main store with its displays of fresh fruit and vegetables, meats, cold cuts, and baked goods. The shelves spill piñatas, gloves, hats, pruning shears, and loaves of Bimbo white bread. The wall of Pacifico and 16-ounce cans of Bud is rebuilt daily. Vicente Fernández, the king of ranchera music, is crooning to no one, but it won't be this way in thirty minutes, Hussein tells me. Today is *quincena* day, twice-a-month payday, and he needs me to scram because the workers coming in to cash their checks and wire 25 percent back across the border to families in Guanajuato and Guerrero will wonder if I'm with Immigration and Customs Enforcement. If that happens, they'll go down the highway, and he'll lose the $1 he takes for every $100 worth of their checks. "It's a bad day," he says, shooing me out. "You look like Border Patrol undercover."

I sit in my car and wait in the parking lot. They arrive in Chevy trucks and Dodge vans and spill out in groups of four or five under the sweat-stained hats of the 49ers, Penn State, and the Yankees. Each face wears its own weary. The twenty-year-olds look like twenty-year-olds, the thirty-year-olds like forty-year-olds, the forty-year-olds like sixty-year-olds. Summer or not, they're dressed in shirt layered upon shirt and the same no-name dusty blue jeans. Or at least this is what I can glean through the car window. I grab my notebook and walk up to one of the vans.

Inside sits a young man named Pablo. The oldest of five children, he came from Mexico when he was eighteen. He had no papers, like so many others, just an image of what this side of the border looked like. When he was told there were fields upon fields, he did not believe there could be this many fields. That was eight or nine years ago. He lives down the road in Wasco, the "Rose Capital of America," though the roses too have turned to nuts. He works year-round for Wonderful. This means he can avoid the thievery of a labor contractor who acts as a middleman between the farmer and the farmworker and charges for rides and drinks and doesn't always pay minimum wage. Pablo prunes and irrigates the almond and pistachio trees and applies the chemicals that cannot be applied by helicopter. He makes $10.50 an hour, and the company provides him with a 401(k) plan and medical insurance.

He's thankful to the Resnicks, especially "Lady Lynda," for that. "I saw her a few months ago. She is here and there, but I have never seen her up close. She owns this place." He goes on to explain what he means by *own*. Most everything that can be touched in this corner of California belongs to Wonderful. Four thousand people— more than double the number on the highway sign—live in town, and three out of every four rely on a payday from Wonderful. All but a handful come from Mexico. In the Wonderful fields, he tells me, at least 80 percent of the workers carry no documents or documents that are not real. U.S. immigration has little say-so here. Rather, it is the authority vested in Wonderful that counts. It was Lynda who teamed up with the USDA to develop twenty-one new single-family homes and sixty new townhouses on a couple of acres of almonds that Wonderful tore out. The neighborhoods didn't have sidewalks; when it rained, the kids had to walk to school in the mud. Lynda built sidewalks and storm drains, the new park and community center, and repaved the roads. So the way Pablo uses *own* isn't necessarily a pejorative. "When I crossed the border and found Lost Hills, there was nothing here," he says. "Now there's something here. We had gangs and murders, but that's better too."

He has come to El Toro Loco to cash his check and buy some beer. I follow him inside to a long line of workers that ends at a plastic window where Hussein sits on the other side, working the cash register like a teller at a racetrack. When it's Pablo's turn, he hands Hussein a check for $437, and Hussein counts out $433 back to him in cash. On the way out of the market, Pablo buys a case of Pacifico. Tonight, feeling no pain, he'll sit in one of the strip clubs in Bakersfield and maybe buy himself a fancy lap dance.

Across the street, the Soto family has built a new Mexican restaurant named Gabby's that dwarfs every other business on the street with its Spanish Mission façade. The Sotos made a name for themselves in Lost Hills by taking their taco trucks into the agricultural fields. Angelica, one of four sisters, runs the restaurant. She tells me her not-so-silent partner is Lady Lynda, who was so bothered that Lost Hills didn't have a sit-down restaurant of its own that she sought out Angelica. Lynda assisted her with the design and color scheme but otherwise has remained hands-off. "She'll check in every so often to see how business is going. But she doesn't dictate this or that." Angelica would prefer not to get into the details of their financial arrangement. It's been more than a year since the grand opening, and they're still operating in the red. So far Lynda has shown only patience. A restaurant built by Wonderful for the purpose of making the company town look better from the roadside may enjoy a more forgiving bottom line than, say, the Subway up the road. But that still doesn't mean that most people in town can afford to eat here. "We're still trying to figure out who our typical customer is going to be," Angelica says. For now, she's playing country-western music on the sound system and trying to lure a combination of oil-field workers, supervisors at Wonderful, and travelers driving the last miles of James Dean.

I leave Gabby's and follow a winding concrete path through the new Wonderful Park. The grass is a color green on the verge of blue, and the cutouts for trees are razor-etched. The 5.3 acres are so flawless and at odds with the town that the whole thing feels like a movie set. Even the community water tank is painted baby-blue with a big sunflower. "You Have Found Lost Hills!!" it says. On the north end sits the Wonderful Soccer Field with its all-weather track, stadium lights, artificial turf, and giant yellow sunburst embossed at midfield. On the south end stands the Wonderful Community Center, where residents are urged to attend thrice-weekly Zumba and core-training sessions, healthy cooking classes, and weekend cultural outings featuring the likes of America's Premier Latino Dance Company.

This is a lot of gestures to unpack, and as I exit the grounds, I keep turning around to get one last look that's true. I don't know how Hershey did Hershey, Pennsylvania, but Lynda is present in every painted sunburst, every planted flower, every blade of grass. The believer and the skeptic do their tussle inside my head. This is a park for the people, to give them a break from their hard lives. Lost Hills finally has something to be proud about. This is an offering of cake handed down from king and queen to serfs. It is one more way to extend the brand. Even Wonderful Park is spelled with the same heart-shaped *O* that stamps a bottle of POM.

The compass in my car says I'm headed east, but that means almost nothing inside a province of 15 million trees. Each square-mile section is divided into blocks, and each block counts a precise number of rows. When a farmer's orchards encompass 186 square miles, finding the field man can be a challenge. Section, block, and row don't compute; he has to direct me by cell phone and guideposts. My dust cloud tells him I'm getting close. He turns out to be a kindly religious man whose short hair is dyed the black of shoe polish. I ask him about his delivery of services—pruning, pesticides, herbicides, fertilizer, water—that can be calibrated and timed to enable the smallest unit to achieve maximum yield. Surely no one does this better than Wonderful?

He explains that Wonderful has grown too big to hassle such precision. Let the smaller grower walk among his trees and farm by the row. Fussing with one input or another, he can produce 3,500 pounds of nuts an acre. Wonderful, by contrast, shoots for the middle. The scale of production—and the ability to process, market, and sell its own crops—allows Wonderful to be mostly mediocre in the fields and remain highly profitable. No one's going to get fired for bringing home 2,500 pounds of nuts an acre. "These trees are pruned by a machine that hedges one side and then the other," he says. "But the smaller farmer still uses a pruning shears to make his most important cuts. If he knows what he's doing, the shears can make a thousand more pounds an acre."

It's the beginning of September 2016, and battalions of heavy machinery dispatched from the Wonderful equipment yards pound the ground and rattle the trees. No picking of crop agitates the earth like the picking of almonds and pistachios. A plume of dust joins up with other plumes of dust until the sky over the valley turns sickly. By the eighth day of harvest, the sun is gone. Not that long ago we used to time our sinus infections by the immense cloud of defoliants sprayed on the cotton fields at the end of Indian summer. Now it's the seven-week nut harvest that brings out the inhalers. All this stirring up is a consequence of mechanization. Because a human picker is not needed in the almond and pistachio groves, the nut harvest doesn't spread around money the way it spreads around dust. Wages that used to go to workers stay in the pocket of the nut growers. Maybe not since the wheat barons has the income disparity between farmer and farmworker been greater. Growers a tenth the size of Resnick flee the dust in their Ferraris to their second houses in Carmel.

I follow one of the engines of harvest as it rolls into an orchard like a tank. Giant pincers manned by a single worker grab the tree by the throat and start shaking. For the next two or three seconds the almonds pour down like hail. The vibration is a stunning piece of violence to behold. It moves in a wave from trunk to limb to nut and back down to earth. The jolt and shudder would tear out the roots of a lesser species. When the clamps let go of the trunk, eight thousand almonds, green outer shells wilted and partly opened, the meat inside a wooden womb, lie scattered on the flat dry earth. Somehow, thirty or forty nuts aren't compelled to drop. The man and his pincers can't be bothered. The rain of almonds has moved on to the next tree. Once each tree has been shaken, the nuts are left on the ground for a few days to dry.

I walk to another part of the orchard and watch phase two. In a swirl of dust, a worker atop a different machine is blowing the almonds from their spot beneath the trees to the middle of the row. The nuts are kept there a few more days—any longer and the ants will attack them—to complete their drying. I then move to the far side of the orchard, where another worker, riding a huge mower, is kicking up an even bigger cloud of dust. He maneuvers down the middle of the row, sweeps up the dried almonds, and throws them into a catcher. The contents of each catcher, 500 pounds of almond meat, are placed on a conveyor 20 feet high and dumped into a big-rig hauler for transport to the Wonderful processing plant.

All told, nine men operating five machines will pick clean this orchard over the next four weeks. They'll take home $11 an hour for their labors. And how will the Resnicks fare? Each tree produces 22 pounds of nuts. Typically each pound sells wholesale for $3.75. That's $83 a tree. By harvest's end, the Resnicks will have put their clamps on 4.4 million almond trees. Nearly $365 million worth of Wonderful almonds will have dropped down from the dry sky.

In the city of trees I find a paved road with speed bumps that takes me to the harvest of pistachios. The bunches of chartreuse-tipped nuts hanging from antler branches never touch the ground. Two men sit inside separate cabins of a small tractor with pincers on one side and a catcher on the other. One man drives and shakes the tree while the other man makes sure the clusters fall into the butterfly opening of the receiver. The vibration here isn't quite as vehement. As the nuts pour down onto the roof of the catcher, the operator shifts the trough so that it becomes a conveyor belt. The continuous rattle feeds the nuts into a series of bins on the backside of the tractor. There's no waiting around. Unlike the almond, the pistachio is moist and combustible. The nut must be hurried from bin to truck to processing plant to keep it from discoloring. "This is a big crop," the field man tells me.

All told, thirty-six men operating six machines will harvest the orchard in six days. Each tree produces 38 pounds of nuts. Typically each pound sells wholesale for $4.25. The math works out to $162 a tree. The pistachio trees in Wonderful number 6 million. That's a billion-dollar crop.

The truck driver hits the wide open of Highway 33 and traces the serpentine of the aqueduct. He's headed to the Wonderful plant, 13 miles north of Lost Hills, to drop off his load. He's carrying 55,000 pounds of crop in two swaggering trailers open to the sun. The load will translate into 18,000 pounds of finished nuts in a matter of days. Whether he realizes it, he's part of the biggest pistachio harvest in history. California growers, in the grip of drought, have produced 900 million pounds of the green nut. That's more than double the crop that Resnick boasted about when I saw him eight years ago. Nearly a third of the harvest—the nuts grown by Wonderful, the nuts grown by hundreds of farmers who belong to the Wonderful brand—will come through these gates.

The new plant, the size of seven super Walmarts and built at a cost of $300 million, rises out of a clearing like an apparition. The eye numbed by the tedium of orchards isn't prepared for the 1.3 million square feet of industrial assault, though the palm trees and roses along the perimeter try for a transition. This is where the pistachios, four hundred truckloads a day, fifty days of harvest, come to be weighed, washed, peeled, dried, gassed, sorted, salted, roasted, packaged, and shipped out to the world.

No whistle shouts mealtime in the modern-day company town. The graders, sorters, and beeping forklift drivers head to an immaculate café, where the Wonderful Salad—roasted chicken, mixed greens, cilantro, pistachios, and slices of mandarin in a blue cheese vinaigrette—sells for $3. Lynda believes that if they're enticed in the right direction, the 1,300 workers might choose to prepare the same healthy fare at home. Sugar kills, she tells them. It takes a life every six seconds. What spikes blood sugar more than a can of Coke? A flour tortilla. Eat a corn tortilla instead, she urges. She's built a grocery section in the back of the café stocked with grapeseed oil and what she touts are "Whole Foods–quality vegetables and fruits that sell at Walmart prices." Why grapeseed oil? I ask Andy Anzaldo, head of grower relations and a fitness buff, who's taken on the added duties of what might be called Wonderful's minister of health. "Research is showing that grapeseed oil is healthier than corn oil and canola oil and may be better for you than olive oil," he tells me.

Anzaldo's grandfather came from Guadalajara in the 1950s as part of the bracero farmworker program. His father worked as a truck driver, transporting crops to the city. Anzaldo grew up in Bakersfield and attended a Catholic high school where he played football and basketball. For college he picked California Polytechnic in San Luis Obispo over the hill and majored in agriculture business. The Resnicks brought him aboard in 1999, and now he works alongside Lynda and consults daily with the company chef. Five years ago they decided to get rid of the nacho chips, french fries, and soft drinks. The workers didn't react well. That's when the Resnicks decided to sell the concept of wellness to their 4,300 employees throughout the valley the same way they sell workplace safety. "We changed the culture of safety, and we think we can do the same with health," Anzaldo says.

The Spanish rice isn't rice but cauliflower made to look like rice. The pizza dough is cauliflower too. A worker can still order a hamburger, but it's half the size of the old hamburger and costs $6 —twice what the wild salmon served with creamed leeks and raw asparagus salad costs. Whichever dish they choose, workers are asked not to take a bite until they have considered Lynda's latest concoction: an ounce of apple cider vinegar cut with ginger, mandarin juice, and turmeric served in small plastic cups like the wine of Mass. Everything about our physical selves, Lynda believes, begins in our guts. To change the microbial life in our digestive tracts and reduce inflammation that leads to disease, we have to reintroduce fermented foods into our diet.

If the workers doubt the benefit of the enzymes from apple cider vinegar, video banners stream a continuous message of bad food habits to be broken and body mass indexes to be measured and met. "Rethink Your Drink" is the latest slogan. Coke, Gatorade, and Monster Energy are sky-high in sweeteners, but don't be fooled by that SunnyD either. "More than half our employees are obese or near obese," Anzaldo tells me. "One out of eight has diabetes. You can't reverse diabetes, but you can control it with a blood sugar level between 6.5 and 8. That's our goal. To manage the disease. Because when we don't manage it, they end up with severe chronic health issues and amputated limbs."

Anzaldo is a man wired for solemn, but he does manage to smile once during lunch, when talking about the 1,150 workers who've earned bonuses of up to $500 for losing a collective 14,000 pounds in two years. That still leaves the majority of the workforce beyond his cajole. "You and I look at this meal," he says. "Wild salmon and all these sides made from scratch. 'Wow. This is only three dollars?' But for a lot of workers, bringing that big fat burrito from home still makes sense."

I had seen what J. G. Boswell had done for the town of Corcoran. The hospital, senior citizens' center, and football stadium all bore the signature of his giving. What the Resnicks were doing for Lost Hills, though, was a level of philanthropy I had never witnessed in the valley. They were hardly the first rich people to use patronage to try to wheedle a citizenry toward their idea of a better life. But this wasn't the Resnick Pavilion at the Los Angeles County Museum of Art. This was Lost Hills, where the people are dependent on the Resnicks from cradle to grave. "There's a lot to commend here," I tell Anzaldo, "but where does persuasion end and coercion begin?"

As a second-generation Mexican American, Anzaldo says he knows the powerful clench of fast food and sugar among his own family. "We are sensitive to that. We can't insist on wellness the way we can insist on plant safety. Being healthy is a choice. Have we gone too far? The feedback we're hearing is 'No.' In fact, some of the workers think that we haven't gone far enough."

The workers aren't around for a quick survey. They've gone back to the nut line. On a Facebook page with postings in Spanish, they offer a glimpse of life "inside pistachio world." They give thanks for a job that provides decent wages and access to a free wellness center next door staffed by a full-time doctor, physician's assistant, registered dietitian, and marriage and family therapist. During paid breaks they do their fifteen minutes of Zumba, take a walk along a designated path, and munch on the free fruits and veggies put out for them. Mostly, though, they can't wait for the avalanche of nuts to end. "One more bin," a post reads. "So so sleepy," says another. "One more hour and I'm outta this fucking place."

On the way out, the voice in their head, Lynda's voice, goads them to give one more hour to the Wonderful Fitness Center. Inside, a trainer watches over a line of treadmills, elliptical machines, and stationary bikes. There's a section stacked with weights and a yoga room with mats on a hardwood floor. When the next shift ends, he tells me, the gym will fill up with workers looking to win the cash bonuses from the company's GetFit program. On the whiteboard in front of the weights, the big boys list their totals. They're all chasing Bobby, whose 325-pound bench press, 335-pound squat, and 455-pound dead lift make him the sole member of the 1,000-Pound Club.

In the maroon of sundown, I follow the workers back to Lost Hills. Their houses made from railroad boxcars have been painted purple, blue, yellow, and gold. The colors turn brilliant in the light made spectacular by the particles of dust. Down a rutted road, one hundred trailers with foundations dressed in plywood back up against an orchard. Even if they had wheels, they wouldn't be going anywhere. The people here have traveled too far. Some of them have paid $12,000 to buy their trailers and spent thousands more to fix them up. The brick-hard ground can't be bought. They're paying $340 a month for its privilege. As farmworker colonies go, this one isn't as grim as others I've visited. There's no garbage piled high and smoldering, no chickens picking at scratch. The Sureños gang has tagged the front entrance but otherwise has left the inside unmarked. The junk scattered about could be a lot worse. It is the ditch up the road, the one that carries no water, that is filled with old mattresses and spent appliances. Twine strung trailer to trailer hangs with the laundry of fathers, mothers, and children. The space for a family's secrets is only a few feet. Here and there a mulberry tree, its canopy pruned back, breaks up the red-smeared sky.

A woman named Lupe is standing above me on the wooden stairway that climbs to the front door of her trailer. She is small with lively brown eyes and a sweet but confident voice. Her husband, Manuel, will awaken in thirty minutes to prepare for his night shift. Under lights he prunes, plows, and irrigates the almonds. Lupe and Manuel, like many of the residents, grew up next to each other in a pueblo called San Antonio deep in the state of Guerrero, a mountainous region of dramatic beauty. They were married only a short time when Manuel decided to cross the border almost twenty years ago. He worked as a gardener in Los Angeles and then heard about the almond trees on the other side of the mountain, where the living was so much cheaper. He landed a steady job with a big grower and a year later paid a coyote $5,000 to bring Lupe and their baby son to Lost Hills.

She remembers handing the boy to her sister-in-law, who carried phony papers, and watching them cross by bridge into California. Because Lupe had no papers, she followed the coyote for many more miles until they reached a steep pass. Lucky for her that the young man was kind. Before he left her to cross alone, he gave her soda, water, chips, and Cheetos. The baby is now a twenty-year-old student at Bakersfield College. Lupe gave birth to two daughters, U.S. citizens, who are now eleven and six. If she has her way, they will go to college too. "We tell the children about the fields when they are young so they don't know the fields when they are old," she says.

More than a dozen family members have followed Lupe and Manuel to Lost Hills. One cousin arrived only last week. Relatives arranged his passage, paying the coyote the new rate of $12,000. A portion of his wages will be set aside each month to pay down the debt. "We send money home each month to our families left behind," Lupe says. "Then some of the money we save goes to pay the coyote. It takes a lot of work to get ahead." She and Manuel were able to buy their trailer several years ago. He spends much of his off hours fixing it up. He has painted the interior and put down two new patterns of linoleum, one to mark the living room and the other to mark the kitchen. The ceiling, all sheetrock and spackling, remains a work in progress.

Lupe excuses herself to prepare dinner. The bowls on her kitchen table are filled with grapes, berries, bananas, and red and green bell peppers. She washes two kinds of lettuce and cuts up fresh papaya to mix into a salad. I notice she keeps the water running for a long time. I ask her if she is concerned about wasting water, given the drought and the distance the water has traveled — 20 miles from a well in Wasco — and that the cost goes up the more they use. Already they are paying $69 a month to the local utility district. She tells me the water comes out of the tap yellow and foul-smelling, and she doesn't trust it. The family takes showers in it, and she washes their laundry in it, and if she runs the water long enough, she will use it to wash her vegetables and cook her rice and potatoes. But she cannot remember the last time she or Manuel or their children drank it. "It comes out like pee," says her eleven-year-old daughter.

The water is filtered for arsenic, boron, and other salts, and the monthly tests show no violation of state or federal standards. This hasn't convinced the people of Lost Hills, however. Lupe says no one in her family, and none of her friends living in the trailer park or on the other side of town, drink the water that comes out of the pipe.

In the kitchen corner, cases of bottled water are stacked halfway up the wall. These are donations from other farmworker families, but they're not for her and Manuel and the kids. Her brother-in-law was killed recently in a car crash along Highway 46. He was headed to the fields at the same time that another farmworker, drunk on beer, was coming home from the fields. The sober man died. What to give a grieving widow and her five children in Lost Hills but drinking water?

In the trailer next door, Lupe's cousin Margarita lives with her husband, Selfo, and their three young children. They were farmers back in San Antonio, growing lettuce, cilantro, and radishes on a small plot of land. Then the drug cartels took over the countryside and planted poppies. One day gunmen mowed down residents with AK-47s and threw grenades at the church filled with parishioners. "I saw horrible things," Margarita says. "My husband would have been shot dead like the others, but he was lucky. He had left for the cornfields a few minutes before the killings."

That was four years ago. They are still paying off the $27,000 debt to relatives who hired the coyote. The relatives try not to press them, but the arrangement still feels like a form of indentured servitude. Selfo works fifty hours a week as an irrigator. He makes $10.75 an hour. It comes out to $2,000 a month. The rent is $540. The food is more. The gas to and from the orchards costs him $80 a week. They spend $50 a month on bottled water. "There's not much left over," he says. "Our relatives have been patient." He worries because there isn't enough water now to properly irrigate the almonds, pistachios, and pomegranates. He wonders what agriculture will look like in western Kern in ten years.

"A bunch of trees are going dry," he says. "The land is turning to salt. In one orchard, half the trees are dying."

I had traveled the fields of Wonderful from one end of western Kern to the other, looking for dying trees. I had not seen any. "Because of a lack of water?" I ask. "The drought?"

"Yes. It's happening." The bosses won't speak of it, he says. If I want to know more, I need to talk to Lupe's brother, Gustavo, who has worked as an irrigator at Wonderful for five years and knows what the company is planning for the future.

Lupe and I walk to the far side of the trailer park to find Gustavo. He is a single man who rents a bedroom from other family members for $150 a month. Lupe knocks on his door, and he invites us in. The room smells of Vicks VapoRub. A cross of Jesus hangs from the bedpost. "Welcome to San Antonio del Norte," he says. "San Antonio south doesn't exist anymore." He is a small, good-looking man with a patch of black hair under his lip. I ask him how the drought has affected Wonderful. He says his bosses have been instructing him to cut the water each irrigation. There are plans, crazy as it sounds, to take out 10,000 acres of almonds. When the rain returns, some of the ground will be replanted in pistachios, a tree that can better withstand drought. "Wonderful is getting smaller," he says.

The next day I drive to a spot a few miles beyond the trailer park where the county road dead-ends in a pomegranate orchard, or what used to be a pomegranate orchard before a Caterpillar came crashing through. Every last tree has been torn out of the ground. Thousands of Wonderful acres lay bare. The juice isn't selling like it used to. The POM tanks, I'm told, are backed up with a three-year supply. The Federal Trade Commission found Wonderful guilty of false advertising and ordered the Resnicks to stop claiming that POM cured heart disease and erectile dysfunction. A balancing of books in an office in the city has decided that this orchard and others around it, covered by too little water, can go. Already Wonderful has bulldozed 8,000 to 10,000 acres of pomegranate trees over the past few years to send more water to its nuts. Across the field a heavy machine is stacking what's left of the trees into giant mounds. Each mound is fed into an even bigger machine, whose teeth pulverize the trees and make sawdust. I park the car and walk across the barren rows. Here and there my boots crunch down on the dried remains of pomegranates that look like small pieces of scat dropped by a coyote. Plastic drip-irrigation lines stick out of the ground at wrong angles. Tender sprouts poke out of the dry soil, and I bend down to feel their prickle. They're baby tumble-weeds that have come home.

IV. The Philanthropist

A giant pistachio nut flashes on the big screen. It cracks open and out pops the head shot of Stewart Resnick in a pistachio-green tie. When he materializes onstage, he is wearing narrow black jeans, a black mock turtleneck, and a dark jacket. Damn, if he doesn't look even younger and more fit than the last time I saw him, eight years earlier. The Ninth Annual Wonderful Pistachio Conference at the Visalia Convention Center is an invitation-only affair, but I managed to sneak in and grab a seat.

He's getting ready to introduce Lynda, the main speaker, but first he wants to address the federal government's recent recall of Wonderful pistachios. Two strains of salmonella found in their pistachios had caused a multistate outbreak of illnesses. The FDA sent a warning letter, and Wonderful pledged to study the chlorine levels in the bathing tanks. As far as the company can tell, no active salmonella has ever traced back to the plant. Even so, Resnick says, he learned a lesson from the 2004 recall of 13 million pounds of the company's salmonella-tainted almonds: don't fight the FDA. "When they get on their high horse, you don't want to argue with them."

He launches into a CFO's riff on the pistachio market. Domestic sales are up 42 percent over the past eight years, but foreign sales have stalled. He blames Iran. Since international sanctions were lifted five years earlier, Iran has been crowding the market with its more buttery-tasting pistachios. The Iranians don't irrigate their trees. They rely only on rain, which concentrates the flavorful oils. China, for one, prefers the Iranian pistachio. So do the Israelis, who go to the trouble of repackaging the nuts so it doesn't appear that they're consuming the product of an enemy. Iranian pista-chios show up in Tel Aviv as nuts from Turkey.

What market share has been lost in Asia and the Middle East the company is looking to get back in Mexico with its spicy Latin line of nuts. Thanks to Wonderful's $15 million "Get Crackin'" cam-paign—the largest media buy in the history of snack nuts—pista-chios now rank among the top ten best-selling salty snack items in the U.S. "We are no longer processing nuts," he says. "We are creating foods." Nothing keeps prices high like a monopoly. In case the growers are fearing the antitrust cops from the Department of Justice, they needn't. For years agriculture has been given a wide berth when it comes to monopolistic practices. The net return on the pistachio proves that Wonderful's dominance in the market has benefited every grower in the room. The price for pistachios has climbed from $4.50 a pound to an unbelievable $5.25 a pound. It isn't going down because he won't let it go down.

Then he motions to Lynda, who's standing off to the side of the light-dimmed stage. I've never seen her up close, never watched her in action. She seems a little nervous waiting in the wings. Six hundred pistachio growers in blue jeans isn't her usual crowd. "We saved the best for last," he says. "As you know, our philosophy at Wonderful is doing well by doing good. About five years ago Lynda started our community development organization in Lost Hills, and the journey has been an amazing one. We produced a short documentary film. Every time I see it, I'm inspired and proud of what we've been able to accomplish in such a short amount of time. We hope you enjoy *Finding Lost Hills.*"

The eleven-minute film opens with a shot of swirling dust. This was Lost Hills before Lynda got involved. "I had no idea what I wanted to do, but I reached a moment in my life where I had to give back in a meaningful way," she tells the camera. "When I started to realize the socioeconomic issues of the Central Valley, I decided to stop writing checks to other charities and bring my business acumen into the project. It took time to gain the respect of the people, and I was afraid. What if I failed? If you're messing with people's lives and it doesn't work, that's serious . . . It had to work." Tens of millions of dollars spent on philanthropy in Lost Hills wasn't just good for the people, she discovered. It was good for the bottom line. Because the more you invested in your employees and their communities, the more productive they became. The film ends with the laughter of kids playing inside the giant sunburst at the center of the soccer field. "I did not name the town," Lynda says. "But I couldn't have picked a more cinematic name than Lost Hills. Because it's so much fun to say that Lost Hills has been found."

The room full of growers applauds. I applaud too. Since it is also true that Lost Hills has belonged to the Resnicks for thirty years, one of us might have blurted out, "What took you so long to find it?" As the film runs to credits, I can see that one credit is missing. John Gibler, a freelance journalist, found Lost Hills a year before Lynda. In the summer of 2010 he spent several days documenting the deplorable conditions of the modern company town. His account appeared in the *Earth Island Journal*, a small environmental quarterly out of Berkeley. Somehow it made its way to Lynda. "There is nothing here," one of the townsfolk told Gibler. "This is a forgotten community. And you know why? Because it is a community of all Hispanics."

The piece, I was told, had left Lynda embarrassed and fuming. It must have wounded all the more because she and Stewart thought of themselves as progressive Democrats. Over the years they had donated large sums of money to political campaigns, and some of it went to Republicans who had pledged to prop up California agriculture. This was how a billionaire who needed more water did politics. At the core, though, the Resnicks were still moved by the duty of social justice, not just as traditional liberals but as secular Jews. Stewart would deny that Gibler's reporting played a part in their philanthropy. "Look, I have no guilt. I've done no big wrong in my life that would cause me to have any. Well, maybe just a little guilt, but that's Jewish." The timing said otherwise. It was only a few weeks after the article appeared that Lynda kicked into high gear their mission to save Lost Hills and several other farmworker towns where Wonderful operated its orchards and processing plants.

They're now building an $80 million charter-school complex in Delano, just down the road from Cesar Chavez High. It looks like no other campus in the valley: a modern, minimalist two-story design that uses paneled wood and fabricated metal, wild colors, and terraced landscaping to create the feel of a high-tech mountain retreat. When all three phases are finished, 1,800 students will be attending the high school, middle school, elementary, and preschool. What Lynda seems to have in mind is a kind of utopian village set amid orchards, not unlike the utopias that were tried by the early dreamers of Southern California. Young men and women from Teach for America will do their two-year stints at the complex and live in village housing. The curriculum is being created by Noemi Donoso, the chief of education for the Chicago public schools before Lynda recruited her to Wonderful. "Lynda isn't just writing checks," Donoso told me. "She's designing the school. She's designing the curriculum."

Lynda is also mapping out a farm-to-food program where students will grow fruits, vegetables, and grains on a plot of village land. A fully equipped teaching kitchen will turn the harvest into school lunches. Already the high school is filled with hundreds of students bused in from farmworker towns that are among the poorest communities in the West. Among the graduating class are kids headed to Stanford, UC Berkeley, UCLA, Dartmouth, and the state and community college systems. When Lynda learned that half the students receiving thousands of dollars in company scholarships were dropping out of school, she wasn't deterred. She's now providing tutors and counselors in every region of California to boost the graduation rate.

For the bright kids who have no interest in a bachelor's degree, she has designed the Wonderful Agriculture Prep Program to serve an additional one thousand students. Selling the farm to migrant families has required Lynda to rebrand agriculture. No longer does it have to be a career that brings Mexicans to their hands and knees. Under her "rethink agriculture" program, the kids will be trained in plant science and irrigation technology, marketing and sales.

Now Lynda herself stands before us, a single light over her head. She is twinkling from earlobe and finger. Whether it's the glint of a fifteen-carat yellow canary diamond ring, a twenty-fifth wedding anniversary gift from Stewart, or one of the pomegranate-colored rubies she says are a girl's best friend, it's hard to tell from the back row. She gestures to the young students in the front row, the ones enrolled in the ag-prep classes, and asks them to stand up and take a bow. "They're our future," she says. She is determined that their lives will play out differently from the lives of their parents, but she means no disrespect by this. "It's not easy to hear, but I'm not going to sugarcoat this," she says. "In Kern County, one in two adults and almost one in five children are obese. And it's even worse for the children in Kings County. Fifty-three percent of our employees are obese, and twelve percent of them have diabetes."

The growers start to fidget. It's not the fidget of boredom. There's an unease about the room. This isn't the Lynda posing for photos with Barbra Streisand. This is the Lynda who now endeavors to see farmhands as something more than workers. To the growers, it must feel like a jab in the stomach. They're listening with their heads bent down. Do they sense the shaming about to come? She delivers it in classic Lynda style. "At Wonderful Health and Wellness, we're educating our employees about this health crisis. At the plant, we built our gyms, and we have stretching and walking activities. Being Wonderful means more than growing, harvesting, and distributing the best of the best. It also means giving back."

She walks off the stage with Stewart. He lingers in the crowd long enough to shake hands with a friend from Bel-Air who's planting thousands of acres of pistachios in the worst ground of Tulare Lake. I walk up and reintroduce myself. His face is blank. I remind him of the time we spent together eight years earlier in his Sunset House. His face is still blank. His partner in the mandarins once told me that when Stewart is done with you, he's done with you. He and the Resnicks had fought an ugly legal battle that tore their Cutie brand in two. The partner kept the Cutie name but only after paying the Resnicks tens of millions of dollars. Stewart and Lynda created a new brand, the Halo, from the same variety of mandarin. The Cutie and the Halo are now warring in the fields outside the Visalia Convention Center. Inside, a Wonderful media specialist sees that Resnick needs to be rescued. She deftly places her body between him and me. When I tell her my name, she whispers into his ear. "Ah," he says, "so you're the one who's been snooping around." She grabs him by the wrist, and they make a beeline for the convention hall door.

V. The Secret Pipeline

I catch Highway 99 in rare somnolence. The miles clock by not as road but as story. This is the route my grandfather, one of a legion of fruit tramps, took as he drifted from farm to farm in the 1920s picking crops. He saved up a down payment for a raisin ranch west of Fresno, where my father was born in the worst of the Great Depression. My grandfather lost the farm to vine hoppers is the story he told. My grandmother said it was his leftist politics that ate up that vineyard and the ones that followed. One way or the other, we got rid of our last farm a few years before I was born and moved to the Fresno suburbs.

The men and women who planted, irrigated, sprayed, and picked our crops were phantoms. On our trips to Disneyland, I must have blinkered my eyes heading down 99. I didn't see the tumbleweeds along the roadside and the strip of parched earth that separated what remained of the desert from the perfect rows of irrigated agriculture. I didn't see our creation, much less the figures bent under the canopies of vine that our creation counted on.

This was the same road that took me to Selma, the raisin capital of the world, to pack peaches and plums for Mel Girazian, my father's old friend. I was sixteen, and his packing house was my first job, a baptism into the "money, money, money" world of the men who grew fruit and the men who sold it. The growers would stand in front of the cull line and never stop moaning about how much of their fruit got rejected by Girazian's graders. I learned back then that our farmers thought the whole world was out to screw them.

Maybe this explains why the United Way could declare the valley one of the nation's skinflints, a place where the wealthy farmers donated to the children's hospital or Fresno State athletics but almost never to the communities filled with Mexicans where their crops grew. As a class of people, the farmers and real estate developers harbor a deep-down contempt for what they have built. They hide from the fact that it relies on the subjugation of peasants from Mexico they themselves have brought here. It exists as one thing they can almost rationalize out in the fields. It becomes something else as soon as they encounter their workers in another guise—as a fellow shopper at Costco or as the parents of the kid who goes to school with their kid. It becomes scorn because they can't allow it to become pity or self-hatred.

I cross the Tulare County line heading south into Bakersfield, and there in front of me, for no eye to miss, stands the Wonderful Citrus complex with its four-story storage building designed in the shape of an almighty box of Halo mandarins. Conceived by Lynda, it cost one fortune to build and a second fortune to light up. I doubt the Resnicks have any idea of the fester that eats at this place, the shame piled on shame.

On this same stretch of 99, I once wrote a story about farmworkers who moonlighted as meth cookers to make ends meet. Bruce Springsteen turned it into a song on his *Ghost of Tom Joad* album. More than one ballad was about the valley, so he came to Fresno. The William Saroyan Theatre was packed that October 1996 night. Halfway through his solo performance, he interrupted his set to tell us a piggy bank had been set up by the exit to donate money to the "hardworking men and women in the fields." When the concert was over, I took my wife and children backstage to meet him. As we sat down to chat, one of his assistants leaned over and whispered into his jewel-studded ear. Springsteen shook his head and smiled a thin, ironic smile. Then he turned and faced me. "Tell me," he asked, though it wasn't entirely a question. "What kind of place is this? Not a single penny was put in that piggy bank."

I cut across Twisselman Road to the pipeline gliding along the aqueduct like a silver snake. I thwack both lines. They thwack back. Yes, they're still delivering water. If I follow them north through Resnick pomegranates, I can find out where the water is coming from. If I follow them south into Resnick almonds, I can see where the water is going. Either way is a trespass. I steer toward the almonds, past a row of worker housing and a main gate. I enter an equipment yard where a Wonderful farmhand is standing next to a tractor. He doesn't wave me off or give chase. He knows what I don't know. This road ends abruptly at the rise of a second fence. Nowhere to turn, I turn back around and roll down my window. He's smiling but speaks only Spanish. He doesn't know what *pipeline* means. But if it's the *tube* that I'm looking to follow, I must drive through the almond grove. A road will pick up and connect me to where the tube is going.

"Why is the tube here?"

"To carry water from someplace far away to another place far away," he says. I thank him and hurry down the dirt road through the almonds, eyeing the rearview mirror to see if a Resnick truck is following me. I'm driving too fast for the ruts in the road. My head keeps hitting the sunroof. A minute later I reconnect with the pipeline and pursue its length for a football field. Each section of pipe is 40 feet long. I try to calculate how many hundreds of aluminum sections need to be linked seamlessly, or at least watertight, to cover the distance of a mile. Just ahead I can see the last section of pipe throwing a cascade of white water into a main canal belonging to the Lost Hills Water District. I hop out of the car.

RAIN FOR RENT, the pipes say. If Resnick retains every drop, he might squeeze 25 acre-feet of water a day out of both pipes. He needs nearly 1,000 acre-feet a day for 165 days—the length of nut-growing season—to hang a good crop across his acres in western Kern. This last-ditch water in Lost Hills won't make every-

thing right. But there's no denying his desperation. It is flowing
to a place of dire thirst. For as far as I can see, the water in the
canal runs inky through the orchards. Because the road ends here,
there is no physical way to follow the canal's flow. I take out my cell
phone and swipe across Google Maps. The image of water moves
on and on through miles of western Kern. This is one of the ways
the Nut King and the Pomegranate Queen are defying the California drought. This is how the land of Wonderful is keeping alive its
trees.

I call the manager of the Lost Hills Water District. He used to
work for the Resnicks before Stewart put him in charge of the
district. He's a decent guy making $216,000 a year who doesn't
pretend that he isn't beholden to Wonderful. As the head of a
quasi-public agency, he knows he can't completely blow off my
questions. He doesn't feign surprise when I tell him about the
pipeline, but he dismisses it as a private matter between private
parties. It takes my visiting the irrigation district office during a
public meeting for him to cough up more details. Yes, the pipeline
belongs to Resnick. It's bringing water from the Dudley Ridge Water District in Kings County. He's using it to irrigate his almonds
and pistachios in Lost Hills.

I find a former partner of Resnick. He doesn't know about the
pipeline. What he knows is that Wonderful is buying up to 50,000
acre-feet of water a year in a series of hidden deals. The sellers
include farmers in the Tulare Lake basin who are pumping so
much water out of the ground that the levees protecting the town
of Corcoran are sinking, not by inches but by feet. During the
drought the Boswell Company has drilled fifty-two holes into the
old lake bottom—seven of these wells reaching a depth of 2,500
feet. To fix the subsidence and keep the town dry in the next flood,
residents and the state prison are having to pay $10 million in extra
taxes. Altogether Resnick has purchased 300,000 acre-feet of water from farmers and water districts—at a cost of $200 million—to
cover his shortfall during the drought.

I meet up with the Wonderful field man who first tipped me off
to the pipeline. He says he doesn't feel sorry for Resnick. He got
himself into this jam. "This is a company that runs its resources to
the max," he tells me. "When Resnick plants, he plants his trees
wall to wall. That's why he's in trouble."

"So he makes a deal for private water?"

"Yep. That's why he built the pipeline. He needs every drop he can get."

"Whose water is it?"

"Don't you know? It's John Vidovich. Billionaire comes to the rescue of billionaire."

"But those two guys hate each other."

"Not anymore. They're drought's best buddies."

John Vidovich will tell you he's the interloper who came over the other mountain, the Coast Range. His father grew grapes, cherries, and apricots in the Santa Clara Valley back when Stanford University still had a reason to be known as the Farm. He sold a chunk of land to the builders of Sunnyvale and decided he could develop the rest himself. His real estate empire became big enough to bring aboard each of his four children. By the time he died an old man on his tractor in the Cupertino Hills, where he had planted grapes again and was making wine, the transformation of his valley by the silicon chip was complete.

John, his oldest son, had served in the military as an intelligence officer and graduated from Santa Clara law school. He had none of his father's sentimentality. He paved over the last orchard in the Santa Clara Valley with some apartments and then went looking for another valley where he might build his own empire. That's how he came upon the San Joaquin. "There's a lot of people who don't like me," he said after his father's death. "But nobody didn't like my dad."

It was a curious statement but true. The son, 5-foot-6 and thin, with closely cropped blond hair and blue eyes that fix on you, isn't concerned about ingratiating himself. In a timespan even shorter than Resnick's, the sixty-one-year-old Vidovich has bought up more than 100,000 acres of farmland scattered across the valley. He's planting ground that no one has ever planted before. If you study his moves, you can see a method to the acres he is accumulating. Whether it's Fresno or Kings or Tulare or Kern County, he's grabbing land where the groundwater is plenty or a river runs through it or the aqueduct spills its north-to-south flow. Don't let his boots, blue jeans, and ball cap fool you, the old-timers say. He isn't farming dirt. He's farming water.

In the winter of 2010, Vidovich put up for sale half his draw of state water from the Dudley Ridge Water District. This amounted

to 14,000 acre-feet. Everyone knew where it was going. It was going
to houses. California had passed a law intended to stop the rising
of new towns in the middle of nowhere. Developers now had to
identify a source of water before a city or county would green-light
their projects. So off the developers went in search of farm water.
Resnick himself had sold 5,000 acre-feet to a proposed new town
in the farm fields of Madera. Vidovich didn't have to wait long for
a buyer to come calling. The Mojave Water Agency in the high
desert needed a backup supply to serve its growing communities of
Barstow and Apple Valley, Hesperia and Victorville. The agency did
not balk at the price tag: $5,321 an acre-foot. Vidovich went home
with $74 million in his pocket.

The sale got under the skin of valley farmers. It was true that
agriculture had been selling state project water to cities for two decades. But those deals were one water district selling to another water district. This sale made headlines because it was engineered by
one farmer—an outsider from the city—for his benefit only. To top
it off, the "greedy SOB" (farmers rarely uttered Vidovich's name)
intended to keep his 7,000 acres of nut trees in Dudley Ridge. He
only needed to find groundwater from another basin to replace
the state aqueduct water he had just sold.

Vidovich went on a shopping spree. He bought 20,000 acres
in the Tulare Lake basin—land that not even Boswell dared farm.
He had no intention of farming it either. But those 20,000 acres
near the town of Pixley came with an endowment: a little spit of
earth that produced endless amounts of groundwater. Never mind
that this is one of the most overdrafted basins in California or that
the land is sinking a half foot a year. Vidovich digs seventeen new
wells, several to the depth of 1,400 feet, and pumps groundwater
into ditches and canals that move the flow across miles of flat lake
bed. Where does the water end up? Right there in the big canal of
the Dudley Ridge Water District. He's not only able to irrigate his
nut trees with an imported flow of groundwater—40,000 acre-feet
in some years. He can mix this private water with his leftover state
water and ship it to at least one stranded neighbor who will pay the
price.

Who would have thought the two of them in cahoots? Not long
before, Vidovich was trying to grab water from Resnick, not give
it. He accused Resnick in 2008 of using various shell companies
to monopolize control of the Kern Water Bank. A public resource

had been privatized for the purpose of growing tens of thousands of acres of nuts, he charged. The matter was headed to court when Vidovich paid a visit to Resnick. His ego had gotten the best of him, he conceded. What if he dropped his lawsuit and the two of them worked together to solve their water problems? That's all fine and good, Resnick replied, but what about the $1 million-plus he'd spent on lawyer's fees? Vidovich wrote out a check for the full amount, then went looking for the water to prop up Resnick's monopoly. He found it.

By car and foot, I trace the silver pipeline as it creeps north through Wonderful pomegranate orchards. One mile, two miles, three miles, four—it keeps going until it reaches another county and back to one of the main canals in the Dudley Ridge Water District. A pump is shooting water out of the canal and into the RAIN FOR RENT pipes. The water is cold, clean, and salty, though not too salty for a desperate man. Or at least that's the way Vidovich puts it when I finally reach him.

"This drought has brought Stewart to his knees. What can I say? We've had our battles in the past, and I don't agree with everything he's doing. But when your neighbor is going to lose his crop, you do what you can to help him."

I tell Vidovich this sounds almost charitable. "How much water are we talking about?"

"I'd rather not get too specific. It isn't a lot of water."

"What's the cost?"

"I'm not going to give you the numbers. Neighbors don't tell on neighbors."

Vidovich has more than one reason to be evasive. Farmers near Pixley already have sued him once for taking too much water out of their ground and moving it. The court settlement allows him to take the water to Dudley Ridge, but it can't go outside Kings County. Yet the Resnick pipeline is doing just that.

"Resnick picks up the water in Dudley Ridge," Vidovich says. "It's his pipe, not mine. Where he takes the water is none of my business."

"He's taking it into his orchards in Kern. That breaks your agreement with those farmers. You can't be exporting groundwater from one basin to another."

"Whatever water he's taking, it's too little, too late."

I try again to pin him down, but he's a man who likes to think of himself as wily. So I ask about the big picture.

"Let's call it what it is," he says. "It's gambling. Stewart gambled and won for many years. He gambled on the price of nuts going up, and he gambled on the water never going dry. He kept planting more and more trees. But he got too big. Too many pistachios. Too many almonds. Too many pomegranates. Like a lot of empires, it comes to an end."

"So what about you?" I ask. "What kind of empire are you trying to build?"

"I'm here to show the farmer that ag's footprint needs to get smaller."

I chew on his answer for a second. The calculation and hubris inside it. The truth a mercenary has landed on. "I get it. You're the one who leads the way on selling agricultural water to the cities. Fallowing the farm until the footprint gets smaller and smaller. Making hundreds of millions of dollars in the process?"

"It can't be farmed like it was," he says.

VI. The Aftermath

Six hundred and forty acres don't look like 640 acres—a square mile—until they start ripping out the trees. The white flowers have set into buds, and the buds have become baby almonds covered in fuzz. Now it's the Bobcat's turn. The biggest farmer of them all is tearing out 10,000 acres because he doesn't have enough water to cover the nuts to harvest. Since the middle of the drought, the price of almonds has dropped almost by half. In a region of wall-to-wall plantings, one of the walls is crashing down. The way the Bobcat goes full steam, it takes but a few seconds of splendid violence to uproot a tree. The farmer isn't here to smell the cracking open of wood, the ripping open of warm secret earth. No farmer ever is. The sentimental ones stay away. The bloodless ones stay away. On the day the trees fall quietly upon the orchard floor, no one is here but the Mexican on his tractor.

Then the autumn of 2016 arrives with the strangeness of clouds. The rain starts to fall, big, fat, slashing drops that feel like electricity on my open palm. It hardly ceases for the next five months. Drought turning to flood—it is the story of California. The wildfires can't be far behind. The winter goes down as one of the wettest in recorded history. So much snowmelt comes down the mountain that it nearly takes out Oroville Dam. The dam ends up holding, and the levees too. All the new water pours into the delta, and what doesn't go out to sea fills up the aqueduct again. The State Water Project, for the first time in six years, delivers surplus flows. The tule fog sets down again in the valley. The great drought is officially over. California is free to return to its amnesia.

Wonderful has enough water to irrigate its orchards in Lost Hills and park tens of thousands of acre-feet in the water bank. The Resnicks are growing again. From the east side of Tulare County to the west side of Fresno County, they're planting more nuts and Halos. Of the 22,000 acres they ripped during the drought, 18,000 acres are being replanted in pistachios. Along a fan of the Kings River, a raisin farmer in Selma shows me his well that's coughing up sand. He points to the young almond trees that envelop his 20 acres like a siege. "Resnick," he says. "My old well can't compete with his new wells. I'll have to go deeper if I can."

On Sleepy Farm Road outside Paso Robles, the Resnicks were looking to add 380 acres of wine grapes and build a small reservoir with groundwater. One of the neighbors watched in disgust as the bulldozers tore into the hillside. Thousands of California oaks were felled. Only after the media were alerted did Stewart and Lynda claim to have discovered the clear-cutting. Up and down the Central Coast, restaurants are boycotting their wines.

"When we learned of the terrible situation, not to mention our poor reputation within the community, we were ashamed and are sorry," their official statement reads. "We were asleep at the wheel. We are horrified by the lack of regard for both neighbor and nature, and we hope that the community will accept our deepest and most sincere apologies and find it in their hearts to forgive us." They pledge to donate the 380 acres to charity.

I write an email to the Wonderful PR team. A day later I get a call from Mr. Resnick. It's been more than a year since he gave me the cold shoulder at the pistachio conference. He tells me to meet him in Lost Hills.

He's dressed Italian chin to foot—Loro Piana jeans and Hogan tennis shoes. "I would have worn my Levi's," he says, "but Lynda's here, and she thinks I dress like a bum." We're standing in the sun outside the plant's corporate office, a building whose clean lines and retro furniture wear the imprint of Lynda too. He's surrounded by a half dozen of his top men and women, the same ones who've been artfully dodging me for the past three years. They greet me with smiles and handshakes. A van pulls up to the curb, and the door slides open. Resnick has saved the front seat for me. "You're the one who needs to see."

We pull out of the parking lot, past the palm trees and roses, and head up the thin ribbon of Highway 33 into the dust-swirling tunnel of nuts and fruits. The big man with the goatee behind the wheel is Bernard Puget, a Basque sheepman's son who oversees these orchards. As we hop down from the van to inspect the pomegranates on the eve of harvest, Resnick motions to Bernard's belly. In his best Borscht Belt nasal, he takes a jab. "Bernard, what's happened? You get exempted from the company's wellness program?" Bernard has actually lost a few pounds. "I'm down, Stewart," he protests. "I'm down."

The leathery skin on the fruit has turned a nice orange-red. Each bush is saddled with more than a hundred pomegranates the size of softballs and baseballs. The softballs will go to market as whole fruit or as seedpods in a package. The baseballs will be crushed into juice.

"These are loaded," Resnick says. "It sure looks heavier than last year."

Bernard smiles and nods to the others. "He's fishing right now. He thinks I've understated the crop."

Resnick grabs at a pomegranate that might win a blue ribbon at the fair and tries to twist it free. No luck. He yanks and pulls, and it finally comes off, throwing him a foot backward. "You sure this isn't eighteen tons an acre?" he says, goading.

"It's loaded," Bernard says. "But for every good-sized fruit, there's a bunch that never sized up." Resnick is giving him one of his looks. "What? You don't believe me?"

"No, I believe you," Resnick says. "It's going to be what it's going to be. We'll still make money."

We pile back into the van and head up the road. Then it hits me. This isn't any road. This is Twisselman. Bernard, hard to believe, is driving straight toward the aqueduct. The knoll begins to rise. I gaze out the passenger window, looking for the glint of the pipeline. It should be right here, but I don't see it. It's gone. I look back at Resnick. He's oblivious, or so it seems. Bernard's eyes are fixed straight ahead. He's trying to play dumb, but I can see the sliest of grins peeking out from his mustache and goatee.

"It's gone," I say. "How come?"

"We don't need it anymore," he whispers.

Back at the plant, Lynda is meeting with Wonderful doctors, nurses, and farmworkers. They're coming up with ideas that might lead to an even bigger drop in the number of employees with diabetes. Stewart tries to interrupt, but he's not the boss in this room. "Thirty-five percent of our prediabetic population has gone into the healthy range," she tells the team. "They're no longer in danger. Now they have to keep that up, right? So how do we do even better next year?"

He guides me to the café, and we grab our lunches from the buffet. He unfolds a $20 bill from a wad he keeps inside a bent paper clip, and we take a seat in the far corner. For a silent minute we dig into our bowls. I feel his gaze going past me, his voice turning oddly sentimental.

"When I look around here at what we've built and then look back at my life in New Jersey, I think, 'How did it happen?' For one man and woman to build something like this would be almost impossible today."

One hundred and twenty thousand acres of nuts and fruits and berries in California and still counting. They had survived the drought. Did it teach him any lessons?

"Lessons?" he says, sounding perplexed. "Who knows when a five-year drought is coming? Who anticipates that you can't fill a water bank for six or seven years?"

"Come on," I say. "It's California."

"Sure. But you take some risks in business. And when you've been as lucky as we've been, you start to think you can ride out drought too."

He did learn one lesson. You can plant only so many acres on ground that has no groundwater. From now on they'll grow on land that offers a double protection against drought. "State or federal water isn't enough. We want good groundwater too."

"You mean no more pipelines carrying water in the dead of night?"

"The pipeline . . ." He stammers a bit. "Look, I delegate a lot of things, obviously. I'm sure I knew we had a pipeline in there. But that's not an issue I deal with."

"How much water was it bringing in?"

"I don't even know what it was, to be honest with you."

I take a last bite of cauliflower rice. I know there's a more forceful way to ask the question, but to what end? This was the same distance—geographic, psychic—that allowed him and Lynda to clear-cut the oaks and to kill the independent pistachio commission, to grab a water bank that belonged to the state and to pretend for thirty years that Lost Hills wasn't a place of dire need. It was the same distance that allows them to control more land and water —130 billion gallons a year—than any other man and woman in California and still believe it isn't enough.

"I know I can't do this forever," he says. "I'm eighty years old. Problem is, I feel like I'm fifty. I feel too good to give any of it up."

His oldest son is retired in Seattle. His second son is a psychiatrist. His daughter, who used to own a restaurant, is busy raising her one son. Lynda has a son who works as a musician and a son who suffered a birth trauma and lives in a care facility. The four grandchildren have visited the orchards once or twice. Not a single one of them wants any part of Wonderful.

"Who gets the keys to the kingdom?"

"I don't know. All I know is I don't want to split it up or sell it in some leveraged buyout. I want to know that what we built will continue into the future."

He takes a look at his watch. He's got another meeting to attend. As he walks away, I notice his $400 sneakers. They're dusty with San Joaquin dirt.

I retrace the road I came in on and cross old Tulare Lake, which rose by flood and sank by drought. Four tribes of Yokut lived along its shores. On the shallow bottom, the women fished mussels and clams with their toes. The nets of the Chinese during the Gold Rush caught terrapin that was served as turtle soup in the fanciest restaurants of San Francisco. Then the men of cotton, driven out of the South by the boll weevil, put the five rivers into canals and dried up the lake. They made a new plantation here. Before he died at age eighty-six, J. G. Boswell told me what a fool he and his forebears had been for wasting water, sun, and soil in California to raise fiber, of all things. Cotton still grows on the lake bottom, but less and less each year. Thousands of acres of pistachio trees now await the next flood. Boswell pumps reach 2,500 feet into the earth looking for water to grow crops, looking for water to sell. For now they're selling to farmers like Resnick who can pay the price.

The extraction of water beneath the lake bottom won't last forever. The state of California has adopted a new law that finally regulates the pumping. When it goes into full effect, in a decade or two, more than a million acres of cropland across the valley will have to be retired. By then Wonderful, if it still exists, will be a portfolio run by men even farther away than Beverly Hills. The water will be stripped from the land and sold to developers of new towns both here and over the mountain. In my lifetime alone, California has gone from 13 million people to 40 million people. Nothing will stop the houses. The Wheat King begets the Cattle King, and the Cattle King begets the Cotton King, and the Cotton King begets the Nut King and Pomegranate Queen. Like the waters of the lake, the indent of the Resnicks will recede from the land too. The Yokut had a saying that when the farmer drained the last drops of snowmelt from Tulare Lake, the water would return. It would return as tule fog to remind the white man of his theft. The fog is our history.

YEMISI ARIBISALA

The Girls Who Fainted at the Sight of an Egg

FROM *The New Yorker*

I LOVE THE congeniality of eggs, how quintessentially composed they are, the way they snuggle into the cupped hand. The way the eye is compelled around the ovalness, the different coffee-and-milk complexions, recycled-manila-envelope pores, the fragility. Yet it feels slightly pretentious to be a Nigerian and muse about eggs; we are supposedly too no-nonsense for that. I think, for instance, about our national disdain for sell-by dates. How we might drolly concede their significance when heads of lettuce left in the fridge turn to black mush or green peppers melt into slime. But as far as the egg sitting in the average Nigerian fridge is concerned, it is so perfectly composed, so cool when we are not, that we are reassured that all we believed about those *òyìnbós*, those global northerners and their hangup about dates, is true. I have never seen a sell-by date on eggs in Nigeria. And maybe I never will. Our point of view on the matter is that if the egg has salmonella, it is too bad for the egg!

My maternal grandfather bred farmhouse chickens. He introduced me to guinea fowl, duck, and turkey eggs, all as food, not as objects of contemplation. As a child I was taught how to carry an egg and how to move protesting chickens gently aside. When we were on holiday in Ososàmì, Ìbàdàn, my siblings and I had to collect chicken eggs as one of our chores. My younger sister, Morótì, has a scar near her eye that looks like the Igbo scarifications given to sickly children for protection. It is nothing so dramatic. We are not Igbo. It was only a furious chicken flying up in the air one day and pecking her for touching her eggs.

I know, in exact detail, what my perfect chicken egg is like. In size it must be average, or even small. When it is broken into hot oil, it must spread no farther than three to four inches. The yolk must have the energetic, luminous complexion of yellow maize, and it must fall into the pan and not budge, like a spoon of àkàrà in new oil. And the egg must smell like an egg. This is not stating the obvious. In 2003, I lived in Houston, Texas, for five months, and in that time I did not encounter one fried egg that smelled like a fried egg, like that lavish, heady, tangy aroma of grease and creaminess calling for onions, green peppers, roasted mushrooms, sausages. It was the clincher, believe it or not, for whether or not I could live in Houston.

Once, on Twitter, with six words, Ruth Reichl broke down my carefully built defenses. All she had to say was "soft custard of slowly scrambled eggs" and I teared up. Longing burrowed from my stomach to my heart. You see, ever since I contracted some unjust metabolic illness, several years ago, my body refuses to quietly digest eggs. After I eat them, I can recognize where all my nerves start and end. They converse loudly, and this goes on for days, even in my sleep, painful electrical currents firing across my head and my arms. So I can no longer eat eggs, no matter how excruciatingly I long for them.

I could never cook eggs with sardines as well as nostalgia can. Two tablespoons of coconut oil or King's groundnut oil in a frying pan. One tin of Titus sardines; the original thingamabob with the curly-headed bust of someone (surely Titus) on a maroon-and-sepia tin. Six eggs. A few thin slices of onion. Maybe one tomato, half a green pepper, and one yellow, scented-not-hot Scotch bonnet. The Scotch bonnet is chopped extremely fine and tamed in the hot oil for a minute. The oil will have the powerful fragrance of hot pepper, which will linger tantalizingly well past the end of cooking. The tomato is chopped roughly and added to the frying Scotch bonnet with the onion slices and green peppers, and stirred until the onions are translucent. The sardines are broken up into large pieces with a fork and added to the beaten eggs with a good pinch of salt and a splash of water. The heat is turned down completely, and the mixture is added to the pan. As the eggs cook, the edges are lifted carefully, the pan tilted, and the uncooked eggs directed under the cooked parts to form a thick crust.

I suppose there is something about not being able to have eggs that compels another, more acute level of obsession: staring at them, obsessing about shades of khaki, reading egg recipes that taste fabulous in my head, and collecting egg stories. My favorite was told to me by a friend who, as a child, had to go and live with his grandparents after his parents' marriage broke down. His father was a proud man who did not believe that men should say they are sorry. His mother had another suitor. The matter had gone well past the attempts to pretend all was well. My friend's grandmother was an extraordinary woman. She was willing to embrace other people's children and care for them, but she was famous for her uncompromising views about everything, especially matters of discipline. Many relatives sent their daughters to live with my friend's grandmother, for an unequivocal induction into life by a no-nonsense matriarch. These girls had to learn to keep a home, farm competently, and take care of children. Their parents believed that at home the girls were too comfortable to take instructions to heart.

The grandmother apparently saw through everything—doors, walls, closed lips—and she read minds and bodies too. She could tell by the angle of a woman's bottom whether she was "fornicating" or "contemplating fornication." If you were on your way out of her room and your head caught a cobweb, you would be grounded and made to sit with her the whole day. The web was a sign that if you were allowed out, something bad and irrevocable was going to happen. The grandmother also administered a homemade virginity test to all the girls and young women in the house. That's where the eggs came in.

On the relevant morning the girls would be made to wait outside the testing room, not in a formal queue but in a reluctant mass, apprehensive bodies sitting, standing, leaning, fainting from fear. The apprehension was not unreasonable. In those days mothers told their daughters all manner of stories to try to get them to abstain from sex. If you kiss a boy you immediately become pregnant. If a man sees you naked, you become pregnant. If you see a naked man, if you are fondled, you become pregnant—with twins. Some girls had become pregnant just by having a man brush against them on a busy street. It was dangerously contagious, this pregnancy business.

By the time a young woman had spent long hours on the farm, fried a vat of *gari,* taken turns to cook meals from scratch, and cared for the younger children in the household, sex was possible, desirable, hormonally pertinent, but not a condition that was acted upon. To be sure, there were girls who knew everything and had done everything, but they dared not live in my friend's grandmother's house because they would never pass the test.

The grandmother's instrument of investigation was a small free-range egg. You would have to lie back, hitch up your dress, close your eyes, for goodness' sake, and instinctively clench. You hoped for the best with what little you knew of your body or of rudimentary biology or of the phenomenon of contagious pregnancy. Whether you liked it or not, whether you were willing or not. Whether you thought it was unfair that the boys in the house could do what they liked and fondle whomever, or wondered why pregnancy seemed to be the punishment for sex. If your body reverse-hatched that egg, your life was not going to be worth living. The excuse that your hymen "broke during physical and health education" was never going to fly with this omniscient grandmother. All hell would break loose if the egg passed from the grandmother's hand into that dark part of your anatomy you knew so little about. Before the week ran out your parents would come to get you even if they were coming from Kotangora.

It never happened, though. Not in all the years my friend lived with his grandmother did a girl fail the egg test. The fear of that egg was overwhelming. And afterward you never look at an egg the same way again. The egg is such a ubiquitous object that you are reminded constantly of contagious pregnancies. You reach for warm eggs laid by chickens and you think of the mysterious regions that produced eggs. Of what it is like for a chicken to pass an egg and whether it is the effort that makes them so irate. You do not hold it and feel consoled by its khaki blandness. You do not tear up with longing at the sight of eggs.

Even when your wedding night comes and goes, and you have permission to fondle and be fondled, the sense of shame will remain ingrained. You will wonder about the shape of things, the discrepancy between that which is oval and that which is long and tubelike. You will think of the wages of sin. By then, of course, you will understand that there is no such thing as a Bluetooth pregnancy, and you will feel both ashamed at your own foolishness and angry that you allowed yourself that degree of ingenuousness. When you are bearing your children, you will wonder if this is a good or bad thing. You will wonder if perhaps that is why chickens are so foolish and confused—too much coming and going, too little understanding of the reasons why. You will sleep and imagine yourself turning into a large chicken, but you won't tell anyone because of the shame.

Bean Freaks

FROM *The New Yorker*

THE BEST MEAL of my life, or at least the most memorable, came from a can. I was thirteen at the time and living in France, so that may have had something to do with it. But I credit the beans. My older sisters and I were at a hippie camp in the Alps that summer, not far from the Italian border. My parents had stashed us there while they went home to Oklahoma to check on our house, which they'd rented to some graduate students while my father was on sabbatical. The camp was the cheapest one they could find, and they seemed to have done next to no research before signing us up. My mother just loved the name: Jeunesse du Soleil Levant, Youth of the Rising Sun.

As it turned out, we rarely woke before noon. The camp had promised a vigorous program of crafts, hikes, and team-building games, but the counselors were usually too hungover, or too caught up in their tent-hopping romances, to bother. (On the last day of camp, I found a stack of unopened boxes behind the mess tent; they were filled with modeling clay and watercolor paints.) We spent most afternoons playing cards and plunking guitars, killing time till after dinner, when we'd hike down to the village to drink beer with grenadine and dance to French disco music.

It was paradise, mostly. The exception was the few mornings when our counselors, seized by a spasm of conscience, would roust us from our tents and lead us on forced marches through the mountains, declaring that this was what summer camp was all about. It was on one of those trips, on the shore of a frigid lake, that

I had the meal of my life. I was famished by then and wobbly with fatigue. I'd spent too many days lounging around, and a counselor had stuffed two giant cans of cassoulet in my backpack before we left. French trail mix. When we pried them open for dinner, there were only white beans inside, flecked with salt pork. They had one flavor, one texture, one purpose—to fill my stomach—but that was enough. Hunger is a simple thing, an alarm bell in the brain. Sometimes there's nothing better than shutting it off.

I thought about that meal last spring, when I first met Steve Sando. We were standing at a table heaped with hibiscus flowers, at an outdoor market in the town of Ixmiquilpan, three hours north of Mexico City in the state of Hidalgo. It was a Thursday morning in May, and the stalls were full of women gossiping and picking through produce: corn fungus and cactus paddles, purslane and pickling lime, agave buds and papalo leaf that smelled of mint and gasoline. Sando, who is fifty-eight, ambled among them in a white guayabera shirt, untucked at the waist. He had on loose jeans, tennis shoes, and a bright-red baseball cap that said RANCHO GORDO above the bill. He could hardly have looked more American, yet he fit in perfectly somehow. He was built like a giant bean.

That may seem too easy, beans being Sando's business. But people are often shaped by their obsessions, and in Sando's case the similarities are hard to miss. His body is mostly torso, his skin both ruddy and tanned, like a pinto. He makes a colorful first impression, gets a little starchy if you crowd him, then slowly softens up. Fifteen years ago, when Sando founded Rancho Gordo, he had no food-retailing or farming experience. Now he's the country's largest retailer of heirloom beans and a minor celebrity in the culinary world. He's a side dish who's become a staple.

"This to me . . . it just makes me so happy," he said. He was holding a bag of rayado chiles smoked over an oak fire. He stuck his nose deep inside and inhaled. Weeks later, in my pantry at home, a jar of these chiles would abruptly blossom with black moths, hatched from eggs embedded in their flesh. But Sando was just thinking how great they'd be with a mess of beans. We passed tables of epazote, an herb said to prevent flatulence, and bowls of a greenish gray soil with a vaguely vegetal smell. "Pond scum from Lake Texcoco," Sando said. "We use it to soften beans." To Sando, everything in Mexico seems to connect to beans, and through them to the rest of world cuisine. When he's at home, in Napa, California, he sometimes gives talks at local elementary schools. He starts by asking the kids where pizza comes from.

"Italy!"

"*Wrong*. Mexico! That's where tomatoes are from. What about chocolate?"

"Switzerland!"

"Nope. Mexico! That's where cocoa beans are from. How about vanilla?"

"Mexico?"

"That's right! And chiles, corn, and squash too." Many of the staples of European and Asian cooking came from Mesoamerica via the Spanish, he explains. It's called the Columbian Exchange, but it wasn't much of a trade for the Mesoamericans. They got turnips, barley, and spinach.

Sando is a rather sheepish addition to that history. He's uneasy about import regulations, fretful of cultural appropriation, and well aware of his fumbling grasp of Mexican custom. "I'm not the Indiana Jones of beans," he told me. "I'm the Don Quixote." Every year he takes one or two trips to Mexico to look for rare varieties and farmers who might grow them for him. He was in Ixmiquilpan to search for an especially elusive quarry: Flor de Durazno, the Flower of the Peach. This was a dainty pinkish brown bean of uncommon taste and velvety texture, grown in Hidalgo. Sando had seen it once in his life, in a package sent to his office by a farmer not far from this market. He was hoping to buy 2,000 pounds for his Bean Club.

I happen to be a member of the Bean Club, though I'm a little reluctant to admit it. Not that it isn't a pretty exclusive thing. Anyone can buy beans from Rancho Gordo, but the Bean Club—which sends members six rare varieties and a few other oddments, like blue hominy, every three months—closed its rolls last year. Sando couldn't keep up with demand. Still, admitting that you're obsessed with beans is a little like saying you collect decorative plates. It marks your taste as untrustworthy. I've seen the reaction often enough in my family: the eye roll and stifled cough, the muttered aside as I show yet another guest the wonders of my well-lit and cleverly organized bean closet. As my daughter Evangeline put it one night, a bit melodramatically, when I served beans for the third time in a week, "Lord, why couldn't it have been bacon or chocolate?"

Beans are the middle child of American cooking, the food we forget we love. Back in Oklahoma, after my father's sabbatical, they always seemed to be covered in cheese, coated in ketchup and molasses, or tossed into a three-bean salad like so many protein pellets. The closest I came to the cassoulet was the Sea Island Red Peas that I had in Charleston one spring thirty years later. They were an heirloom variety, reintroduced by the food historian Glenn Roberts at Anson Mills—potent little field peas possessed of an unreasonably rich brown broth. But Anson Mills had only the one variety to offer, along with some Purple Cape beans from time to time. Then I found Rancho Gordo.

The beans on Sando's site look like gems in a jewelry case: crimson, violet, black, and gold; stippled, striped, and swirled. They bear evocative names—Eye of the Goat, Yellow Indian Woman—and range in size from tiny Pinquitos to Royal Coronas the size of a baby's ear. There is, admittedly, some risk of false advertising. Once the beans have cooked, the colors run and fade, leaving a soupy pot of brownish seeds. The inky depth of a black bean, or the grassiness of a flageolet, is easy to taste. But most varieties aren't nearly as distinct as their bright costumes portend. Cooking beans is like going to see clowns and sword swallowers at a circus, only to find them all sitting inside the tent playing canasta. "It's God's little joke," Sando told me.

Sando knows how it is to have a divided nature. How a flashy exterior can conceal a modest but hearty interior. As a boy growing up in Sausalito in the early seventies, he had his share of social handicaps. He was gay in an era of reflexive homophobia, overweight long before the body-positive movement, and, as a child of divorced parents, always shuttling between homes and schools. He felt both anonymous and glaringly conspicuous. "I was so tired of being the fat new kid," he told me. "I remember in sixth grade, just after my parents divorced, I sat down next to this girl in summer school, and I heard her say, 'Well, I guess we have a fat fag on our hands.' It was like I could hear the violins going backward." His father, a former Disney animator who'd worked on *101 Dalmatians*, wished him sleeker and more successful; his mother, a nurse, wished him a little more conventional. When he first told them that he was gay, at eighteen, "they let it be known that this was not

okay," Sando recalls. "But they came around. My father marched in
the gay pride parade a few years later."

In his late teens Sando lost weight and found his crowd, learned
to improvise on the piano, and discovered, to his great surprise,
that he'd become rather good-looking. "What we call a twink now,"
he says. Although he never found a true, long-term partner, he
married a friend of a friend in his late thirties and had two boys
with her, now nineteen and sixteen. "I'd had every lesbian on the
planet ask me for sperm," he says. "But there was a side of me that
said, 'I can't do this as a passive bystander.'" They raised the boys
in adjacent houses for a few years, then divorced. "*There's* a sitcom
waiting to happen," he says. But he tells the story flatly, without
grievance or irony, as if giving a deposition. "The truth is that your
sexual identity is just about the least interesting thing about you,"
he says. "Do you play an instrument? That would be interesting."

Sando now lives with his younger son in the hills above Napa
Valley, in a former Seventh-Day Adventist church that he's decorated with Mexican colonial art and religious icons. (The icons
seem to be working. A few weeks after I visited, when wildfires
ripped through Northern California, Sando sent me a video of his
property: the house was untouched, the trees around it burned to
charcoal and ash.) When he's at ease, he can be loose and self-dep-
recating, with a mildly sardonic wit. But he's never quite lost his
childhood wariness. His default mode is a kind of prickly joviality,
a gregarious misanthropy. He likes people just enough to spend
a lot of time with them, at which point he realizes that on second
thought, he'd rather be alone.

In the years between high school and having children, Sando
drifted between gainful and fanciful employment. He took a few
courses at San Francisco State and at the College of Marin, spent
six months backpacking through India, moved to Santa Fe, then
London, then to San Francisco again, where he landed a job with
Esprit in 1982. The company was in its heyday, selling bright-col-
ored clothes for the notionally idealistic. Sando started out answer-
ing phones and was soon overseeing multimillion-dollar accounts.
He was a natural salesman, he found, with a gift for turning that
striped blouse with pearl buttons into a story that buyers wanted
to hear. Esprit's hip corporate culture—its non-hierarchical of-
fices and upward mobility, free Italian lessons and half-price op-
era tickets—left a mark on him, he says. But what really stuck was

the shrewd branding. The way a luxurious dress could cast a halo over the rest of the line, so that customers felt good getting what they really wanted: the rainbow T-shirt. "They wanted it because the fashion line made them want it," he says.

Sando left for Milan after five years, thinking that he'd eventually take a job in Esprit's Italian office. Instead he wrote to a local radio station offering to host an hour-long jazz show, and to his shock, the station agreed. The show, which he called *Mr. Lucky,* mixed ambient cocktail sounds with classics from Frank Sinatra and Sarah Vaughan ("My listeners pronounced it 'Vo-gon'"). It developed a following but paid next to nothing, and a year later Sando was back in San Francisco, broke. There followed a string of near-misses and half-successes: music reviewing, music licensing, a zine, a website, a website-designing business—the dot-com hopscotch of the late nineties. "Always hand to mouth, always just about to make it," as he puts it. His mother's family was well off, and in the back of his mind Sando had long assumed that if nothing else worked, an inheritance might bail him out. But his grandmother willed everything to his stepgrandfather, who willed everything to his nurse. "I was turning forty by then, and I thought, Okay, you're a major fuckup," Sando says. "Just start a garden and get a job at Target."

The gardening, at least, was a success. In 2000, Sando moved to a house outside Napa, on two and a half acres of land. He planted heirloom Mexican tomatoes at first, then some rare bean varieties he'd found in seed catalogs, and was soon overwhelmed with produce. "I thought I had a gift," he told me. "But really it was Napa. Anything can grow in Napa." When the farmers' market in town wouldn't have him, he settled for the scruffier one in Yountville, nine miles to the north. But sales were slow. The beans were pretty enough, but a little intimidating: pebbles somehow to be made edible. Shoppers were always mistaking them for candied nuts. "They weren't part of the standard repertoire," Sando says. "People would ask, 'What's your best bean?' And the subtext was 'Beans are bad. Which is the least bad?'" Most of the time he'd suggest Good Mother Stallards—gorgeous purple-and-red speckled beans that make a rich broth. But they'd usually shake their heads: "Oh, no, I don't like dark beans."

Then one day, in 2003, Thomas Keller came by. His restaurant, the French Laundry, which would later earn three Michelin stars, happened to be in Yountville. "I remember he had probably a dozen different beans on the table," Keller told me recently. "To get something that freshly dried was a revelation." The bean that caught Keller's eye was a greenish yellow thing with a red-rimmed eye, like a soybean with a hangover. Called the Vallarta, it was on the verge of extinction when Sando found it, but it had a dense, fudgy texture and gave a good broth. "Steve had taken something that used to be just a dried bean and raised it to a new level, where the flavor was really intense and it cooked so much more consistently," Keller said. Within a month it was a staple of the French Laundry. Within a year every chef in California seemed to be serving beans.

Sando had got it all wrong. He'd been selling beans as a health food, a sop for the meatless. He'd even named his company with the intent of pitching a bean-based diet: Rancho Gordo, Fat Ranch. But all that earnest salesmanship had just made beans seem unappetizing. "People don't buy moral food," Sando told me. "They think they do, but they don't. It's all about the flavor." It was another version of the halo effect he'd seen at Esprit: "You start with the chefs and you work your way down."

The real problem was supply, not demand. Sando had reached the limits of his bean-farming abilities. "I'm very good at the early stages," he says. "I'm like, Oh, yeah, I've controlled nature. She's my bitch. But by August I'm thinking, Please, let this be over." Not long after Keller's visit, Sando began looking for a farmer. He tried hiring some wonky young guys with "groovy ag ideas," but their results were as unreliable as his. He approached a few industrial growers, but they said his beans weren't worth the bother. Heirlooms were too finicky, the yields too low, the orders too small—10,000 pounds from farmers accustomed to growing 2 million. Sando's prices could more than make up for all that: his beans retail for $6 a pound, about three times the cost of ordinary varieties. But to cover the perceived risk he still had to guarantee some contracts. The farmer got paid even if a crop failed. Finally, in 2012, Sando handed the crop management over to James Schrupp, an agronomist and former commodities trader who's married to the food writer Georgeanne Brennan. Most of Schrupp's growers are in California's San Joaquin and Sacramento Valleys and in Washington's Columbia Basin, though Royal Coronas are grown in Poland. "Jim speaks farmer, which turns out to be a universal language," Sando told me.

Rancho Gordo now sells half a million pounds of beans a y
The chefs have been followed by other celebrities—bold figu
like Andy Richter and Emilio Estevez, unafraid of legumes—an
then by ordinary customers. Sando's beans have sent their tendrils
into the *Saveur* 100 and *O, the Oprah Magazine,* and he has published
four cookbooks. A few years ago he was looking through a list of
orders on his computer when he found one from Marcella Hazan,
the doyenne of Italian cuisine in the United States. He sent her an
inscribed copy of his first cookbook, *Heirloom Beans,* published in
2008, and they struck up a correspondence. Soon he had tracked
down Hazan's favorite bean: the Sorana, a type of cannellini that
grows along the Pescia River in Tuscany. This is a bean so tender,
with a skin so vanishingly thin, that Rossini once accepted several
pounds in exchange for correcting another composer's score.
Sando found a farmer to grow it in California and renamed it the
Marcella. When the *Times* ran a piece about it two years ago, after
it went on sale at Rancho Gordo, the orders crashed the website.

"This is how all our bean adventures go," Sando said. *"Mercado,
iglesia, comida, siesta."* Market, church, food, sleep. We were sitting
in the cool confines of San Miguel Arcángel, the coral-colored
church that looms over Ixmiquilpan. We'd eaten a great deal of
mutton *barbacoa* at the market, then spent an hour exploring the
deserted sixteenth-century convent next door. I was ready for the
siesta. Sando, though, wanted to see the sanctuary first. He loved
these old colonial buildings, with their bare stone cells and dusky
chapels, their peeling saints and tin retables crimped with wonder
and pain. But like so much in Mexico, they left him discomfited,
unsure of his role. Was he a tourist? An amateur art collector? A
fair-trade emissary who'd volunteered for Cesar Chavez while still
in high school? Or was he just "the gringo elephant in the room"?
Ixmiquilpan was one of his favorite towns in Mexico, but it didn't
always ingratiate itself with outsiders. Its name means "place where
the pigweed cuts like knives." In 1548, when Augustinian friars arrived to convert the local Otomi, they used forced labor to build
this church. The results may not have been what they expected. All
around us in the sanctuary, crumbling frescoes reached up into the
nave: centaurs and griffins, eagle knights and coyote warriors. The
Otomi hadn't just repurposed Christian imagery; they'd replaced
it with their own. Instead of angels and saints, there were soldiers

beheading one another; instead of Madonnas and Christs, there were pregnant women sprouting from acanthus buds. Sando shook his head: "Every time I come to Mexico, I feel like I know less than I did before."

Next to him on the pew, Yunuén Carrillo Quiroz gazed up at the altar with a look of mingled pride and disquiet. She and her husband, Gabriel Cortés García, manage all of Rancho Gordo's operations in Mexico. They are Sando's fixers, farm managers, production coordinators, and fellow bean researchers. Quiroz, forty-two, is from Mexico City, the daughter of a logistics supervisor at Ford; García, thirty-nine, is from a village near Ixmiquilpan, the eldest son of a social worker. Quiroz is the urban sophisticate, bright and articulate, with a round laughing face and connections with the best restaurants in Mexico City. García is the savvy local, quiet and watchful, with a broad-shouldered frame and a good head for numbers. "It took the right gringo and the right Mexicans to make this happen," Sando said.

And yet the three of them straddled two cultures as uneasily as the Otomi. The frescoes were ostensibly about the tribe's battles against the Chichimecas to the north, but Quiroz saw a different message. "They're a call to war for all indigenous people," she said. "Even the eagle above the altar is wearing a native headdress. When Christ's blood is served at communion, it's a kind of blood sacrifice." Quiroz told me the story of La Malinche, the infamous native woman who served as Cortés's translator and adviser during the conquest. As Rancho Gordo has expanded its Mexican operations, some chefs in Mexico City have accused Quiroz of being a culinary La Malinche. "They say, 'Why are you telling him about these beans?'" Sando said. "'Why didn't you tell us first?' Well, the beans were there all along."

"It's true that a lot of the really good Mexican products get exported," the chef Enrique Olvera told me. "But if you keep some here and export the rest, there's no problem. Food migrates." Olvera is the owner of Pujol, in Mexico City, which is often cited as one of the best restaurants in the world, and of Cosme and Atla, in New York. He met Quiroz ten years ago and has been a Rancho Gordo customer ever since. The Columbian Exchange is less lopsided than it used to be, he pointed out. Mexican cooks use cilantro and cheese from Asia and Europe. Why not share their beans?

Mexico is the cradle of the common bean. It's where *Phaseolus vulgaris* first evolved, 2 million years ago, and it still has the greatest bean diversity in the world. "I always had a fantasy of bringing beans from here," Sando told me. But when he first came to Mexico, in 2001, he had no import-export experience, no real connections. Although he spoke a little Spanish, he'd never mastered the accent and had a disconcerting habit of mixing in Italian words. ("It's like music, really," he says.) Worse still, he had no idea where to find the best varieties. He kept getting wrong-footed. At one point, at a market in Mexico City, he came upon a basket of beans as bright and various as a designer's color wheel. *Revuelto,* the seller called them. It was only later, after Sando had bought several pounds, that he realized that these weren't some magical rainbow-colored variety; they were random beans tossed together. *Revuelto* means "scrambled."

When Sando did manage to locate a bean that he wanted to grow in the United States, the locals wouldn't sell it to him. "They were appalled," he told me. "They were like, 'Seeds are life.'" Why would they give their greatest asset away? Sando asked if they could grow the beans locally, then export them to the United States. But that still made no sense to them. For decades agronomists had been telling Mexican farmers to get with the program, to grow the latest high-yielding varieties in order to compete with China and Peru. Now here was this strange, excitable American saying he didn't like modern beans. He'd much rather have the ones their grandparents grew. "They were incredulous," Sando says. He was paying them to regress.

Sando met Quiroz and García in 2008. A year earlier the couple had started exporting dried prickly pear cactus fruit and other local specialties from Hidalgo. They were young, childless (they now have a six-year-old daughter, Yunuéncita), and as hungry to explore their country as Sando was. A pattern was established: Sando would fly down and they'd pile into a truck with a few bags. Then they'd set off for Michoacán, Oaxaca, Veracruz, the Yucatán—anywhere with a great bean-cooking tradition. Which seemed to be everywhere. They'd start in the village markets, then zero in on the older ladies at the periphery, in the indigenous section, with small sacks of produce from their gardens. If they found an interesting bean, García would talk to the farmers, Quiroz would talk to the women, and Sando would stay out of the way till the deal was done. "We try not to irritate people," Quiroz says.

Everywhere they went, they found new beans. Some were spectacular, like the delicate, rose-colored Lila that grew in Morelos, in the shadow of an active volcano. Others never caught on, like the Ron bean from the Yucatán, with its thick ochre skin and bland flesh, or the Veronico, from the town of Tecozautla, which looked like a pine nut but tasted like a cowpea. There were always new varieties to take their place, though. "It was like Ali Baba," Quiroz told me. "We discovered an explosion of beans."

Late one morning at the hacienda where García grew up, in the thorn- and blossom-covered hills southwest of Ixmiquilpan, Sando made me a pot of beans. The hacienda has an enormous wood-fired stove in the center of the kitchen, with seven burners of volcanic stone. When the building was a Jesuit monastery, in the eighteenth century, the stove was used to feed the brethren and their servants. After the Spanish Crown evicted the Jesuits from Mexico, in 1767, the hacienda was bought by wealthy silver miners. While the kitchen served them and their guests, ranks of campesinos grew crops, tended cattle, and fermented pulque on the surrounding land. When the revolution came, the hacienda was looted, its chapel burned, and its water lines shattered. What was left was half mansion and half ruin, still shunned by the local villagers. A precinct of ghosts.

The stove is rarely used now. García's mother and her best friend, Lupe, whose family bought the hacienda in the 1930s, prefer the gas range. Both women are exceptional cooks in the elaborate Mexican home style. In the days when I was there, they laid out dozens of dishes in the hacienda's formal dining room: black-bean rolls with sardines; chilaquiles with tomatillos and Oaxacan cheese; slender local avocados with edible, anise-flavored skin; and sweet, buttery slices of mamey, the fruit of a tropical evergreen tree. Lupe's cow's-foot soup was made with pieces of stomach, Puya chiles, and dried prickly pear cactus fruit. It had a deeply funky flavor and a mucilaginous texture that was off-putting at first—it was like sipping a whole cow—then weirdly addictive. But the beans were different. The beans were dead simple.

Sando and Lupe began by building a fire on the covered porch that encircled the hacienda's courtyard. She balanced a slender clay pot above the coals, then Sando poured in some olive oil and dropped in a handful of chopped onion. When they'd cooked awhile, he put in a few cups of water and a bowl of Moro beans, speckled black and gray like a starling's belly. He added two whole cloves of garlic, a few crystals of Mixtecan salt, which contains natural softeners, and a bay leaf. Then Lupe set a small bowl of water on the pot, to serve as a lid and to replenish the beans, and left it to simmer.

Easy enough, yet everything they'd done was debatable. Lupe would have used lard instead of olive oil and raw instead of sautéed onion. She preferred avocado leaves to bay, and epazote to the oregano that Sando used. And those were just matters of taste. The thornier debates were technical. Should beans be soaked? (Yes, most cookbooks say, but that's only because store-bought beans are often years old.) When should they be salted? (After they're cooked, most recipes insist; but tests have shown that soaking and cooking beans in salt water both plumps them up and helps them hold their shape.) How should they be cooked? (Simmering is the rule, but Sando recommends a brief hard boil first, "to let them know you're the boss.") Is pressure cooking allowed? (The French Laundry swears by it; Sando says it kills the broth.) The simpler the food, the more every variable counts.

Watching Sando and Lupe cook, I realized what I'd been doing wrong. I'd been trying so hard to make my family love beans that my dishes had got more and more complicated, like the ones in Oklahoma. I'd added bacon, brown sugar, kielbasa, and southern ham, whole heads of garlic and bunches of sage; I'd made minestrone, *pasta e fagioli,* and Brazilian feijoada. Good recipes, but poor psychology. Instead of showcasing the beans, I'd camouflaged them, turned them into a suspect food—an element to be rooted out, like the spinach that parents hide in pizza. "I hate recipes," Sando said. "I always tell people to cook beans simply, and they always say, 'Oh, I did. I just used a ham hock and chicken stock.' Well, in that case you might as well use commercial pintos."

The best staples make a virtue of blandness. They quiet the mind. The nuttiness in rice, the mineral in a potato, the hint of chocolate in a Rio Zape bean are all the better for being barely there. They make your senses reach out to them. (That's why turnips, sweet and faintly bitter, don't quite cut it; they have too much going on.) The conundrum, for a seller of heirloom beans, is that those qualities are the opposite of what he's advertising. To get people to pay three times the cost of store-bought beans, Sando needs to convince them that his are dramatically different. That canned beans are a travesty by comparison. Yet to expect a burst of flavor from a Moro is to miss the point.

Sando fished a few beans from the pot with a wooden spoon. He blew on them to see if their skin split and curled back—the sign that they were done—then gave them to me. They tasted like a cross between black beans and pintos, with just a trace of the oregano. Had I made them at home, I would have added more salt. Maybe some cumin. And then maybe some cilantro and a squeeze of lime. But they turned out to be just right as they were: the perfect foil for the cow's-foot soup. "There's something miraculous about turning this rock into something that tastes good," Sando said.

Sando likes to tell a story about a field trial at the University of California, Davis, a few years ago. The school's agronomists had laid out test plots of hybrid beans bred for every possible attribute: shelf life, yield, insect resistance, disease resistance. They scanned the fields digitally with drones, then counted the percentage of green pixels to quantify each variety's growth. They used infrared cameras to show how much water the leaves were retaining—an indication of heat and drought resistance. But when Sando asked about taste, the agronomists drew a blank. They hadn't tested for that.

To Sando, this was unforgivable. But how different are heirloom beans, really? How much do Lupe's Moros owe to the cook and the setting—to the skylit dining room and the green Oaxacan pottery, the colonial architecture and the swallows in the fig trees—and how much to their untampered genes? Sando's chief counterpart in this debate is Paul Gepts, a professor of plant sciences at Davis. Gepts is a small Belgian man of seemingly indeterminate age (he is sixty-four), with a bottlebrush mustache and bespectacled eyes that glint with suppressed humor. Physically, he's a smaller, paler version of Sando—the navy bean to the other man's lima. When I asked Gepts if beans were his primary focus, he smiled and murmured, "I am Mr. Bean." The following week he gave the keynote address at the International Bean Conference in Brazil.

Gepts takes a fatherly pride in his subjects. On the bookcase in his office, jars of beans sit side by side with pictures of his son. He keeps an eye on Rancho Gordo's website, he told me, to see which beans are selling and to intervene in the forums sometimes, to correct an especially wrongheaded post. But he doesn't segregate beans as Sando does—into heirloom and industrial, authentic and engineered varieties. To Gepts, their entire history is a genetic experiment. His research has shown that beans were domesticated twice: in Mesoamerica, where their wild forebears evolved, and in the Andes. Mesoamerican beans are smaller and rounder, Andean beans more kidney-shaped. Mesoamerican varieties tend be more prolific, Andean varieties more colorful. Pinto, navy, and black beans are Mesoamerican. Cranberry, cannellini, and large lima beans are Andean. "I can see just by looking at them which ones are which," Gepts said.

To a bean breeder, the difference is more than academic. Mesoamerican and Andean beans have different yields and tolerances; they get different diseases and thrive in different climates. Crossbreed them one way and you can consolidate their best traits in a single bean; crossbreed them in another way and you may get a "lethal line" that withers on the vine. (Mesoamerican and Andean beans tend not to cross well.) Building better beans is more than just a commercial enterprise, Gepts says. It's essential to feeding the world. In some African countries, beans represent almost half of the protein that people eat, and they're sometimes smuggled across borders to meet demand.

Later that day Gepts drove me out to the university's experimental farm, where some new breeds were being tested for drought resistance. Eight bean varieties had been crossed with one another for three generations, producing 960 genetic lines, each marked by a little stick in the dirt. Half the plots were well watered and green; the other half were parched and yellow. Gepts stepped over to a row of scraggly-looking tepary beans and cracked open a pod. "This is the bean that can most beat the drought," he said, pointing to the hard black seeds inside. "The question is, why don't people eat them?"

The answer seems obvious to Sando. "Have you tasted those beans?" he asked me later. "Blech!" But Gepts says it's not that simple. Four years ago he and some colleagues conducted a taste test of garbanzo beans. They asked a panel of ten plant breeders, seed brokers, food technicians, and other professionals to rate sixteen varieties according to seven criteria: size, flavor, texture, color, consistency, wholeness, and skin condition. The only things they couldn't agree on were flavor and texture. The loss of flavor to industrial farming can be "an issue," Gepts admitted. But it's hard to quantify. Unlike tomatoes, say, which are picked green and bred tough for transport, beans can ripen on the vine and stay sturdy once dried. A mealy pink tomato tastes nothing like the crimson fruit at a farmers' market. A store-bought bean still tastes like a bean.

Sando says that he can easily tell the differences among varieties —some black beans are creamy, for instance, others more starchy or meaty—not to mention the difference between freshly dried beans like his and those that have languished on a supermarket shelf. "And if your point of reference is the canned kidney bean at a salad bar, I totally understand if you hate beans," he said. The chef Enrique Olvera goes further. A bean grown in an industrial field tastes nothing like the same bean grown at a small farm where crops are rotated, he says. Yet those differences may have little to do with how much we like a bean. When I asked chefs about their favorite bean dishes, they invariably went back to their childhood. Olvera talked about the black beans that his grandmother cooked with a little lime, amachito pepper, and Mexican coriander. David Breeden, the chef de cuisine at the French Laundry, recalled the pinto beans and corn bread that his mother made in eastern Tennessee. (The version that he served me at the restaurant was the single best thing in a meal of small astonishments.) Even Thomas Keller, a famously fastidious cook, waxed nostalgic about the white-bean soup that his mother used to make. "She would just take some canned beans and chicken stock and purée them," he told me. "It didn't require a lot of attention, because the beans didn't have a lot of integrity, but it made this wonderful, velvety soup."

Bean-eaters are creatures of habit. "It's very marked," Gepts said. "In Colombia they like big red beans. In Venezuela they like small black beans. It's all about which beans you grew up with." For a breeder, that means the one trait you can't mess with is appearance. "With wheat, the husks may look different or the seeds may be different shapes, but they'll get ground into flour eventually," Gepts said. "That's not true with beans." He stepped over to another row of plants and snapped open a pod. "Not white enough," he said. Then he reached across to the next row. These plants were especially lush, and their seeds were among the most beautiful I'd seen: glossy and olive-brown, with a shimmering stripe like a tiger's-eye gem. Gepts shook his head. "It's not a commercial plant," he said, tossing a pod into the weeds. "People want beans to look the way they've always looked."

The Flower of the Peach was like no bean Sando had ever seen. This made it irresistible to him—"I'm a whore," he told me. "My favorite bean is always the last one I ate"—but not necessarily to his customers. For all his efforts on behalf of Mexican beans, three-quarters of his sales are still for European varieties. His top sellers are Royal Coronas, followed by cassoulet, flageolet, cranberry, and Marcella beans. "There are total Mexican-bean addicts, but a lot of people will never buy them," he said as we drove to meet the Flor de Durazno farmers. "Which irritates me. They're twenty-five percent of my sales but forty percent of my time."

If anything can grow in Napa, very little seems to grow in most of Hidalgo. It's Mexican cowboy country, though cattle seem to like it no better than crops do. In the small towns between ranches, lanky men in straw hats lean in shady doorways, waiting for their feed orders to be filled, their boots to be reheeled. It's a landscape of relentless sun and little water, where the fields look like empty lots scattered with gravel. In Napa, the fog rolls in from the Pacific every morning to wet the plants, then parts obligingly for the sun in the afternoon. In the San Joaquin Valley, beans are harvested by a machine called Big Bertha, which can pick and thresh 50,000 pounds a day. In Hidalgo, the harvests are done mostly by hand. When I asked one farmer if it was hard to plant in such rocky soil, he said, "No, no, we like the rocks. We pile them around the seedlings to shield them from the sun."

Sando's growers lived in a village north of Ixmiquilpan, past a small school for indigenous Nahuatl-speakers, on a dirt road with goats scampering about. The compound was hidden behind a tall palisade of cactus and purple bougainvillea. When we arrived, three men in jeans and denim work shirts came out to greet us: a father, son, and uncle, with a few small boys peeking from behind them. They'd stretched a blue plastic tarp above a picnic table in the courtyard, and their wives and daughters were setting out charro beans and fresh tortillas. There followed a good deal of halting, touchingly formal talk about harvests and the maddening

intermittence of rain. The toughest part of working with Mexican
farmers, Sando had told me, is their circumspection. "They're so
polite, and we're used to being so direct," he said. "If my book-
keeper forgets to pay for a crop, the farmer might say, 'It's been
really hard lately. We've been eating a lot of cactus.' It's only after
a while that I'll realize, 'Oh, you mean you didn't get the check!'"

Rancho Gordo pays its Mexican farmers anywhere from 5 to 30
percent above the market rate, Quiroz says. But when I asked the
farmers about their prices and yields for the Flor de Durazno, an
awkward, side-glancing silence ensued. "It's universal among farmers," Sando interjected. "Yield is connected to self-worth." García
huddled with the men for a moment, then whispered something to
Quiroz, who came over to us. "Would you mind if we all had a beer
together? Gabriel says they're getting nervous."

These were tentative, fragile relationships, Sando told me later,
with men who'd been screwed over again and again by buyers. The
best way to keep their trust was to bring money year after year and
not to ask too many questions. "At some point it'll be nice to look
back and say we helped them pave their roads, but we're not there
yet," he said. "We're still in the middle of this. They're not stable,
we're not stable. And it's been ten years. So it's the farmer's job to
get as much as he can, and I need to get the price as low as I can.
We both need to win." He shrugged. "I'm not a saint. I'm here to
make a profit. I don't want to save the world with beans."

After the jugs had been emptied and the plates cleared, the farmers clapped García on the back and climbed into a pickup truck.
Aside from a small cup of peach-colored beans that they'd passed
round, there had been no sign of Sando's order. We followed the
farmers out to a small storage shed on the outskirts of the village,
and they motioned for us to join them. Inside, ten bulging nylon
bags stood stacked in a corner, each filled with 200 pounds of Flor
de Durazno beans. They'd been there all along.

Driving back to the hacienda that afternoon with Quiroz and
García, Sando seemed, for just a moment, content. His sales were
growing by a steady 15 to 20 percent a year. The Bean Club had
a waiting list of more than five hundred, and he was thinking of
reopening it in the spring. (When he launched a Facebook group
for the club last August, it was flooded with recipes and pictures.
Sample comment: "HOLY CRAP, these beans were good.") Yet

Sando still mistrusted his success. "My father always said, 'If you're coasting, you're going downhill.'"

These bean adventures were getting harder to organize, he said. In the early years, the three of them could travel wherever they wanted. The goal was just to get lost. Now drug violence had reached such a pitch—nearly 30,000 murders in 2017, higher even than at the peak of Mexico's drug wars, in 2011—that entire states were off-limits. "Parts of Michoacán aren't safe at all," Sando said. "Same thing with Veracruz. I have friends in Puebla, but for the first time I don't feel comfortable going there at night." Two years earlier, on their way to an indigenous sugar cooperative in San Luis Potosí, they'd been pinned down for four hours by federal agents, who were pursuing some narcos ahead. More recently, the skulls of more than 250 people, probably victims of drug cartels, had been found in a mass grave in Veracruz, near a house the trio used to rent. The last time they stayed there, Sando said, the electricity went out inexplicably one night. "And I thought, Oh, this is how I die."

Perhaps the wiser move was to pare down Rancho Gordo's offerings, focus on what sold best. "New strategy!" Sando said. "Just please the bean freaks." Yet he kept dreaming of new varieties: Icatone white beans from the Tarahumara peoples in Chihuahua, or pearl-gray Frijolon de Zimatlán from Oaxaca, or, best of all, the Rosa de Castilla from Michoacán. "It's my Moby Dick," he said. "Just to look at those beans makes my knees buckle. And they're absolutely delicious—velvety but light, with a great bean broth." The narcos were a problem, true. But García might be able to source the beans through an avocado grower he knew, or a local restaurant owner. Or maybe they should go to the city of Juchitán, on the Pacific Coast, where some Zapotecan men identify as a third gender, known as *muxe*, and dress and behave like women. They have a four-day festival every November, called La Vela de las Auténticas Intrépidas Buscadoras del Peligro, or the Vigil of the Authentic, Intrepid Danger-Seekers. Sando grinned. "And they have great beans!"

A few months later, back in Brooklyn, a small box arrived on my doorstep. The label bore the Rancho Gordo logo, with a Mexican starlet licking her lips. I found the usual Bean Club bounty inside: one-pound bags of Alubia Blanca and Domingo Rojo, Yellow Indian Woman, and, buried at the bottom, the Flor de Durazno. I cooked them simply, as Sando and Lupe had taught me—though I made an ancho chile salsa on the side, just in case. When I served them later, Evangeline glanced down at her bowl with a familiar look of resignation. She took one bite, then another, then turned to me with her eyebrows slightly raised. "They're really delicious," she said. "For beans."

Salty Tooth

FROM *The New York Times Magazine*

IN JANUARY 1940, in the pages of this very magazine, a correspondent by the excellent name of Hudson Strode published a piece with the headline "Sisu: A Word That Explains Finland." A Finnish concept that's tricky to translate into English with any real precision, *sisu* represents somethin like a deep well of inner fortitude. The Wikipedia entry includes links to *stiff upper lip, cojones,* and *chutzpah,* but none of those phrases or words quite capture it. "A special kind of strong will" is the definition Strode goes with, something drawn upon by the stoic in order to persevere in the face of extreme adversity—say, winter, if you live in Lapland.

At one point in the article, Strode visits a Finnish town near the Russian border and meets the local sheriff. For sentimental reasons, this sheriff carries around a dagger, which he hands to Strode. Apparently the previous owner used the blade to fend off six attackers. "They fought for an hour," the sheriff says. "He cut the six to pieces. I saw the finish of the fight—it was a glorious display of *sisu.*" Strode doesn't record his own response, but he seems impressed. The sheriff slips the knife back into its leather holster and gazes to the east. "We shall have need of *sisu,*" he observes gravely, "to face what may come shortly."

Reading about Strode's journey—which took him to Finland at the start of World War II, only months before the Soviet invasion—I thought about my own rapidly approaching trip to the same country, for the same magazine, seventy-nine years later. I smiled at the pleasing symmetry. Granted, my surname does not double as an active verb, not even in Italian. Also, I was going to Finland

to report an article on salty licorice. But otherwise our tasks were
not dissimilar. Strode had introduced his readers to a word that
explained a distant country and its underlying values. I would try to
do the same, only with a really weird flavor of candy.

There would be need of *sisu* to face what might come shortly.

Throughout much of the world, licorice remains one of our most
divisive confections. Hervé This, one of the food scientists who
coined the term *molecular gastronomy*, likes to use licorice to attack the notion that humans possess four basic tastes. You might
reflexively think of licorice as sweet, but it's not, really, nor is it
salty, sour, or bitter. (Or umami, for that matter, This adds.) The
confounding nature of licorice's flavor has given rise to a sharp
partisanship. Licorice candy has been compared, astutely, to the
Grateful Dead, by none other than the Grateful Dead singer Jerry
Garcia, who allowed in an interview, "Our audience is like people
who like licorice. Not everybody likes licorice, but the people who
like licorice *really* like licorice."

To extend Garcia's simile, albeit imperfectly, that would make
salty liquorice — *salmiakki* in Finland, where they consume the most
potent flavors — the candy equivalent of a forty-seven-minute version of "Dark Star." Meaning, for superfans only.

With *salmiakki*, that fan base is clustered almost entirely in
northern Europe, in what Jukka Annala, the author of a book on
salmiakki and the founder and president of the Finnish Salty Licorice Association, refers to as the seven "salty-licorice countries":
Sweden, Norway, Denmark, Iceland, Finland, the Netherlands, and
Germany (in its north). I should explain here that if you read *salty
licorice* and think, "Well, I enjoy a sea-salt chocolate chip cookie;
how bad could this stuff be?" the salt used in *salmiakki* is not sea
salt or even iodized table salt but ammonium chloride — *sal ammo-
niacum* in Latin, *salmiac* in English — an astringent, extremely bitter
chemical compound formed, like all salts, by mixing a base and an
acid, which in the case of salmiac are ammonia and either hydro-
choloric acid or hydrogen chloride.

At this point you might wonder, "How is this different from the
deeply unpleasant sour candies my own beloved children torture
themselves with?" The thing is, in salty-licorice countries, *salmiakki* is not some niche product marketed exclusively at kids. It's
a respectable treat option for all ages and demographics. In Hel-

sinki, I scouted at least a dozen convenience stores and groceries, and every candy section therein contained at least one full display rack, sometimes several, dedicated exclusively to *salmiakki*. Certain brands packaged themselves like breath mints, in stylish cardboard packs, to appeal directly to adults. Your classic Finnish *salmiakki* comes in the shape of a black diamond, but you can also find salty-licorice dragster wheels, pirate coins, farm animals, "witch whistles" (which look more like gray cigarette butts), pacifiers, pastilles, skulls, hockey pucks, octopi, long flat strips resembling squid-ink fettucine, and, of course, traditional Swedish fish.

Amid the set of country-themed emoji released by Finland's Ministry of Foreign Affairs in late 2015, there's one for *salmiakki*—an ecstatic woman clutching a pair of black diamonds—described on the English-language website as "something Finns can't live without." "It's sort of the national candy," Annala told me. Which is saying something, because tiny Finland tends to punch far above its weight when it comes to candy appetites overall. A 2017 study by the London-based market-research firm Euromonitor International ranked the country fifth worldwide in per capita candy consumption. Three other salty-licorice countries, Sweden, the Netherlands, and Norway, placed third, ninth and tenth. (The United States didn't even crack the top ten.)

Here's another interesting statistic: Finland just scored the top spot on the 2018 World Happiness Report. It's produced by a United Nations initiative based on global polling data, and you can make of the methodology what you will, but Finns reported themselves happier than any other nationality on earth, and they were followed on the list by three Nordic neighbors: Norway, Denmark, and Iceland. Americans, meanwhile, came in at a dismal eighteenth. Correlation does not mean causation, but come on, this is totally causation, right? All those salty-licorice countries clustered at the very top? Maybe it's not so crazy to think about reported national happiness in relationship to something like a favorite national candy, because what is candy, after all, if not an elemental signifier of happiness and also something extraordinarily culturally specific and wrapped up in nostalgia and childhood memories and, by proxy, national identity?

So when considering the romanticized notion of Scandinavia that's taken hold of the non-Nordic imagination in recent years—a land of a happy citizenry, of generous social welfare programs and prisons nicer than our schools and schools nicer than even that, a land of *hygge* and Noma and Björk—could examining their love of salty licorice be one small but crucial means of unlocking a secret to living the rest of us, particularly those of us all the way down at number eighteen, gorging ourselves on king-sized Snickers bars like overgrown children unable to handle complicated flavors, haven't figured out?

Annala had offered to arrange a salty-licorice tasting for me in Helsinki, as well as convene a meeting of the FSLA's *Salmiakkikonklaavi* (*Salmiakki* Conclave), the ruling body that awards an annual Salty Licorice of the Year honor at the group's spring gala. The first gala took place in 1998, shortly after the founding of the FSLA, whose membership numbers about eighty. One year, Annala told me, "some people misunderstood that the word *gala* was an ironic thing and came in gowns."

I was grateful for Annala's offer. Though it's no longer especially popular in America, I happen to enjoy black licorice, or at least I used to as a boy, when it came in the shoestring-length "whips" more common back then. (These had the added bonus of really stinging if you managed to snap, say, a younger brother's arm or cheek just so. What can I say? *Indiana Jones* had just come out. We dug whips.) By Nordic standards, however, my licorice palate lacked sophistication. In the United States, our favorite licorice snack, far and away, remains the crimson middle finger that is the red Twizzler, which is technically not even licorice—those Twizzlers are strawberry-flavored, not licorice-flavored, contain no licorice extract, and offer all the masticatory pleasures of an edible candle —and which I'd imagine for licorice purists is akin to stuffing a loaf of Wonder Bread into a poster tube and calling what comes out the other end a baguette.

Annala, diplomatically, made no mention of Twizzlers when we met for lunch at one of Helsinki's most venerable restaurants, the Ravintola Sea Horse, which has been around since the 1930s and is still a haunt of artists and cultural figures. The house specialty, fried Baltic herring, comes stacked like kindling on an oversized plate. Annala greeted me from a booth. In picturing him, a middle-aged professional obsessed enough with his favorite candy to start a fan club, I'd expected some combination of zany and plump, but he turned out to be a trim man with a neat graying beard, pale blue eyes, and a slight air of Nordic melancholy. He apologized for his low energy: he was just recovering from the flu. By day Annala works as an editor at the Finnish News Agency STT, the main wire service in Finland. *Salmiakki,* his handsome and lavishly researched coffee-table book, was published in 2001.

In the book, Annala traces the origins of salty licorice back to early-twentieth-century pharmacies, when chemists in Finland and parts of Scandinavia began selling *salmiakki* as a cough medicine. (Ammonium chloride acts as an expectorant, which adds credence to the commonly cited theory that the people in certain colder climes were initially drawn to salty licorice for health reasons.) The *salmiakki* most often came in powdered form in little envelopes, though syrups and diamond-shaped lozenges were also available. *Salmiakki,* like traditional licorice, is made from licorice root, which is mixed with wheat flour and turned into a paste that is generally dyed black. (The natural color of licorice-root extract is closer to the ocher shade of powdered *salmiakki.*) Additional flavors can be added to the paste—ammonium chloride in the case of *salmiakki,* but also anise, toffee, menthol—before it's molded into candy shapes.

Even before the addition of ammonium chloride, licorice had been used as a respiratory and digestive aid for millenia. It turns up in the *Charaka Samhita,* an ancient Hindu medical text, and Theophrastus's *Enquiry into Plants.* And at least according to citations in the *Oxford English Dictionary,* "lycuresse" is both "good for the voyce" and "doth loose fleume." (The *OED* also quotes the English writer R. D. Blackmore's 1869 novel *Lorna Doone: A Romance of Exmoor:* "I cough sometimes in the winter-weather, and father gives me lickerish.") Sometime around 1760 an English apothecary named George Dunhill receives credit for being the first to add sugar to the licorice lozenges he sold at his shop, in the Yorkshire town of Pontrefact, cementing the herbal medicine's off-label use as a sweet. So-called Pontrefact cakes are still sold in the United Kingdom, though now they're manufactured by the German candy giant Haribo.

After our meal Annala unzipped his backpack and removed a jar of salty licorice produced by one of his favorite *salmiakki* manufacturers, Namitupa, a small-batch label out of Ilmajoki, a town in southwestern Finland. The licorice was in powdered form, in the old pharmacy style, which Annala adored. The FSLA named it Salmiakki of the Year for 2012. Annala unscrewed the lid, instructed me to hold out my hand, and tapped a modest pile into the center of my palm. "It's a bit messy, but this is the traditional way to do it," Annala explained. Then he shrugged, apologetic. "Not so hygienic. Not so aesthetic."

I glanced around anxiously, feeling like we should have maybe skulked off to a toilet stall before getting into this part of the interview. The powder was extremely fine and looked like ground cumin. I'll note that before my investigations into *salmiakki*, I had never tasted it, and my original plan had been to meet Annala in a virginal state. But then a friend heard about the article and ended up bringing some Dutch salty licorice—a gift from a Scandinavian ex-girlfriend—to a bar one afternoon, so I broke down and tried it. Having watched a series of YouTube videos involving non-salty-licorice-country children being tricked into eating salty licorice, I have to admit: I expected worse. The Dutch candy, a coin-sized black disk, had a mild saltiness that canceled out the licorice flavor, but just barely, leaving me feeling like I was gnawing on a savory leather button. So, not my first choice of things to put in my mouth, sure, but also not the makings of *Jackass*-style reaction videos.

"This is different," Annala assured me. "This is real Finnish *salmiakki*. Quite strong stuff." Heaping some of the powder into his own palm, he said, "Now you lick it."

Had I expected things to proceed more in the fashion of a genteel tasting at a Lexington whiskey distillery and less like, say, a scene from a William S. Burroughs novel where the characters ingest weird, made-up drugs? Yes, I had.

Anyway. I licked it. The *salmiakki* tasted as if someone had made a bouillon cube out of a briny licorice stock, then crushed it into a powder. My tongue immediately tingled. After my experience with the underwhelming Dutch licorice, I hadn't been prepared for how—what's the tasting note I'm looking for?— *ammonium-chloride-forward* Finnish *salmiakki* would be. It was pungent, in a saltier-than-salt way that brought some heat. The licorice had an aggressive presence as well, which might sound like a good thing, potential balance, but it seemed only to intensify the curdled chemical aftertaste, some combination of diet cola, fennel toothpaste, and MSG that multiple sips of water wouldn't flush.

Across the table, Annala seemed lost in a reverie. "Mmm," he murmured, closing his eyes for a moment, as if to shut out all senses but taste. "So delicious."

Over the course of the next seven hours, at multiple locations, we consumed a considerable, perhaps unhealthful, amount of *salmiakki*. I tasted brittle black tokens strong enough to make my eyes water. Annala happily crunched several at once, as if he'd just plucked his favorite bits from a sack of trail mix, announcing, "It's like eating iron!" We drank shots of salty-licorice vodka, a popular spirit throughout Scandinavia. (In *The Nordic Cookbook,* the Swedish chef Magnus Nilsson, whose restaurant Faviken Magasinet is an internationally lauded purveyor of New Nordic cuisine, writes about teenage friends making bootleg versions of the stuff by packing salty licorice into a three-quarter-filled bottle of vodka and running it through the dishwasher.)

We met two members of the *Salmiakkikonklaavi,* Juha Hellsten and Kaija Collin, at a bar with red carpeting and white plastic-laminate bistro tables that felt like someone's idea of the future in 1967. Annala placed a mixed bag of loose *salmiakki* in the center of the table and tore down its sides so they looked like the petals of a giant flower, the pile of licorice now a teeming black bulb. Choosing a subtly flavored Swedish fish, Annala twisted it between his fingers, then took a bite and nodded approvingly. "It's mild but has just enough salty licorice to make it acceptable. And the structure is very good and playful."

Hellsten, who works in management at the telecommunications company Ericsson and has been known to partly fill a suitcase with *salmiakki* when traveling to non-salty-licorice countries, agreed: "It's not a top scorer. But a reliable defender on the team." Annala said one of the things he loved about *salmiakki* was the "drama of the candy," by which he meant that the flavor evolved as you experienced it, like different acts of a play. "Sometimes there is a shock effect on the surface, then it is sweet inside," he explained. "What's happening changes from the first to the middle to the end to the aftermath."

Collin, who works at her family's asbestos-removal company, bit into a black licorice alligator with a white belly and frowned. "This is not *salmiakki,*" she said.

Annala tried one and determined the belly was in fact marshmallow. "It's a crime to call this salty licorice!'" he said, throwing down the candy in disgust.

Collin handed me a black lump and said, "Now I want you to try this one. No one else does it. Tar candy!"

It was a *Tervapiru* ("Tar Devil"), and it did indeed smell like a black-market cigarette with the filter torn off. I felt as if it also tasted strongly of tar, though I can't say for sure, not having knowingly tasted tar before. (Finns add tar, derived in their country from wood rather than coal, to various foods as a smoky flavoring agent.)

"I remember tasting pure ammonium chloride," Hellsten said. He had pushed up the sleeves of his cardigan and was rooting around in the licorice pile.

"Did you like it?" Annala asked.

"*Like* is perhaps not the right word," Hellsten said.

At a certain point I hit a wall. When someone shook a couple of strong *salmiakki* mints into my hand, I popped only one of them, palming the second and slipping it into my shoe while pretending to scratch my ankle.

Someone brought up a 2012 move by the European Union to sharply curb the allowable per-gram amount of ammonium chloride in food, which would have effectively banned *salmiakki* and possibly triggered a Finnexit. A Finnish EU bureaucrat helped intervene in the end, and candy was exempted from the rule. Annala invited the bureaucrat to the FSLA gala, but she never responded.

Fazer is the unofficial candy brand of Finland, the national equivalent of Hershey or Cadbury. Its founder, Karl Fazer, was born in Helsinki in 1866, one year after Jean Sibelius. His father, a Swiss immigrant, worked as a furrier, but Karl, the youngest son of eight children, always loved baking with his mother, and after an apprenticeship in St. Petersburg, he opened a French-Russian confectionery shop in Helsinki in 1891. By 1922, Fazer had begun mass-producing the milk-chocolate bars upon which he would build his fortune, their patriotic "Fazer Blue" wrappers a nod to the cross on the Finnish flag. (The country achieved independence from Russia five years earlier.) The company remains in the hands of the Fazer family, with 15,000 employees worldwide. Some of the products introduced in Karl's day are still on the market, including Mignons, handmade Easter delicacies that require deyolking actual eggs, then refilling the intact shells with hazelnut chocolate.

Fazer is also the largest producer of licorice in the country. In 1927 the company bought a British-Finnish biscuit and licorice company, and it released its signature line of sweet licorice the following year. The wrapper design featured a racist "golliwog" caricature, the British equivalent of a Sambo doll, which, depressingly, was not uncommon in itself—you can find historic examples of noxious candy packaging throughout the world—but which Fazer failed to jettison until 2007, in part under pressure from the European Union. (Why the company took so long to act is a "good and hard question," a Fazer spokesperson, Liisa Eerola, told me in an email. "Culturally, Finland was quite isolated for a long time . . . Looking back, it is easy to say that we moved far too late.") Fazer has been making *salmiakki* since 1938, and its portfolio of salty offerings now includes products like Super Salmiakki, Panterri ("Panther"), and Tyrkisk Peber ("Turkish Pepper"), so spicy that it's ranked like hot sauce, with a flaming-star rating system.

All these treats are made at the Fazer complex in Lappeenranta, two hours from Helsinki by train and about 16 miles from the Russian border. The factory is a century-old redbrick building with a series of modern additions, built along the shore of the largest lake in Finland. It has three hundred employees and runs three to five shifts, depending on the candy needs of the nearest holiday. In 2017 the factory produced 19,200 tons of candy: Mariannes (white peppermint pearls with chocolate centers), Tutti Fruttis (variously flavored gummies), Avecs (petite "French"-style pastilles), Amerikans (much larger "American"-style pastilles, which my tour guide enjoyed teasing me about), and all manner of *salmiakki*. Fifteen percent of Lappeenranta's output is salty licorice, translating to roughly 3,000 tons of the stuff last year.

The factory was very much a typical factory in certain ways (vast, noisy) and more specifically a candy factory in others (my shoes stuck to the floors from the sugar, and there was a pleasant, lingering odor of fruit more or less wherever I went). As thoroughly automated as any car plant I'd visited in Detroit, the place felt, as those factories did, like both an extraordinary human achievement and an allegory for human redundancy in the form of a mechanical tableau vivant. Stamping presses pounded candy shapes into sheets of starch powder; licorice or sugary fillings were squirted into the molds; robot arms hoisted trays onto drying racks. In one room a lone human employee manually plucked misshapen candies from a conveyor belt, tossing them into a plastic hopper at his feet. I found myself hoping the belt would accidentally speed up and force him to begin gobbling candy Lucy-and-Ethel-style. But apparently there's an optical scanner also checking the candy shapes, and if anything goes wrong, an alarm will sound.

As the tour continued, I couldn't help wondering how future international demand might affect the facility. After all, we're living in a time when fashionable omnivorism and a growing hipster monoculture have conspired to make even the most previously obscure regional delicacies available, if not everywhere, then at least far from their natural habitats. Hawaiian poke is no longer served solely on the Big Island; Detroit-style pizza has migrated well beyond Eight Mile Road. Nashville hot chicken, East Harlem chopped-cheese sandwiches—we could go on. Why not *salmiakki?*

But when I met Petri Tervonen, Fazer's marketing director at the time, he smiled when I asked if the company had made any big push to export salty licorice outside Northern Europe. *Salmiakki*'s "taste profile," he explained, was "much more intense" than the average consumer in a non-salty-licorice country was accustomed to. "So you have a natural kind of barrier."

We were eating bowls of salmon soup in the cafeteria of a different Fazer facility near Helsinki, a building whose curved glass walls and blond wood ceiling made it look like a UFO conceived by a team of Scandinavian designers. Tervonen had moved to Fazer eight years ago from another of Finland's iconic brands, Nokia. He told me Fazer was planning to launch a line of premium dark chocolate called Nordi in the United States next year and gave me a sneak preview of the bars. The sleek packaging nodded toward chic, aspirational Scandinavian lifestyle trends, featuring scenes of Nordic splendor: pristine mountain rivers, the candied glow of smoke from a cozy sauna. "Here our brand awareness is one hundred percent, but if you were to rank all confectioners worldwide, we're probably number forty-something," Tervonen said. "So we're competing with giants. What is typical for the category as a whole is it's an impulse decision. Not many people write down 'Buy chocolate' on their shopping list. So how do you get people to stop in front of what you're selling, make them curious, and then get them to try it?"

I kept pushing on *salmiakki*. Wouldn't a shopper at Whole Foods at least be curious? Secretly I pictured a series of alternate sleeves for a Nordi brand of premium salty licorice, scenes that might reflect the darker side of Scandinavian culture, thus preparing potential buyers for what they might be getting into. A black-metal band burning down a church? Max von Sydow playing chess with Death?

Tervonen said the trend experts they worked with in the States had tasted salty licorice in the past and found it "interesting," which Tervonen pronounced in a way that did not sound promising. He shrugged. "Salty licorice is a taste that divides opinion, even here." He said he had two sons: the eight-year-old loves *salmiakki,* but the eleven-year-old can't stand it.

The worst licorice I tasted during my epic night with the *Salmiakkikonklaavi* turned out to be a candied heart. I'd instinctively reached for one, the color (red as a raspberry) and shape tricking my brain into momentarily believing I'd selected something sweeter. It turned out to be the saltiest and most abrasive item on the menu, a flavor assault only heightened by the dissonance of the delivery mechanism.

A plastic twist bag of those hearts has been sitting at the foot of my desk since I returned from Helsinki, buried within a larger grocery bag of *salmiakki* I'd hauled back to my apartment. Reijo Laine, the owner of Namitupa, the producer of the hearts, had recommended I make a present of the candy to my wife. "She will be happy with you for six weeks," he added, with a mysterious precision.

That had struck me as a poor idea. But back home, as I struggled to account for the appeal of *salmiakki,* I thought again about *sisu.* Was the defining Finnish attribute really as noble as Hudson Strode had made it out to be? What if in fact it merely represented a national tendency toward masochism, some understandable but aberrant quality born of endless winter nights that wound up manifesting itself in a fanatical love of saunas and Turkish peppers?

Yet I couldn't shake my memory of the blissful expressions on the faces of the members of the *Salmiakkikonklaavi.* To pathologize such a love felt narrow-minded, unfair. So maybe the answer hinged on flipping the question. Forget about the salty-licorice countries for a moment: Why does *salmiakki* feel like such a category error to the rest of us? And was the answer to that question right in front of my face? Could one of the secrets to Finnish happiness simply come down to not always expecting hearts to be sweet?

Dumping the bag of licorice onto my desk, I began to dig around, pushing aside a Super Salmiakki lollipop, a packet of Dracula Piller (*salmiakki* with a creepy vampire mascot), a box of peppered *salmiakki* pellets (actually called *Sisu!*), before finally extracting what I'd been looking for. And what do you know? With the foreknowledge of what was coming, it didn't taste all that bad. I mean, certainly no worse than any of the rest.

I resealed the bag of hearts and replaced them in the shopping bag. I haven't touched any licorice since.

In the Twin Cities, Asian Chefs Feel the Sting of Andrew Zimmern's Insults. They Say His Apology Isn't Enough.

FROM *The Washington Post*

SITTING AT A large round table at Grand Szechuan, its lazy Susan loaded with plates of mapo tofu, dan dan noodles, and other Szechuan specialties, Eve Wu says she's done with Minnesota nice. She's angry, and her pique is directed at one of the Twin Cities' most powerful personalities, Andrew Zimmern, the bespectacled chef and TV host who recently insulted Chinese American food during a widely circulated video interview.

Eve and her husband, Eddie Wu—she's a baker, he's a chef with a Korean-influenced diner—are so incensed they've partnered with Hmong American chef Chris Her to host a series of pop-ups to foster conversations around the issues raised in Zimmern's interview: white privilege, cultural appropriation, and casual racism. About one hundred people showed up for the first pop-up, on December 7, at Eddie Wu's Cook St. Paul, where they dined on kimchi fried rice, mandu dumplings, Hmong sausage, and other dishes served in a box stamped with the word *horse*— —, a derogatory term that Zimmern used to describe the mall-level cooking often foisted off as Chinese food in America.

If you're wondering what Hmong and Korean fare have to do with Chinese cuisine, you need to understand how Zimmern's insults landed with Her and the Wus. When Zimmern dissed Chinese American food—P.F. Chang's in particular, which Zimmern labeled a "rip-off"—they say he dissed the culinary efforts of all Asian immigrants and Asian Americans who have tried to find their way in the U.S. mainstream.

"I'll back P.F. Chang's and their family any day of the week. Asians forever!" says Eve Wu. "If we have to be the generation that is going to be calling out problematic behavior, because in the past it hasn't been, then I'm going to do it . . . I will do a hundred-year war with him."

Eve Wu's indignation is just the most vocal example of the responses generated by Zimmern's interview with Fast Company, which was published to coincide with the debut of Lucky Cricket, the *Bizarre Foods* host's two-hundred-seat Chinese restaurant and tiki bar in a Minneapolis suburb. The interview has shaken the faith that some had placed in Zimmern, a former drug addict who cleaned up his act in the Twin Cities and become one of the region's brightest lights. He is, after all, a guy who has spent much of his career exalting the food of foreign countries, not denigrating immigrants' attempts to assimilate into America.

In the interview with Mark Wilson, Zimmern said he wanted to introduce midwesterners to Szechuan chile oil, hand-cut noodles, and Peking duck. Lucky Cricket, Zimmern suggested, could even morph into a two-hundred-outlet chain, kind of like P.F. Chang's but for "authentic" Chinese cooking. Zimmern, a fifty-seven-year-old white man from New York, set himself up as the savior of Chinese food in the Midwest.

"I think I'm saving the souls of all the people from having to dine at these horse——restaurants masquerading as Chinese food that are in the Midwest," Zimmern said.

Looking back on that interview, conducted this summer at the Minnesota State Fair, Zimmern is at a loss to explain how those words could have tumbled from his mouth.

"I let myself get carried away and have too much fun as opposed to realizing that I was working," he says at Szechuan Spice in the Uptown neighborhood. "You stop being mindful, and you say something flippant. You're not being precise with your words."

Zimmern would spend the better part of a stone-cold Tuesday with me in the Twin Cities, where the temperature never cracked freezing. Wearing a knit cap and a thick yellow parka, Zimmern led me on a tour of some of his favorite Chinese restaurants, ending with a stop at Lucky Cricket.

Zimmern's affection for Chinese food, he says, began in childhood. He remembers being three years old and occupying a window seat with his father at Bobo's in New York's Chinatown, coming to grips with a lettuce wrap of minced squid and shrimp. Over the next fifty-four years, when not grappling with his addictions, Zimmern says, he became a serious student of Chinese cookery, learning its history, its techniques, its leading practitioners.

"I believe Chinese cooking and Mexican cooking are the two great cuisines in terms of depth and breadth. They outpace French and Italian," he says, navigating his white Mercedes E400 rental into the parking lot at Mandarin Kitchen in Bloomington.

During its weekend dim sum, Mandarin Kitchen is as packed as a subway station at rush hour. But on this afternoon Zimmern quickly secures a table without needing to pull his hat down low to hide from selfie hunters. He's on the prowl for whole king crab, but there is none today. Zimmern settles for a whole lobster, with ginger and scallions, and half a roast duck.

As if on cue, the Reverend Stephen Tsui, an eighty-five-year-old retired Lutheran minister, approaches Zimmern, clutching a copy of the *China Tribune*. The paper had just published a story about Zimmern's interview and the fallout. Tsui, a longtime Zimmern fan, is indignant. "They don't know that he's promoting [Chinese] culture," Tsui says. "I defend on him. I understand him more than many other people."

Zimmern is grateful for the unsolicited support. He also swears it's not a setup for a visiting journalist. "I didn't tell the restaurants I was coming," he says.

At other Chinese restaurants in the Twin Cities I visited without him, the reactions to Zimmern's comments are more reserved, a mixture of forgiveness, frustration, and the kind of resignation that comes, perhaps, from hearing one too many authenticity hounds bad-mouth your menu. At David Fong's, a Chinese American landmark in Bloomington, third-generation restaurateur Edward Fong says Zimmern was simply trying to distance Lucky Cricket from previous generations' efforts to integrate Chinese cooking into their communities. Fong views Zimmern's remarks as little more than self-interested, poorly conceived marketing.

"I think he understands that he didn't just insult Chinese independent restaurants like ourselves," Fong says, "but he really insulted people who like to come to our restaurants, which is a lot of people." Then he allows himself a good laugh, perhaps a last one.

Over at Rainbow Chinese on Nicollet Avenue—a stretch widely viewed as a culinary destination—chef and owner Tammy Wong stands in her spotless stainless-steel kitchen outfitted with high-powered woks. She's laying out her magnificent life story: she's the oldest daughter born to ethnic Chinese parents living in Cho Lon, Vietnam, which has long been a magnet for Chinese immigrants and refugees.

Wong's family fled Vietnam after the fall of Saigon, landing in New York City and eventually settling in Minneapolis in 1983. Four years later her father decided to open a restaurant, even though no one in the eleven-member clan knew the first thing about running such a business. Wong had to improvise, cobbling together a menu from dishes she spotted at other Chinese American restaurants. The food leaned on her family's Cantonese traditions but was modified to appeal to the Scandinavian palate of the region.

Ingredients weren't always available (eighty-four-year-old David Fong recalls growing bean sprouts in his basement and ordering canned tofu from San Francisco), and minds weren't always open to new flavors. Early Chinese menus, by necessity, included General Tso's chicken, chop suey, and even hamburgers.

Over time both Fong's and Rainbow Chinese developed loyal followings based on their personalized takes on Cantonese cooking. If reluctant at first, Wong came to embrace her role as chef. She constantly tinkers with her menus, whether incorporating produce from farmers' markets or reengineering sauces to feature fresher, more healthful ingredients. These days she also tries to cater to Minnesotans who grew up eating Thai, Vietnamese, or Laotian dishes.

"I would not call [my food] Chinese American," Wong says. "If it's anything, I would call it Chinese Minnesotan."

Both Wong and Edward Fong view their food as a legitimate expression of Cantonese cooking, informed by local tastes and available ingredients, like any other regional cuisine. They don't take kindly to having their efforts—and their family's efforts—diminished by Minneapolis's favorite son.

"I was not right away totally offended" by Zimmern's comments,

Wong says. "But I just felt that, 'Oh, my God, this maybe offended a lot of other people.'"

*

As he offers quick reviews of the dishes before him at Szechuan Spice—generally positive, by the way—Zimmern stops cold when I relate what Wong and the Fongs had told me. Zimmern had already read a fair number of comments online. He knew his words had offended. But hearing from people whom he knows, and respects, hits him hard.

"Welcome to how awful I feel," he says, tears welling in his eyes. "Who wants to hurt someone that you care about? And to do so just out of flippance and stupidity?" he continues. "That's the kind of stuff I used to do before I learned that mindfulness and words matter."

Zimmern says he wants to do more than apologize to the people close to him. He wants to make amends, and one way to do so, he says, is just to shut up and listen. He wants to hear their truth and their opinions on such topics as cultural appropriation. (For the record, no one I spoke to cares much if Zimmern cooks or profits off Chinese food.)

Eve Wu would like Zimmern to listen too. The celebrity chef was invited to the first Horse— — pop-up, but he never showed. (Zimmern says he never saw the invite.) Wu wants Zimmern to reconcile two seemingly incompatible positions: a man who has made a career out of elevating foreign foods, and a man who would call some Chinese American food "horse— —." She wants him to square his affection for immigrant culture with his view of immigrant Philip Chiang, cofounder of P.F. Chang's, whom Zimmern described as Chinese on the outside but a "rich American kid on the inside." (Chiang's email response: "I am not going to get involved in his muck. I am totally comfortable with who I am and with who I am not.")

Although she's angry, Wu is also sympathetic. She knows it's hard to confront your contradictions. She's living proof of it: she's Korean by birth, adopted by a conservative white family. She's experienced the sting of racism while at the same time dealing with the "inner monologue" of a white woman who calls the police on any perceived threat.

"It's like, dude, I get it," Wu says. "I get it, Andrew Z. It's tough [stuff], but I just did it. You can do it."

Maybe Zimmern can start the unpacking at Lucky Cricket, which has already drawn criticism for its awkward amalgam of Chinese fare and tiki culture. As Zimmern trots out some dishes to sample —Szechuan wontons, crispy glazed eighteen-hour ribs, soy sauce noodles—we begin to dissect the establishment, from the food on the table to the Easter Island–like heads in the bar.

With each element that we analyze—Zimmern points out the chicken-and-waffles riff on the menu, I note the thin layer of chile oil beneath the wontons, which traditionally swim in the hot stuff —it becomes clear that Lucky Cricket is not the temple to authenticity that he intended. It's fusion. It's a sexier, twenty-first-century version of the Chinese American establishments that he had dismissed in the first place. They both meet customers where they are.

"I happen to think of it as fusion too," Zimmern says. "That's why I regret so much the flippant way I described the restaurant . . . Words matter, and the imprecision of that matters. My imprecision matters."

Imprecision may explain another twist in the Lucky Cricket saga: its next location may not be in the Midwest, the land Zimmern wants to save from inferior Chinese fare. Among the cities where Zimmern and his business partner, McDermott Restaurant Group, are scouting locations is Las Vegas, that neon beacon in the desert where image, not authenticity, is the coin of the realm.

The Food of My Youth

FROM *The New York Review of Books/Economic Hardship Reporting Project*

WHEN YOU ARE always on the run, from the bill collectors or the Man, or people in suits checking up on you, you need foods with a long shelf life. When the lights went out in our apartment and so did the electric stove, we lived on saltines with peanut butter and beans from a can. We ate like miners. There was a certain pride to be had in eating like men who were prospecting for gold, because the prospect of a better future is what had brought my family here to Northern California. Later, in the early eighties, Ma's pursuit of higher education plopped us in our small apartment in Los Angeles along the 405 freeway.

Meanwhile my grandmother's garage back in Seaside was lined with MREs—Meals Ready to Eat. I fingered those army-colored cans and felt safe. Their sturdiness, the security my Filipino grandfather gave us by earning them when he was in the U.S. Army. He'd brought us from the hungry jungle to a decent house in a small town by the ocean.

Growing up, I drank powdered milk and ate Spam, Vienna sausages, "new potatoes" (small peeled potatoes in a can), and rice with butter, salt, and pepper. The vegetables were jaundiced, green beans made salty and chewy in chicken stock or sweet, thick creamed corn. For dessert we had Halo-halo, an array of tropical sweet beans and chewy strips of orange jackfruit served over ice, with sweetened condensed milk, a Filipino treat—the most complicated act of love. To get the ingredients we had to go to a special Filipino market, but once we had them, they would last on the shelf all year long.

We did our best to get enough food. We tried to get in front of the hunger by eating casseroles, greasy noodle dishes, and white bread covered in that sweetened condensed milk. Or SOS—"shit on a shingle," toasted white bread with white gravy—ground beef when we could afford it, a block of Velveeta cheese in the freezer, and a plate with softened butter on the table.

We ate quickly and with our hands. Raised plates to our mouths and made a trowel out of chopsticks. We lived as people without money do, with a sense of impending doom that everything as we knew it could end at any time. Despite the end-time anxiety, we ate as often as possible. Ma and I left my *lola*'s house for Los Angeles so she could go to college. When we ran out of money one Christmas, we ate the free, sticky vegetarian treats handed out after dancing with the Hari Krishnas.

We ate at people's homes in the evening before reciting the rosary, in soup kitchens, outside churches—sometimes after playing musical chairs around a cake, it was called the cake walk . . . a game played at street fairs. And we drank coffee at all hours to quell our appetites. Not real coffee but the International Delights kind, a powdered sugary drink. I'd say that this felt like junk or that I felt like I had a strong stomach, or that it felt like decades of poverty running through my veins, but I don't have much else to compare it to. I knew other kids in our apartment building who walked around with a sandwich baggie filled with Kool-Aid crystals, we'd lick our fingers and dip them in, suck the pink, purple, blue powder off, all of us a gaggle of dyed tongues. It wasn't until later that I felt ashamed of the things I put in my body.

When I was fifteen, I was taken out of Ma's care. There was abuse and there was resistance and there was a single parent trying her best, but her best wasn't the same as Department of Children and Family Services' best. I walked into my first group home. After scavenging through a bin of donated clothes, worn T-shirts with summer-camp slogans of places I'd never been, I encountered in the kitchen a new world of locked refrigerators with dated food in plastic containers. On the doors was affixed a detailed meal plan:

> Monday: meatloaf, rice, and green beans
> Tuesday: spaghetti with garlic bread and salad
> Wednesday: hamburgers
> Thursday: taco night . . .

It was lonely there, but at least I didn't have to worry about going hungry. I didn't like to eat food prepared by other people—I was afraid I would taste their emotions—so I learned to cook the food provided by the county. It was largely frozen, prepared in bulk. Salad was a sturdy iceberg with sliced carrot slaw; the ground beef came in a fat tube. The group-home kitchen, with all its canned food and dates on plastic containers, resembled a bunker in the Midwest, as if we were all preparing for the apocalypse.

Only for us the explosions had already happened. The places we'd called home had been lit up and burned to the ground, with nothing left save for the blackened foundations of our past. We kids were screaming for love, for touch, for home. But we found ourselves in limbo, guarding our hearts, biding our time before the Unknown, waiting to see where we would end up. In that place of permanent temporariness, food was the only thing we had some control over; the rest was all court dates and social workers and group therapy and anger management.

It was there that I became a numbered girl. No longer Melissa, or Missy, or Missy Ann, or a girl who preferred the name Randy or Andy, but a girl with a case number, a file, a social worker, and a court date.

Hunting season didn't begin when I became a numbered girl. Hunting season began way back in the sixties when my family bought property in the U.S. and earned paychecks. Then again when we moved to L.A. in the eighties and I tested as a gifted child in my class, when I began competing against the Joneses' child, competing and surpassing, being noticed. It was at this time that I started hearing about "deadbeat dads" on talk shows and getting called to the front of the class for lunch tickets. Just me and sometimes one other poor child. This is when the lights were cut off; this is when the collectors started calling.

Or to my child's mind, that's how it seemed—not coincidence, but some grand conspiracy. I felt that my classmates—girls with names like Cindy and Sara with bright shiny shoes, whose daddies owned the businesses Ma and I begged at—were all in on some secret my family wasn't privy to. I'd look longingly at my white friends' granola, brown rice, and multigrain bread. Trips to the grocery store were always loaded with feelings of shame and desire. Fresh produce was the most extravagant, exotic thing on the shelves, even though it was my people who had picked it in the

Central Valley. I feared I would taste the sweat and tears of a cousin or the impatient plucking of a woman who wanted to get home to watch soap operas.

Even though the food of my youth was largely county food, I also had my fill of food in foster care. Dry chicken dinners. Water. Salad. Three-course meals. Yet it tasted hollow, as if it had a hole in it or was seasoned with longing. Longing was not a feeling I could afford to have.

This has been the cruel irony of America to me: it is the place of dreams, yet to long for anything in this country is to be an object of shame and repulsion. Because our fathers who joined the military were half lost to the violence they were sent to commit in other countries, or to the women they sought comfort from, or men, or to the booze or drugs, or to the new and unburdened lives . . . because of all that, army brats like me stood beside our then-single mothers in line at the supermarkets, arguing with the cashier about the high cost of our groceries. And when the Man handed over our food stamps, we were called moochers, a drain on our country. It's no different now—worse, even, as those people on the Hill try to pass a bill that would make people earn their food stamps. Tacking on work requirements—implying that foster kids are too lazy to pay for their own food, that mothers like mine, whose husbands went off to serve and never came back quite the same, are just not trying hard enough to make ends meet.

I don't know how I got so lucky to be here today. Most likely it has everything to do with the help I got along the way: treatment through Medi-Cal from the county, my ma's food stamps, the affordable housing, the books—all those books (from libraries and teachers and charities and every saved penny from my paychecks). The generosity and kindness and mercy of everyday people. Today I get to live like there's time. I long. I plan. I have the pleasure of walking to the farmers' market and inhaling the bright scent of the peaches and plums. Like a mama hen, I pluck produce and jam, olive oil, hummus. I turn brown eggs over up beside my ear and listen to their yolks. I let the juice from fresh fruit break open in my mouth. I tell my wife that I'm cooking L-O-V-E for dinner.

But sometimes I feel that familiar feeling—as though I'm under attack. It's that same threat that pervaded my childhood, from a small but powerful group of people demanding tax cuts for themselves and taking away what little everyone else has. They are the

Hunters. When I hear about *millions of people* losing access to food stamps and children no longer able to eat those free lunches I had the luxury of hating; when I see a young man, not unlike all the young men I knew, getting shot in the street, or when there's talk of a wall being built, or when my media stream fills with the sound of children crying out for their parents, that distinct wail that only a broken-hearted child can make . . . it's then that I reach for the food of my youth. Corned beef hash. Spam. Fried bologna sandwiches. It's a conversation I've been having in my head with America, the one where I'm told I'm bad and I believe it, just long enough that I have to prepare for the end of the world.

CHARLEE DYROFF

In Kotzebue, Alaska, Hunters Are Bringing Traditional Foods — and a Sense of Comfort — to Their Local Elders

FROM *Pacific Standard*

TWENTY-SIX MILES ABOVE the Arctic Circle, in Kotzebue, Alaska, there's a plain white metal trailer in the center of town that blends in with the snowy tundra during the winter. From the outside it looks like an office or a perhaps a single-family home, but it's actually a modern-day ice cellar, or *siglauq*, where hunters from across Inuit villages throughout northern Alaska can donate meat to be inspected, packaged, and served in the northernmost nursing home in the United States.

"The main source of meat that we have is caribou," says Cyrus Harris, who is in charge of the *siglauq*. Harris can slice and prepare caribou, moose, musk ox, ptarmigan, you name it, almost with his eyes closed. The Alaska native has been hunting for as long as he can remember, providing meals for himself and his family by learning the patterns of the tundra and the animals that make it their home. He inspects all of the food that goes through the *siglauq*, making sure it's safe to be offered in the nursing home, called the Utuqqanaat-Inaat by the Inupiat Eskimo people.

Securing access to traditional foods for Kotzebue's elders has been a difficult process, but the effects on the individuals in the facility are noticeable and significant. Not only does the meat serve as an important source of fat to help them maintain a healthy body weight and remain mobile, but the taste of familiar foods brings the elders comfort.

"I see the difference that it's made for the elders," Harris says. "They are much happier, they communicate better, they're moving around better."

By making an effort to bring native foods and the soothing smells and tastes that come with them into the long-term-care facility, the community of Kotzebue is practicing a unique model of medical care called "person-centered care." This approach takes into account people's own values, preferences, and experiences as part of their health-care program.

"[The Hunter Support Program] is a beautiful example of person-centered care," says Laura Mosqueda, dean of the Keck School of Medicine at the University of Southern California. Mosqueda specializes in family medicine and elderly neglect and abuse. In 2015 she and her team released a study in partnership with the American Geriatrics Society solidifying a definition for person-centered care that can be used as a starting point to measure the effects of it, which have so far proved encouragingly positive.

In a review of seventeen studies pooling data from more than a thousand patients at different nursing homes across the country, two specialists, Sun Kyung Kim and Myonghwa Park, found that person-centered care reduces agitation and symptoms of depression and improves the overall quality of a patient's life. "[The goal is] to take a holistic approach, to understand that a person is not just their blood pressure number or, you know, some metric that we can measure, but that those metrics and organ systems, et cetera, are attached to someone," Mosqueda explains.

For the town of Kotzebue, the push for traditional food in the nursing home began in 1993, when Harris founded the Hunter Support Program, a group that convinced the federal government to allow funds allocated for food in long-term-care facilities to be used to buy fuel and ammunition for hunting instead.

However, not long after the program started, Harris experienced an unexpected roadblock. Nursing homes are generally prohibited from serving food that is not obtained from an approved federal, state, or local source. Because traditional Inupiat foods are wild, they are difficult to categorize with U.S. Department of Agriculture guidelines and often violate standards for long-term-care facilities. In the case of the Utuqqanaat-Inaat, any meat that hunters brought in was not legally permitted to be served, so the federal government retracted its funding for the program.

But Harris was determined to find a way to keep the Hunter Support Program alive. He and the community found a loophole in the system by hosting monthly potlucks, or *niqipaqs* (translation: traditional food), where they could offer restricted dishes as gifts to the elders: baked salmon, steaming caribou, sheefish, and tart wild berries lined long makeshift tables in the Utuqqanaat-Inaat on the first of each month. For years they'd hunt and prepare food to serve to the elders once a month and watch how just a small taste of familiar foods changed their overall attitudes toward life.

The results were so hard to ignore that in 2000 the Maniilaq Association, a nonprofit that provides health and social services to twelve tribes in the northwest of Alaska, adopted the program, and it has been supporting and expanding it for the past eighteen years. At first the association provided funds to keep the Hunter Support Program running, but when Valedeko Kreil arrived as an administrator in 2013, he began working toward finding a way for traditional foods to be inspected and approved so they could be on the menu each day, rather than relying on monthly potlucks.

Kreil and Harris partnered with Chris Dankmeyer, the environmental health manager at the Maniilaq Association, as well as Alaska's Department of Environmental Conservation and Social Services to design a plan for a processing center that could evaluate the meat and approve it. The plan eventually evolved into the construction of the *siglauq*.

But the Maniilaq Association wasn't the only group that understood the value of native foods for the elderly. Ted Mala, an internal medicine physician, was also pushing for the same foods to be allowed in the Anchorage hospital. With a combined effort between the two, along with cooperation and support from Alaska senators, an amendment titled "Service of Traditional Foods in Public Facilities" was passed on February 7, 2014, changing everything for the elders of Kotzebue and for many other Alaska natives. It was the first time that the U.S. government acknowledged traditional foods as a necessary part of the food system. A year later the facility received a permit to serve food inspected, processed, and packaged inside the modern-day ice cellar in the long-term-care facility's kitchens.

In Kotzebue, the dedication to traditional foods represents more than a link to the past. The meat, berries, and fish are ingrained with their culture, in which there's an element of respect for older generations. When members of the community learn to hunt, they're taught to share their first caribou with an elder instead of keeping it for themselves. Kotzebue is the kind of community willing to have conversations with those in the long-term-care facility to see what they are missing, what they need more of, and what could bring them comfort in their last years of life.

"We have all of these people that the community loves," Kreil says. He's worked in geriatric care for over thirty-five years and has never seen anything else like Kotzebue's long-term-care program. "I wish I knew how to translate [respect] to the Lower Forty-eight."

But Harris, Kreil, and Dankemeyer aren't done yet. Next on their list of foods they'd like to see approved for the long-term-care facility is seal oil. Seal oil is essentially seal blubber that's cut up into chunks and broken down over time. In Kotzebue seal oil is like salt and pepper; you can find it on every table, whether to preserve foods, dip raw meat in for flavor, or for cooking. But it's currently restricted to be served in elderly-care facilities because of concerns that it may cause botulism. Kreil is currently working with researchers at labs in Wisconsin and Alaska to create a testing mechanism that will allow seal oil to be served in the facilities. They're hoping for new results to come in this summer.

"There's a good chance I might end up in the long-term-care, you know?" Harris admits. "So how am I going to be able to live in a facility where I'm restricted from having my seal oil?"

Why Do Poor Americans Eat So Unhealthfully? Because Junk Food Is the Only Indulgence They Can Afford.

FROM *The Los Angeles Times*

THE VERDICT IS in: food deserts don't drive nutritional disparities in the United States the way we thought. Over the past decade, study after study has shown that differences in access to healthful food can't fully explain why wealthy Americans consume a healthier diet than poor Americans.

If food deserts aren't to blame, then what is?

I've spent the better part of a decade working to answer this question. I interviewed 73 California families—more than 150 parents and kids—and spent more than 100 hours observing their daily dietary habits, tagging along to grocery stores and drive-through windows. My research suggests that families' socioeconomic status affected not just their access to healthful food but something even more fundamental: the meaning of food.

Most of the parents I interviewed—poor and affluent—wanted their kids to eat nutritious food and believed in the importance of a healthful diet.

But parents were also constantly bombarded with requests for junk food from their kids. Across households, children asked for foods high in sugar, salt, and fat. They wanted Cheetos and Dr Pepper, not broccoli and sweet potatoes. One mom echoed countless others when she told me that her kids "always want junk."

While both wealthy and poor kids asked for junk food, the parents responded differently to these pleas. An overwhelming majority of the wealthy parents told me that they routinely said no to requests for junk food. In 96 percent of high-income families, at least one parent reported that they regularly decline such requests. Parents from poor families, however, almost always said yes to junk food. Only 13 percent of low-income families had a parent that reported regularly declining their kids' requests.

One reason for this disparity is that kids' food requests meant drastically different things to the parents.

For parents raising their kids in poverty, having to say no was a part of daily life. Their financial circumstances forced them to deny their children's requests—for a new pair of Nikes, say, or a trip to Disneyland—all the time. This wasn't tough for the kids alone; it also left the poor parents feeling guilty and inadequate.

Next to all the things poor parents truly couldn't afford, junk food was something they could often say yes to. Poor parents told me they could almost always scrounge up a dollar to buy their kids a can of soda or a bag of chips. So when poor parents could afford to oblige such requests, they did.

Honoring requests for junk food allowed poor parents to show their children that they loved them, heard them, and could meet their needs. As one low-income single mother told me, "They want it, they'll get it. One day they'll know. They'll know I love them, and that's all that matters."

Junk food purchases not only brought smiles to kids' faces but also gave parents something equally vital: a sense of worth and competence as parents in an environment where those feelings were constantly jeopardized.

To wealthy parents, kids' food requests meant something entirely different. Raising their kids in an affluent environment, wealthy parents were regularly able to meet most of their children's material needs and wants. Wealthy parents could almost always say yes, whether it was to the latest iPhone or a college education.

With an abundance of opportunities to honor their kids' desires, high-income parents could more readily stomach saying no to requests for junk food. Doing so wasn't always easy, but it also wasn't nearly as distressing for wealthy parents as for poor ones.

Denying kids Skittles and Oreos wasn't just emotionally easier for wealthy parents. These parents also saw withholding junk food as an act of responsible parenting. Wealthy parents told me that saying no to kids' pleas for candy was a way to teach kids how to say no themselves. Wealthy parents denied junk food to instill healthful dietary habits, such as portion control, as well as more general values, such as willpower.

Both wealthy and poor parents used food to care for their children. But the different meanings they attached to food shaped how they pursued this goal.

Poor parents honored their kids' junk food requests to nourish them emotionally, not to harm their health. Similarly, wealthy parents who denied their kids processed foods did so to teach them healthful lifelong habits, not to deprive them.

Nutritional inequality in the U.S. has more to do with people's socioeconomic status than with their geographic location. Living in poverty or affluence affects more than just our access to healthful food: it shapes the very meanings we attach to food.

Tackling nutritional inequality will require more than putting supermarkets in low-income neighborhoods. These interventions won't change what food means to the poor families I met.

But lifting them out of poverty could. If low-income parents had the resources to consistently meet their kids' desires, maybe a bag of Doritos would be just a bag of Doritos rather than a uniquely potent symbol of parental love and care.

The Maraschino Mogul

FROM *The New Yorker*

ARTHUR MONDELLA IS mourned. Up until the moment of his death, on February 24, 2015, he ran his family's company, Dell's Maraschino Cherries, in the Red Hook section of Brooklyn. His daughters Dana Mondella Bentz and Dominique Mondella, who run the company now, miss him every day. They remember him in their prayers and wish he could see how they've done with the business. Their great-grandfather Arthur Mondella Senior and their grandfather Ralph founded it in 1948. Dell's Maraschino Cherries processes and sells nothing but cherries—about 14 million pounds a year—from its single Red Hook factory. Dana, the president and CEO, is thirty, and Dominique, the vice president, is thirty-two.

One might not expect that Mondella's death also would have saddened many of New York City's beekeepers, but it did. People in the beekeeping community, or their bees, had crossed paths with Mondella in 2010, less than five years before he died. In fact, the complications in Mondella's life that led to his demise had a minor but significant bee component. The first small signs that all was not right with him arrived buzzing in the air. Though circumstances put Mondella and the bees on opposite sides of an issue, the beekeepers still speak admiringly of him and express regret at his unhappy end.

The summer of 2010 was the hottest ever recorded in the city. By July heat reflected from the pavement had scorched the leaves of street trees, creating a false, uncolorful fall. In gardens blossoms dried and withered, and the weeds by highway entrances took on the appearance of twisted wire. As summer progressed, to add a further touch of the apocalyptic, bees returning at the end of the day to hives in Red Hook began to glow an incandescent red. Some local beekeepers found the sight of red bees flying in the sunset strangely beautiful. All of them had noticed that their honey was turning red too.

What next? they wondered. Bees go through a lot. Colony-collapse disorder—the decimation of entire hives—has been a worrisome problem worldwide. Pesticides, parasites, lack of flowers and other forage, erratic weather, and disease have caused drastic declines in bee populations. Hornets sometimes get into a hive and eat bees, honey, honeycombs, and all. Because the red bees were city bees, nobody took the sudden change in the color of their honey as a promising development.

Until March of that year it had not been legal to keep bees in the city. A few beekeepers had evaded the ban by camouflaging their hives with faux-brick contact paper or otherwise making them blend in with the rooftops. The outlaws got a kick out of defying former mayor Rudolph Giuliani, who had initiated the ban. Immediately after the Board of Health voted to lift it, the number of beekeepers multiplied. According to David Selig, a restaurateur who began keeping bees on the roof of his Red Hook apartment building in 2006, the number of hives in the area went from about three to more than a dozen. In the summer's unprecedented heat, water and nectar became harder to find.

At Added Value Farms, a public garden and composting site in Red Hook, Tim O'Neal, who teaches biology in middle school and at Brooklyn College, looked into the problem. O'Neal also keeps bees and writes a blog, Boroughbees. In it he speculated that the red honey might be connected to the nearby service depots for MTA buses and to a substance called ethylene glycol. Bees, pets, and children have been known to sample motor fluids that contain ethylene glycol, because it tastes sweet. The results are sometimes fatal. He thought the bees might be bringing back spilled transmission fluid or antifreeze from the depots, and he advised his fellow beekeepers not to taste any red honey until it had been tested. Cerise Mayo, a food and farm consultant who kept bees both in the garden and on Governors Island, just off the Red Hook shore, wondered why her island bees, separated from land by six hundred yards of water, were also producing red honey.

No one is sure who first began to think of the cherry factory.

Bees were observed flying in its direction and visiting puddles of red juice around it on the sidewalk. In early September, O'Neal took chunks of honeycomb from hives in and near the garden, put them in 50-milliliter sample tubes, and mailed them to the state apiculturist in Albany for testing. About a month later he received the results: the honey tested positive for FD&C Red No. 40, a food-safe dye, which is an ingredient of the maraschino syrup used by the Dell's factory.

In November the *Times* broke the story, which ran on the front page, under the headline "In Mystery (and Culture Clash), Some Brooklyn Bees Turn Red." Cerise Mayo was quoted, voicing her distress that her bees were getting their honey from the syrup. Because her name sounded possibly made up and her first name means "cherry" in French, a *Times* researcher had called her to make sure she was real. The story considered the problem in the context of the gentrification of Red Hook, with the factory standing for the old neighborhood and the beekeepers for the new. The idea of the red bees somehow clicked with readers, and scores of news outlets picked the story up. David Selig, whom it also mentioned, turned on his computer the morning the story came out and found "three thousand emails—from people I'd never heard of and from everybody I ever knew."

The *Times* story contained no quotes from Arthur Mondella, who had not returned phone calls asking for comment. It noted that Mondella had been in touch with Andrew Coté, the founder of the New York City Beekeepers Association, to try to find a solution. Coté is the most famous beekeeper in New York. He keeps bees at several city sites, including on the grounds of the UN, and sells New York City honey at the Union Square Greenmarket. He is a handsome, hazel-eyed man of French Canadian parentage, with a suave black beard going gray. Coté's life has included many adventures, such as hanging upside down nineteen stories above Times Square to remove a swarm of bees from a window washer's stanchion with a special low-suction bee-vacuuming device he built himself, and securing hives on a roof at the request of Secret Service agents who planned to position snipers there and did not want any bees getting into a sniper's ear.

"The red honey tasted terrible, by the way," Coté told me one afternoon at his market stall. "It was sickly sweet, kind of metallic-tasting, and watery. But after the story went all over the place online,

I could've sold a ton of it. I had dozens of customers asking for it. And all that red honey ended up being thrown out, and those bee-keepers lost a season of production." He showed me a few vials of the red honey he had kept as souvenirs.

"I really liked Arthur Mondella," Coté went on. "Arthur was gen-uine, a true Brooklyn guy, and he had that accent. Out of the blue, before the newspaper story, he got in touch about the bee situation and asked me to come to the factory. I didn't go until right after the story appeared. I knew there would be a lot of reporters around, so I asked if he could be there really early, like five a.m. He said, 'I will make it my business to be there.' I'll always remember that. I showed him how to put some screens up, make the lids of his bins tighter, control the spills. It was not a difficult adjustment at all, and we solved the problem. Afterward I sent him an invoice for my services, he paid it, and that was that. Throughout the whole thing he was a gentleman."

No other beekeepers dealt as extensively with Mondella; all were grateful for his levelheaded response. "We had been legal for less than a year," Selig said. "He could've made a fuss about why he had to deal with all these local bees. We appreciated that his first reac-tion wasn't to call the exterminator."

Meanwhile, also taking an interest in the story, the authorities saw an opportunity. According to later news reports, there had been rumors starting in 2009 that Mondella was growing mari-juana. Law enforcement hoped that the attention being directed at the cherry factory might reveal more about what went on inside it. Quiet inquiries were made about the factory's floor plan.

Arthur Ralph Mondella was named after his grandfather Arthur and his father, Ralph. The family came from Naples, though Ralph was born in America. In Italy, Arthur Senior had been a baker, and he wanted to get out of that business because he did not like work-ing seven days a week. He and Ralph began making maraschino cherries in a small factory on Henry Street, in Carroll Gardens. The cherries, which traditionally embellish ice cream sundaes and cocktails, were not steeped in maraschino, the Italian wild-cherry liqueur. (Since Prohibition, most maraschino cherries have not contained maraschino.) Instead the Mondellas used a secret rec-ipe involving sugar, citric acid, red coloring, and a curing process that never subjected the fruit to hot water. The cold-water-only approach preserves the cherries' crunch, the family says. All of the production was small-batch and hand-done. The hours turned out to be just as long as those in a bakery.

Arthur, of the second American generation of the family, was born in 1957. He grew up in Bay Ridge, attended Xavierian High School, and got a full scholarship to New York University. After graduating with a degree in finance he went to Wall Street, where he found a job with an investment firm. He did not want to work in the cherry factory at all, but in 1983 his father had a heart attack and Arthur set aside his financial career to take over the company.

Arthur Senior was long dead by then. When Arthur, the grandson, examined with an ex–Wall Streeter's eye the company he had inherited, he saw room for improvement. In the 1970s it had moved from Carroll Gardens to Dikeman Street, in Red Hook. Mondella set about expanding that location into two adjacent buildings, and eventually the factory occupied a total floor space of 38,000 square feet. He scaled up what had been essentially a mom-and-pop operation; his mother and his sister, Joanne, worked there too, but he ran the show, increasing production capacity and acquiring large-volume food-service clients. In 2014 he made a $7 million investment in automation so that one day the place would "run itself," as he told his daughters.

Despite automating, he wanted to keep his human workforce intact. By all accounts he cared about his employees. Lots of ex-offenders had jobs at Dell's. The Red Hook Houses, a nearby low-income housing project, supplied him with workers who needed the paycheck. Mondella was known for giving salary advances and loans whose repayment was not vigorously pursued. He hired a homeless man, provided him an advance for a deposit, and let him use a company truck to move into a new apartment. Gang tattoos could be seen on the muscular, maraschino-red-stained arms of guys on the factory floor.

The most commonly used news photo of Mondella shows him leaning into a cherry-processing machine, small and serious-looking behind the mass of bright-red cherries in the foreground. He is wearing a white lab coat, and a plastic shower cap covers his hair. ("A terrible picture of him," his daughters say.) He was a slim man, not tall, with dark eyes and a seamed, careworn face. He used "colorful language," according to several accounts. In his office he had a video monitor that showed the factory floor, and when he saw something going wrong he would appear suddenly and yell at those responsible. Unless he was meeting a customer, he dressed in jeans and a T-shirt, but he always wore white sneakers, and asked for new pairs every year from his family for Christmas. He always ended up getting red stains on his white shoes, and he went through a lot of them.

He lived on Staten Island, in a distant neighborhood called Graniteville, until he and the girls' mother divorced. Dominique and Dana and their mother stayed in Graniteville, and Mondella moved back to Brooklyn, where he eventually married a Ukrainian woman. They had a daughter, Antoinette, who is more than twenty years younger than her half-sisters. Later Mondella divorced again and moved in with his new girlfriend. But during all this time he spent most of his life at the factory.

Dominique and Dana both went to Moore Catholic High School, on Staten Island, and then to St. John's University, where Dana got a degree in accounting and Dominique got a degree in finance. Mondella said that after college one of them had to work for him. Dominique had worked off and on at the factory since high school, doing many jobs, from billing customers to booking flights for her father's business trips. After she graduated she went back to the company full-time. Dana was hired at PricewaterhouseCoopers, the international accounting firm, and began a job at its midtown office right out of college, often putting in sixteen-hour days. She met a man in banking, Tom Bentz, and they married in 2013. He also works for the family company.

Dana and Dominique share an office next to the one that used to be their father's. Last year I visited them there. Dominique is pretty and dark, Dana is pretty and blond, and both intensify their eyes with mascara. "My father was just a very, very smart man," Dominique told me. "He wasn't an engineer, he wasn't a mechanic, but the guys on the floor said that he could fix any machine himself. Like, I could ask him, 'Dad, how do I fix my phone, how do I back it up?' and he knew. He would always introduce me to the latest technology."

Dana said, "He didn't have hobbies, he wasn't into sports. He was into movies, a movie buff. When we were little kids, my parents were divorced, so he would pick us up, and we would go to Blockbuster, and we would pick out a bunch of movies and just watch movies. He used to cook these huge barbecues for us, and I'd be like, 'Dad, there's only four of us, we could have a meal like this for like twenty-five people.'"

"He was really specific in what he liked," Dominique said. "If he had a salad, it had to be only oil and vinegar on it, or if he wanted to have this brand of rice, it had to be this specific brand of rice. Potato chips always had to be crinkle-cut."

Dana described going on an errand to buy her father bread. "So I drive from Staten Island to Brooklyn, to Thirteenth Avenue, where my dad wanted me to get the bread. So I call him. I'm like, 'Dad, I can't find the bakery.' He's like, 'What? You don't know where it is on Thirteenth Avenue?' — *click!* — so I found a bakery on Fourteenth Avenue. So I get to his apartment, he breaks the bread open, and he's like, 'This isn't from Thirteenth Avenue! This is from Fourteenth Avenue!' And I'm like, How does this guy even know?"

The smell of maraschino cherries, not unpleasant but eye-water-ingly strong, fills the factory, and the floors remain sticky even though they're constantly mopped. Sometimes neighbors in apartments overlooking the building caught a few whiffs of marijuana along with the cherries. David Selig thought the smell of pot might be the result of workmen smoking it on their breaks. Later news stories said that a postal employee had told authorities that marijuana was being grown on the premises. But the police had failed to find suspicious signs. An increase in energy consumption consistent with the use of grow lights had not been detected, possibly because the factory had its own gasoline-powered generators, and a drug-sniffing dog had not been able to discover a definitive scent of marijuana. Independently, environmental investigators, acting on a tip, began to look into possible violations in the dumping of wastewater from the cherry-manufacturing process into the sewer. Meanwhile the Brooklyn DA's office more or less forgot about the marijuana investigation.

Inquiry into what might be going on at the cherry factory did not proceed much beyond rumor and speculation. The heightened attention caused by the bee episode had increased the factory's visibility. In 2013, Brooklyn elected a new DA, Kenneth Thompson, who set out to clean up pollution in the borough. His office decided to take a look at some stalled environmental cases.

*

"My father was a funny man in that he didn't share much," Dominique said. "That was just the way he was. We've come to find out only after his death what a pioneer he was in this business."

Dana said, "He was very private. We'd ask him questions when we were little and his response would be, 'Whaddya, writin' a book?'"

"Don't get us wrong—he wanted us to learn, but at the factory he would've wanted to make the decisions for us," Dominique said.

"The capacity that we're working at now, he would be so impressed," Dana said. "But I don't know if he would've been able to see that—not in his lifetime, because it wasn't in his nature to see it, to allow us to run with an idea, especially as it pertains to here. He was the type of person that did everything on his own."

"It's not that he didn't have confidence in who we were," Dominique said. "He knew that he raised two smart girls."

"A lot of Dominique's and my growth didn't occur until after his passing. Like, if my father were here, I would not be here. I would still be at PricewaterhouseCoopers doing audits."

"I think you would be here."

"Maybe down the road, but not this early. Our father could be really hard on you, but when he was nice you would forget about that. He gave us everything financially that we could've asked for, but we were not spoiled."

"Dana, see if you have the picture of you and him and Antoinette at the wedding."

"My dad gave me the most impressive, gorgeous wedding I could've ever asked for. It was a hundred and forty-five people, at Our Lady Queen of Peace in Staten Island, and we had the reception at the Palace, in Somerset Park, New Jersey. I wore a white silk dress. D'Pascual, at Nelson and Amboy on Staten Island, did my hair. I watch the video of the wedding sometimes and it's nice. My dad is in it."

"We were just very proud of him, proud of our parent."

When the raid finally happened, it was a surprise. On February 24, 2015, a Tuesday, during working hours, officers from the Department of Environmental Protection, the New York City Police Department, and the Brooklyn District Attorney's Office came to the cherry factory with a warrant to search parts of the premises for evidence of illegal dumping of wastewater. A lawyer for the company later described the action as a "guns blazing" raid, which it was not, but the officers did arrive in numbers. Their warrant hadn't allowed for the searching of Arthur Mondella himself. As the officers moved through his factory, he became more and more agitated. While examining some shelves, they found what appeared to be a false wall. They told him they were going to send for a warrant to search behind it. As they waited for the warrant, Mondella excused himself to use the bathroom. Once inside, he locked the door and would not come out.

The police tried to persuade him to unlock the door. He refused and asked them to bring his sister, Joanne. They did. Through the door, he said to her, "Take care of my kids." Then he shot himself in the head with a .357 Magnum pistol he had been carrying in an ankle holster.

To have strangers going through his factory must have seemed, for such an inward and self-created man, as if invaders were rummaging around in his brain. The factory was his world, he had thought out everything in it—he was it. When he suddenly could not control what was occurring in it, or what was about to occur, he could erase the nightmare only by erasing himself. Experience has shown that the revealing of a secret life can be a motivation for suicide. But nobody saw the catastrophe coming, or imagined the aloneness of this man.

"The day it happened, Dominique called me, and I was like, 'What? What do you mean? Was he depressed?'" Dana said. "I mean, I didn't understand. Then all the news about the marijuana came out. We never knew."

"Reading the articles that came out, that was how we knew," Dominique said. "I guess he was protecting us."

"I remember I was actually out sick that day," Dana said. "And then I came here and I saw that there was a lot of police activity, and I didn't understand, because if somebody killed themselves why would there be this many police?"

Behind the false wall the officers discovered a ladder leading down to a large basement, 2,500 square feet, and space for about a hundred marijuana plants in a well-set-up system of hydroponic cultivation under LED grow lights. They also found about 100 pounds of harvested marijuana, $130,000 in cash, and a small office containing a desk with books on plant husbandry and a copy of *The World Encyclopedia of Organized Crime.* In a garage area they came upon a collection of vintage cars, a Bentley and a Rolls-Royce among them, which suggested that Mondella led a flashier life when not at the factory. Later reports mentioned his use of co-caine, his boat, his lavish spending in restaurants, and his fiancée, a former *Penthouse* model.

Had Mondella lived, he could have gone to jail for two or three years; more likely he would have received probation. The DA charged the company with criminal possession of marijuana in the first degree, a felony, and with failing to comply with laws relating to wastewater dumping, a misdemeanor. The company pleaded guilty to both charges and paid a fine of $1.2 million. After that judgment, no further charges were filed. The DA did not want to destroy a successful local business that provided a number of Brooklyn residents with jobs. Also, investigators had been unable to find evidence to prove that the marijuana was being sold, nor had they tried very hard to find such evidence. The volume of the operation, obviously larger than was needed for personal use, im-plied that Mondella had been selling it. How, and to whom, and who helped him build the farm—who serviced the plumbing, the wiring, the grow lights—remained intriguing questions he was not around to answer.

In his will, Mondella left an estate that included $8.5 million in cash, more than enough to cover the fine. Dana and Dominique received 55 percent of the company between them; Joanne, their aunt, got 20 percent; and 25 went to Antoinette, their half-sister. The older daughters decided to take personal charge of the busi-ness they now controlled. After the news of the raid, some custom-ers dropped Dell's for other cherry suppliers, but by traveling the country to meet with customers individually, Dana and Dominique were able to keep most of them, and later persuaded a few who'd left to come back. Most of their large-volume restaurant chains stayed on.

A young employee, Joshua Sabino, had been hired by Mon-della the day before the raid. Sabino was excited about his new job, but when he saw the police everywhere he figured that the factory would have to close. He had been grateful to Mondella for hiring him. "But the factory closed for only two days," he told me. "They kept all the workers. And we even got paid for the days it was closed. I felt like Mr. Mondella was still taking care of me."

*

In May 2016, Dana and Dominique sued the city for recklessness and negligence in the death of their father, saying that the raid to search for environmental violations had been only a ruse, that officers had obtained a warrant fraudulently, and that the police should have taken their father's gun from him to protect him from harming himself. Their lawyer, Richard Luthmann, of Staten Island, characterized the raid as a "cowboys and Indians" operation that got out of hand and asked for $50 million in damages and penalties. The following April, Judge Leo Glasser, a federal judge in the Eastern District, issued a ruling in which he called the claims "preposterous" and threw the lawsuit out. The officers had no duty to protect Mondella from suicide, Glasser said. The warrant did not call for searching him, he was never in police custody, and no one could have reasonably expected that he might shoot himself over a misdemeanor environmental violation.

When I called Luthmann to ask about Glasser's verdict, he sounded undaunted and said he planned to appeal. Glasser is a famous judge, ninety-four years old, a Bronze Star veteran of the Second World War. "He's a wonderful judge, don't misunderstand me," Luthmann said. "But he's the same guy who put John Gotti away, and I think he may be a little hard on Italians and suspect they're all criminals and in the Mafia. Frankly, I believe this is a decision that could be dangerous to police officers, because here's this potential suspect who was allowed to walk around with a weapon while the investigation of his premises was going on." He added, "If the DA's office had done their homework, they could've found out that this man was licensed to carry a firearm."

As for Mondella's possible criminal ties, his ex-brother-in-law, Salvatore Capece, the former husband of Joanne, served five years in jail for money laundering, and Salvatore's brother, Vincent Capece, had a rap sheet for drug offenses that went back to the 1980s. In 1994, Vincent participated in a smuggling ring that brought $17 million worth of marijuana from California to New York in sealed metal containers, a crime for which he was given a thirty-three-month sentence. Mondella and Salvatore Capece had been known to spend time together. Glasser's decision made no reference to these circumstances.

Despite Mondella's last words to his sister, she was not involved with her nieces' assuming control of the company, or with their later decisions about it, and evidently this did not sit well with her. In March 2017, Joanne sued Dana and Dominique for mismanaging the company, pushing her out, slashing her salary, and ceasing to pay for her leased Mercedes-Benz. Joanne asked that her previous position, salary, and perks be restored to her, or that the company be sold so she could receive her 20 percent. Her mother —Dana and Dominique's grandmother Antoinette—also sued them, asking for restoration of the company car that she had been provided with for more than fifty years, which they had taken away. Commenting on these suits, Luthmann told the *News* that under Dana and Dominique the company was doing "better than ever" and that this family squabbling was a shame. He added, "It was Joanne and Antoinette that fired the first shot."

Though I never met Luthmann in person, I found him helpful on the phone. A follow-up story of December 16, 2017, made me wonder if I had been talking to the same guy. It said that Richard Luthmann—identified as a Staten Island attorney; yes, it was the same guy—and two other men had been arrested for wire fraud, kidnapping, extortion, brandishing a weapon, identity theft, and money laundering. There were eleven charges in all. The alleged scheme involved a scrap-metal-dealer co-conspirator; the sale to foreign customers of shipments of scrap metal that turned out to contain mostly concrete blocks; a blind client of Luthmann's whose identity the conspirators used in order to set up bank accounts and launder almost half a million dollars obtained by this fraud; and the later kidnapping of the scrap-metal dealer for the purposes of extorting an extra $10,000 from him at gunpoint.

Luthmann is a big man who appears in many photos wearing a red bow tie, a tight-fitting powder-blue suit, and round glasses. He once challenged a rival in a lawsuit to settle the issue through trial by combat. Luthmann spent twelve weeks in jail before his release on bail a few weeks ago. He has denied all the charges and is awaiting a May trial. During his incarceration, the deadline lapsed for filing an appeal of Dana and Dominique's suit against the city. Luthmann is currently banned from practicing law, so another lawyer will take over the intrafamily lawsuits, which are still pending.

Every summer Mondella used to host a barbecue for his employees, providing all the food and doing the cooking for everyone. There was no barbecue the summer after he died, but in 2016 the tradition resumed, close to his birthday, June 25, and in 2017 the company continued it. On the day in July when the event took place, I wandered around Red Hook in the morning, checking out the beehives at Added Value Farms, then sheltering under a tent there during a downpour. The rain slackened to a drizzle. Dana was sending me emails saying the barbecue was being delayed until the rain stopped. Red Hook is a waterfront place, with the Statue of Liberty a near neighbor across the harbor and a high, oceanic sky that's larger because none of the buildings are tall. I strolled past businesses that are part of the neighborhood's current incarnation—Fleisher's Craft Butchery, Widow Jane Distillery, Steve's Authentic Key Lime Pie, Flickinger Glassworks. The hot, humid air smelled of the open water it was blowing in from.

Finally the rain quit and patches of blue sky opened up. On Dikeman Street's wide sidewalk, next to a delivery gate for the cherry factory, workmen were sitting on folding chairs beside a table laid with sodas and picnic paraphernalia. Tom Bentz, Dana's husband, was cooking burgers, hot dogs, and marinated chicken breasts on a gas grill the size of a small bus. It had different grilling venues, and ventilator hoods, and shelves, and control knobs of varying sizes. Someone's CD player was blasting rap music with lyrics that did not mess around. Tom, Dana, and Dominique wore black T-shirts printed with the Dell's logo in white. Most of the workmen wore sleeveless shirts, and all were red-spattered and generally a sunburn shade of maraschino red.

Leon Perry, who began his job at the factory after his release from prison twenty years ago, told me how Mondella had loaned him money for rent when he started out. Minnow Johnson, a mechanic, said Mondella had funded his studies at trade school. Arthur Casey remembered when Mondella paid for his $300 cab ride home one night when he had to work late.

Afterward, during the cleanup, Leon Perry pointed to the grill, which Tom was scraping with a metal spatula, and said, "This was his grill." For a moment it was as if Mondella himself had materialized there on Dikeman Street, analogized by this amazing piece of equipment.

Tom looked at the sky. "It cleared up," he said. "That was Dana and Dominique's father looking down." The guys posed for a group photo, smiling, with red arms around one another's shoulders, and then went back to work.

*

I asked Dominique and Dana why they had decided to take over running the company themselves. After all, they could have assembled a committee of consultants, asked for input, done a search for a plant manager, let someone else direct the business day to day. Or they could have sold it; recent years have seen the buyout of other maraschino-cherry companies by large corporations like Green Giant Foods.

"This is all our father left," Dana explained. "He didn't have a home. His cars were taken away by the investigation. I didn't get to sort through his things. He lived with his girlfriend, and it's not really my place to go into her apartment and start grabbing things. What I would've loved would've been like even if I had a pair of cufflinks so I had something that's tangible of his. The only tangible thing that we have left of him is this place."

"This was his life. It was his blood, sweat, and tears," Dominique said.

"When my father came, the business was failing, and he took a risk, he put everything he had into it, and he made it so much better, a real success. When we came it looked as if it was going to fail, because of everything that was happening around it. And we took a risk."

"We put every inch of ourselves into it."

"I lost my father, and I had to come back two days later and go to work. You didn't have time to mourn. He wouldn't't've even wanted that. He wouldn't have wanted us to dwell. He would've been like, 'Get up, let's go, whaddya doin'?'"

"It's definitely been very stressful, but I always think positive," Dominique said.

"I'm more realistic," Dana said. "I try not to think about the factory twenty-four seven, but I'm dreaming about it at night, seeing the cherries, the different sizes, in my head. We sell five different sizes, from small to medium to large to extra-large to colossal, with stems and without, so that's ten different kinds—"

"Also crushed cherries and cherries in halves," Dominique said. "And in different colors. Not only red."

"It's a statistic that a lot of family businesses don't survive past the second generation," Dana said. "My dad was in the third generation, and now we're the fourth. You can make it work, it's just a lot of hard work and dedication."

"Growing up, he always taught us—like, be responsible," Dominique said. "We just knew we had to step up."

Tim O'Neal, who helped solve the red-honey mystery, tends his hives on Saturdays at Added Value Farms. The bizarre events of the summer of 2010 have never happened again. I found him smoking his bees—making them disoriented with smoke from a small handheld device—in order to do hive maintenance. O'Neal is a tall, dark-haired man from Troy, Ohio, and he has the accent of that part of the country. "I felt pity when I heard Mondella died," he said. "What a terrible situation. He was a good neighbor. We all live in a community together—who cares if some dude is growing marijuana? It's practically legal now anyway. I'm sure he was putting out good product. I was shocked the situation turned out so badly."

The fame of Andrew Coté, the beekeeping expert who helped Mondella, has only grown. Lately he has branched out into other countries, riding a surge of interest in beekeeping worldwide. The last time I talked to him at his stall in Union Square, tour organizers from China stopped by to discuss arrangements for his upcoming lectures there. He said that reporters had called him when Mondella died. "It was a dark hour. Arthur was not looking to hurt anybody. He had honesty and integrity, and he made it clear, when dealing with the red-honey problem, that he cared about the bees' welfare." Coté also pointed out, apropos of Tim O'Neal's original ethylene-glycol theory, that recently some hives in East New York had produced a green and poisonous honey whose main ingredient turned out to be antifreeze.

David Selig, the restaurateur who had been the factory's nearest beekeeping neighbor, has created one hit restaurant after another. A recent success, Rockaway Taco, has inspired him to move from Red Hook to that distant part of the city. Selig is another Canadian offspring, a wiry man with dark, Gallic features and a greeter's easy manner.

"I have great admiration for Arthur, and a lot of empathy," Selig said. "He was in his factory morning and night; at one time or another I've slept in every one of my businesses. And after years in restaurants, which in New York City have to be the most regulated industry on the planet, I know what he was facing. If the city and the feds had started in with him, they'd still be on him to this day.

He grew up in this regulatory world and I'm sure he knew how it would go down. What he did was unthinking, like pushing a friend out of the way of a speeding car. He had that boyhood type of loyalty. He gave himself up for his family."

Cerise Mayo, who was one of the first to notice the red honey, no longer keeps bees. She has dark, curly hair and brown eyes, and she wears clothes featuring patterns from nature, such as a shirt with swallows flying wingtip to wingtip. After the summer of 2010, she gave her bees away. The thought of how difficult it is to know what they'll get into in an urban environment discouraged her. If she ever keeps bees again, she wants to be out in the country, in a more pastoral setting. "I felt horrible when I learned of Mr. Mondella's death," she said. "How hard it must have been to carry all the weight he had to deal with. I even saw some follow-up stories that seemed to be blaming his death on the bees. That's crazy. The bees were just behaving like bees."

Black History at Harlem Hops

FROM *The New Yorker*

THE OTHER NIGHT at Harlem Hops, a new beer bar and restaurant on Adam Clayton Powell Jr. Boulevard, a neighborhood old-timer peered at a fellow patron's drink selection and gestured for the bartender's attention. "Interestingly enough, this young lady has, like, four different beers," he observed. The bartender laughed. "It's called a flight," he explained. "A flight?" replied the old-timer. "Like takeoff?" Harlem Hops is a thoroughly modern establishment, with a rotation of sixteen craft brews on tap, geeky tasting notes ("raw wheat, malted oat, milk sugar, lychee" for a sour IPA from the Hudson Valley), and a mostly young, hip crowd.

You'll want to take a picture of the enormous, buttery Bavarian pretzel, flecked with salt crystals, which arrives swinging from the kind of metal stand you might use to hang bananas on your kitchen counter. You'll want to return at least as many times as it takes to try each of the snappy-skinned bratwursts, from Jake's Handcrafted, in Brooklyn, served on griddled pretzel buns. The one made with chicken—laced with sansho peppercorn and sweet soy sauce—and the one that repurposes intensely smoky, burnt-brisket ends are especially exciting.

The owners, Kevin Bradford, Kim Harris, and Stacey Lee, three beer lovers in their forties, were tired of having to leave the neighborhood to get the variety they craved. They wanted to highlight small local breweries, especially those run by brewers of color. They wanted to excavate history too. Did you know that some of the earliest evidence of beer-making, using warm-climate cereals like millet and sorghum, was found in Africa? That ancient Egyptians developed a malting process? That slaves in the American South brewed beer? Bradford, Harris, and Lee, all graduates of historically black colleges and universities, enlisted a historian named Tonya Hopkins, known as the Food Griot, to provide these reminders of the past, which are written in chalk on a pillar at the end of the bar. They also serve a whiskey, made in Tennessee, called Uncle Nearest; Nathan (Nearest) Green was a black master distiller believed to have taught Jack Daniel everything he knew. Where Jack Daniel's is harsh, the bartender argued—"the opposite of that first gulp of water in the morning"—Uncle Nearest moves through your mouth "like a curl. It plays on your lips."

The whiskey went down easy—citrus on the nose, spicy caramel and vanilla on the palate—and paired well with a crispy "Guma pie," a tortilla wrapped like a sharp-cornered package around ground beef seasoned with habanero and African allspice, shipped up from a Virginia-based company started by a Ugandan refugee. The old-timer, who'd taken a phone call, sipped his own whiskey and shared his newfound trivia with whoever was on the other end of the line. "Uncle Nearest got ripped off by Jack Daniel," he said, laughing heartily. "I'd have been looking for him."

KATE HILL

Hearts of Corn — the Women of Yo'on Ixim

FROM *Saveur*

THE TSOTSIL MAYA call themselves the people of the corn. It grows readily in their home, in the foggy cloud forests of Chiapas in southern Mexico, the lush highlands in which their ancestors grew the grain for thousands of years before the first Europeans arrived. According to Mayan creation beliefs, humans were made from corn itself—white corn for men, yellow for women.

Earlier this year I visited a group of Tsotsil, far from their rural homeland, in the central city of Puebla, 65 miles southeast of Mexico City. They are an indigenous people who still speak their own language and maintain much of their rural way of life but have come north temporarily with their families to work, perhaps to help pay medical bills or build a small cement-block house at home. When they make the eighteen-hour bus journey to this sprawling city of 3.5 million, they don't carry much, but they do bring their food traditions. Life is very different here, where the Tsotsil women must shop the local markets for fresh corn and find a local *molinero*, or grinder, to make fresh masa for tamales and tortillas.

I had come as a guest of Yo'on Ixim, a small school and community center on a side street in the Loma barrio, to work with the women and help them share their stories and food traditions in a small cookbook. Yo'on Ixim began as a collaboration between Rosalina Ordóñez, a Tsotsil woman, and Samantha Greiff, a Mexican American born in Puebla. When they met in 2013, Ordóñez was selling chewing gum on a busy street corner. She spoke little Spanish and could neither read nor write it. But soon these two

very different women with barely a common language were working together—Greiff teaching Ordóñez Spanish, Ordóñez teaching Greiff enough Tsotsil vocabulary to learn about their culture
and life.

Five years later, Yo'on Ixim has become a real school, with black-
boards and cubbyholes, three salaried teachers, a handful of vol-
unteers, and sixty students, from age four to thirty-eight. Located
in the same poor neighborhood where the families live when they
are in Puebla, it is also a community center and cooperative, where
Tsotsil women—typically unschooled and married by fourteen—
can study and work together on intricately hand-embroidered gifts
and weavings to sell at the tourist markets and online. *Yo'on Ixim*
means "heart of corn," a reminder that we are what we eat. My
arrival coincided with an end-of-term celebration, and the school-
room had been repurposed for an afternoon of making hundreds
of blue corn tortillas on a coal-heated *comal* (griddle).

In Puebla the men and boys easily blend in, with their modern
clothes, but the Tsotsil women wear their native *blusas*—blouses of
handwoven fabric, laboriously embellished with heavy black wool
and fine, colorful metallic threads—over long black embroidered
skirts, secured by woven cummerbunds, which are worn from the
time the girls are very young. The extensive handiwork in a woman's clothes is her pride and often her most valuable possession.
Outside Puebla these garments could be treasures, but here the
bright colors are a tell that the wearer is a migrant worker, rendering her invisible in many situations. Not all locals are kind, or
open to trying to communicate with women who struggle with
Spanish. Taxi drivers refuse them rides. Even shopping for groceries can become a nuanced cross-cultural dance. But as a unit of
blue and purple, with several children in tow, the women of Yo'on
Ixim moved through the giant Mercado Hidalgo at the southern
end of the neighborhood, inspecting stall after stall of avocados,
chiles, pineapples, *nopales* or cactus paddles, and the prized *pol-
los rancheros,* yellow-skinned, long-necked farm chickens that hang
with heads and feet intact. After the group conferred and carried
out some mandatory haggling with the shopkeeper, they bought
several chickens for soup. Then their shopping bags quickly grew
heavy: 37 pounds of fresh Ayocote beans for tamales, 11 pounds
of tomatoes, 11 more of onions, a bag of green peppers and chiles

for salsa, and a bulging sack of dark green chayotes—small, dense squash—also for the chicken soup.

Upon return to Yo'on Ixim, the women carried in a squat tin coal stove, and the school space became an impromptu kitchen. There was a casual grace to the way they worked together, one holding the pot for another while a third shooed several toddlers away from the fire. An older woman taught a younger one how to wrap the bean and masa tamales in banana leaves; Ordóñez, the cofounder, handled a machete like a paring knife. This way of working together is not traditional for the Tsotsil. In village families the mother-in-law usually rules, but here in the city it is experience and confidence that determine who adds the salt and tastes for seasoning, who sets the rhythm pressing pale blue masa to make tortillas.

Caldo de pollo is at once the simplest chicken soup and a celebration of bounty and community. It is, like most shared dishes the Tsotsil make, really just a vehicle to eat masses of tortillas. Hundreds of the disks, charred from the *comal,* were kept warm in baskets and plastic washtubs lined with clean kitchen towels. The Ayocote beans studded a dense masa for tamales steaming over a tin stove. *Pellizcadas,* a sort of thick tortilla, featured pinched rims to hold in spoonfuls of a simple tomato salsa and crumbled fresh cheese. Each dish celebrated corn, that heart of Tsotsil culture that tethers these families to their homes in the cloud forest so far away.

Do You Eat Dog?

FROM *Taste*

FOR EAST AND Southeast Asians living in the West, especially for those of us who were born here, very few ingredients remind us of our precarious sense of belonging as much as dog meat. We Asians have probably all been asked at least once, perhaps with the inquirer's index finger pointed suggestively at our banh mi or Caesar salads, *Is that dog? Is it true you eat dog?*

Here are the answers we tend to give in sensitive East-meets-West moments like these: *No, never, it's an archaic practice; it's a poor-people thing; it's a myth.* But the more complicated answer is that we come from diverse countries—South Korea, Vietnam, China, the Philippines—where people eat all kinds of regional delicacies that are unknown to the Western palate, not because of poverty or barbarism but simply because they enjoy them. We don't often speak to this nuance because the stereotype has been so damaging that even the discussion feels like a game of hot potato. We do this rhetorical dance because of how the practice of eating dog has been wielded in the past to exoticize and demean us as heartless monsters who wouldn't blink twice at barbecuing man's best friend.

During the 1904 World's Fair in St. Louis, the Philippine Exposition's major draw was an artificially replicated village featuring a group of "primitive" Igorot people grilling dogs on site. Unsurprisingly, this became an object of both scandal and wide fascination. The United States had just won the Philippine-American War two years prior, so exhibiting these people and their culinary habits was a way of celebrating the civilizing effect America was having on the Philippines.

At the time the *St. Louis Republic* reported, "After nearly two weeks of enforced fasting from puppy steaks and dog soup, the famished head-hunters are at last to be regaled with their cherished viands . . . Six dogs have been obtained, where or how is kept a dark secret and the dog-killing time is contingent on how soon the canine victims shall have been fattened for the feast." Spectators viewed the reconstructed village aghast yet relieved that their own country was rapidly whipping the Philippines into shape.

In 1989, as the United States welcomed refugees from Cambodia, Laos, and Vietnam, a dog-eating incident involving two Cambodian men in Long Beach sparked national outrage and a new California law that made it illegal to use any animal "commonly kept as a pet or companion" for food. In an interview with the *New York Times*, Vu-Duc Vuong, then executive director of the Center for Southeast Asian Refugee Resettlement, said, "There have been very few, if any, instances of pet eating. Far more numerous are anti-Asian prejudices and violences based on no more than false or racist stereotypes of Asian Americans."

As recently as 2016, an Oregon senate candidate suggested that taking in Vietnamese refugees was a mistake because, in his words, they were "harvesting people's dogs and cats." Dog-eating has always been political for us.

When I asked Clarissa Wei, senior reporter for *Goldthread*, a digital publication focused on Chinese food and culture, what she thought about dog-eating, she acknowledged the controversy. "Westerners have a tendency to see Chinese people as a monolithic mass," Wei, who is based in Hong Kong, wrote via email. "The people who do regularly consume dog meat are a small minority in a country with a population of 1.379 billion. Yet 'dog-eating' is a dominant topic when it comes to the Chinese."

Because of how the West has obsessed over the practice as a foreign taboo, having a nuanced conversation about dog meat in mixed company is a challenge.

"If anything, eating pig meat or chicken meat or cow meat should warrant the same outrage as dog meat," Wei wrote. She admittedly can't personally stomach it, but it's fairly obvious that the dog is viewed as exceptional for people who aren't normally animal-rights activists.

Last year a bipartisan group of congressional representatives introduced a resolution (H.R. 30) condemning the infamous annual

Lychee and Dog Meat Festival in Yulin, China. If passed, it would be the first time Congress has made a legislative statement about animal-welfare practices overseas; the cosponsors plan to introduce more legislation calling for a worldwide ban on the dog and cat meat trades.

Throughout Asia the practice of eating dog has been a locus point regarding generational differences, class mobility, and the seriousness of Western scrutiny. During the 2018 Winter Olympics in Pyeongchang, South Korea, earlier this year, various news outlets and social media posts put a spotlight on the practice. Alex Paik, managing director of AP Communications, a company that promotes Korean culture, was firm in his response to my queries: "The vast majority of Koreans are grossed out at the thought of eating dog," he said. Since the Korean War, he told me, the perception of Koreans as enthusiastic dog-eaters has haunted them. The truth is, those who embrace the practice have always been a minority; most Koreans, he wrote, are firmly in the "dogs are pets" camp. "Usually we hear about some older folk who believe in it having special, revitalizing properties."

Among Vietnamese people the practice of eating dog meat is a bit harder to shove into a box and stow away, though we also keep that acknowledgment to ourselves. When I was a kid, my mom would joke that our five-pound chihuahua, Bambi, wouldn't make a very good meal if the pantry came up empty: "Maybe one sausage," she'd say. But actually my family, from the seafood-crazy deep south of Vietnam, aren't dog-eaters anyway: it's always been something that we make fun of northerners for. It made sense to me that since the majority of Vietnamese immigrants to the West are from the south, we don't actually know much about the practice. So I called up Andrea Nguyen, renowned author of many pan-Asian and Vietnamese cookbooks and child of northern Vietnam, to have that frank conversation I'd been seeking.

"My dad would tell me, 'Look, if you smell dog grilling, it's so fragrant it'd make your mouth water,'" she recalled. There's a sensory pleasure in fire-roasted dog meat—from the mahogany skin, rendered fat, and pungent aromatics—that activates nostalgia in people who grew up with it as just another potential protein source, like pigs, chickens, and geese, Nguyen told me. But it was a particular kind of dog, a type that isn't normally considered a pet.

"It's not like we're going to watch the Westminster Dog Show and only see a dinner buffet!" she said, laughing.

Nguyen has never eaten dog, but her parents enjoyed it so much that on special occasions her mother would make mock dog stew in their home in Southern California. She'd buy a whole, skin-on pork leg, wrap it in paper, and throw it in the fireplace. "The burning would mimic the smoky flavor they missed, and the ratio of fat to meat to skin in the pork leg is apparently spot on," she said. Her mother would flavor the stew with galangal, turmeric, and *mam tom,* the fermented shrimp sauce.

For Nguyen, mock dog stew was just a tiny, delicious part of her childhood—it wasn't particularly scandalous or desperate. But she's been asked about dog meat so often, she's sick of it. "Why the fixation on this outlier?" she asked. "There are so many other beautiful things in our cuisine."

PRIYA KRISHNA

The Life of a Restaurant Inspector: Rising Grades, Fainting Owners

FROM *The New York Times*

A SHORT MAN in a beige button-down shirt emblazoned with the New York City health department logo walked through the doors of a restaurant kitchen, detected signs of vermin, and called over the owner to tell him the bad news.

The restaurateur started shaking and sweating. He fell out of his chair, hit the floor, and lost consciousness. An ambulance was called.

The most feared and loathed character in the city's restaurant business is not the critic or the landlord. It's the health inspector.

New York's inspectors have long been capable of showing up unannounced, recording violations, and, if necessary, shutting down a kitchen. But in 2010 they acquired a new dimension of power: the ability to assign letter grades (printed on placards that must be visible from the street) and to post their findings in an online database where anyone can scrutinize a restaurant's inspection history. Restaurateurs complained bitterly about the "scarlet letters" and what they saw as punitive enforcement aimed at raising money for the city.

Eight years on, that furor has cooled. The number of restaurants with an A grade rose to 93 percent in April, from 81 percent in that first year. Yet many restaurateurs still feel aggrieved about the rating system; they talk of the health inspectors as arbitrary, unjust —and frightening enough to send an owner to the hospital with a panic attack.

As it turns out, the man in beige who precipitated that crisis is a pleasant, even-keeled individual named Fayick Suleman, who lives in the Bronx with his wife and two children and—like the letter-grading system—is celebrating his eighth anniversary at the Department of Health and Mental Hygiene.

Mr. Suleman was in one of the first groups of health inspectors hired and trained after the department began the grades, largely in response to a widely circulated 2007 amateur video that showed rats scurrying through a fast-food kitchen. (The department wouldn't specify which video, but this one, shot at a KFC/Taco Bell restaurant in Greenwich Village, was attracting attention at that same time.) There are now about one hundred restaurant inspectors.

His experience shows how the inspector's job works and how much it has changed, or hasn't. He says his rounds have become fairly routine—at least for him.

The sight of his distinctive black Casio G'zOne flip phone, the kind issued to inspectors, often sends restaurant staffs into a panic, even when Mr. Suleman goes as a civilian.

He has since switched to an iPhone. Still, chaos inevitably erupts whenever he arrives at a restaurant and announces he is there to inspect it.

"People start running back and forth, throwing out food, picking up mops," he said. "Everyone panics. If you wait too long to do the walk-through, everything is out of your way."

Mr. Suleman grew up in Kumasi, a city in Ghana. He left in 2002, came to New York, and studied biochemistry at Hunter College, hoping to become a brain surgeon. But after the financial downturn in 2008, he realized that with a family to support, he needed a more immediate source of income. One day he met a health inspector at the lab where he worked.

"I had always been curious about health inspectors," Mr. Suleman said. "I always find it puzzling how, when you go to a restaurant and order food, someone disappears and then next thing you know they appear with your food. I always wondered what happened behind the scenes. What do they do with my food? Who is monitoring them?"

The application requirements, he said, were simple: thirty college credits in a biological or physical science. The hard part was the training. Inspectors must attend months of classes, covering everything from how to write violations to the science of food safety.

At a recent food-protection class at the city's Health Academy on

West 100th Street, students were taught all the diseases a customer could contract if different foods were left out for too long. Served at the improper temperature, smoked fish, for example, can carry dangerous bacteria called *Clostridium botulinum.*

"And *Clostridium botulinum* leads to . . . ?" asked Meena Wheeler-Rivera, the instructor and a former health inspector for city swimming pools and saunas.

"Paralysis!" the class of about twenty responded in unison.

"And if you don't go to the hospital . . . ?"

"You die!"

Ms. Wheeler-Rivera knows so much that she rarely eats out anymore. Mr. Suleman still patronizes restaurants, but the potential life-or-death consequences of not writing up a violation are ingrained in him.

On a recent morning he had just shut down a restaurant after finding mouse droppings in the walk-in refrigerator. "You usually won't find mouse droppings in a fridge, because it's a cool environment," he said. "So to have droppings in a walk-in is totally uncalled for. What a way to start the day." He shook his head disapprovingly.

Mr. Suleman conducts three or four inspections a day on average, normally working from 9 a.m. until 5 p.m., or from 3 to 11 p.m. —though a nightclub inspection, say, could keep him out as late as 3 a.m.

His daily schedule is set by a computer that generates a list of randomly selected restaurants in any of the five boroughs. (How often a restaurant is inspected depends on how it has fared in past visits.)

When he shows up and introduces himself, he said, restaurants try various "tricks": Servers press buzzers underneath the host stand to alert the staff that the inspector is there. Sometimes the manager will say he has to go find the manager, and uses that time to get ready.

Inspections can take as little as an hour (a perfect score—zero, for no violations—is possible) or several hours if food-safety conditions are poor. Mr. Suleman has to finish one visit before he can start the next; this means that contrary to the widespread belief that inspectors deliberately show up during peak hours, he has little control over what time he arrives.

"Once we walk in, we can't just say, 'No, you are busy, let's call it a day,'" he said. "No matter the length of the line or how busy a restaurant is, I have to find a way to get the inspection done. It's unavoidable."

Life on the job is lonely. Mr. Suleman travels around the city by himself, carrying a backpack with about 40 pounds of equipment: a Panasonic tablet for typing up reports, a portable Brother printer that allows him to deliver his findings on the spot, two kinds of probes for testing air and food temperatures, alcohol pads for sanitizing the probes, a small flashlight, various types of tags for marking and embargoing food and equipment, and the most important tools of all: the letter grades, printed on thick card stock.

Mr. Suleman carefully pulled out the signs: GRADE PENDING, A, B, "the almighty C," he said. The last one read, "CLOSED BY ORDER OF THE COMMISSIONER OF HEALTH AND MENTAL HYGIENE."

"This is the sign that nobody wants to see," he added with a small chuckle.

Before the grades, when inspection results were not as public, restaurants had little incentive to address health violations, said Christine Testa, who left her job as an assistant director of the health department in 2011 to become president of Early Warning Food Service Solutions, which trains restaurants on food safety.

Without that incentive, many restaurants risked being shut down. "I remember closing ten restaurants in one day," Ms. Testa said. "We were not doing anything but closing people down and taking their money."

Today, before any inspection, every restaurant receives a health department worksheet detailing all potential violations, so owners can preemptively fix problems. Mr. Suleman and others conduct low-cost penalty-free consultations and free workshops for restaurants — measures meant to level the playing field for independent restaurants that lack the resources of larger groups.

But restaurateurs are no less wary about the inspection process; many find it overly subjective, and too ready to write up violations for minor infractions.

"I'm scared of the health department," said Reed Adelson, the owner of Virginia's, a restaurant in the East Village. "Not because I have anything to hide, but I know that if they want to find something, they will always find something. There is always a corner you didn't dust or a light bulb with too high of a wattage."

Virginia's recently received a B grade after an inspector found evidence of mice and foods kept at improper temperatures. The grade was raised to an A after the restaurant addressed some of the violations and successfully disputed others in a hearing with the city's Office of Administrative Trials and Hearings. (Any restaurant can challenge violations before the office.)

But even with the A, Mr. Adelson said he ended up paying about $600 in fines, which are imposed by the office. These penalties —which can range from a few hundred to a few thousand dollars —and other expenses end up being more financially burdensome than helpful in improving operations, he said.

Wilson Tang, the owner of Nom Wah Tea Parlor, in Chinatown, said that while the fairness of inspections has improved overall, "we look at reports, and on one they picked up those couple of things, and the next inspection is completely different.

If the inspector had a great day, cool, they are typically nicer and more lenient," he said. But others "had a chip on their shoulder and rushed into the kitchen like there was something going on."

Mr. Tang also owns a restaurant in Philadelphia, where "it's almost laughable how much more lax it is," he said.

"There is more of a trust in restaurants" in that city, which does not assign letter grades, he added. "They know we are not out to poison people. We are just trying to make a living and provide a service."

The Magnolia Bakery branch in the Bloomingdale's flagship store in midtown chalks up the B grade it received last year to the subjectivity of the inspections. Employees had left scoops in food containers—a potential cross-contamination risk—and the inspector could have penalized the shop only once but instead chose to record an individual violation for each misplaced scoop, said Bobbie Lloyd, a partner and the executive vice president of operations at Magnolia.

"We had to display a B on our door for quite a while, just because of that gray area," she said. "We consider that location to be our cleanest store, but that's going to make customers pause." (The grade was later raised to an A.)

Corinne Schiff, the city's deputy commissioner of environmental health, said there were a number of measures to ensure that restaurants were judged objectively and on the same scale, including an exacting reporting protocol for inspectors to follow and the random assignments.

But the health department still clearly feels the tension that hovers over the process. It would not let a reporter trail Mr. Suleman during his inspections, and limited his interview time. Mr. Suleman would not allow his face to be shown in photographs and was reticent about some details, including his age and his exact salary; the job pays between $42,500 and about $76,000 a year, the department said.

Mr. Suleman often feels frustrated by the perception that inspectors are out to punish restaurants. "I'm not all-powerful," he said. "The power is in the hands of the restaurants" to improve their food safety.

So when he shuts a restaurant down, he said, "how do you expect me to feel bad? You have a set of rules, and if you are not following those rules, you deserve what you get."

For him, the most memorable depiction of a health inspector in pop culture is in the 2003 movie *Deliver Us from Eva,* a modern adaptation of *The Taming of the Shrew,* starring Gabrielle Union as a ruthless health inspector. "She's screaming at people and taunting people," he said.

This, he insisted, is not what his job is like: he tries to be as friendly as possible (but not too friendly, "or they think you will pass them") and communicate openly throughout the inspection.

"I don't think there is any inspector who takes pride in closing down a restaurant," he added. "But imagine food not being cooked to the right temperature and someone getting very sick. That would make me feel even more guilty."

No matter how many customers are protected by shutting down a restaurant, though, the nitpicking, fine-levying bureaucrat will never be the protagonist of the story.

"You want to know why there are only one hundred inspectors for twenty-five thousand restaurants?" Ms. Testa asked. "It is a tough job. You have to go into restaurants knowing they are going to hate you. You have to have a tough skin. It's not warm and fuzzy."

"That's why I left the health department, to be honest."

STEPHANIE M. LEE

Sliced and Diced: Here's How Cornell Scientist Brian Wansink Turned Shoddy Data into Viral Studies About How We Eat

FROM *BuzzFeed News*

IN THE SUMMER of 2013, Özge Siğirci, a young scientist in Turkey, had not yet arrived at Cornell University for her new research stint. But she already had an assignment from her future boss, Brian Wansink: find something interesting about all-you-can-eat buffets.

As the head of Cornell's prestigious food psychology research unit, the Food and Brand Lab, Wansink was a social science star. His dozens of studies about why and how we eat received mainstream attention everywhere from *O, the Oprah Magazine* to the *Today* show to the *New York Times*. At the heart of his work was an accessible, inspiring message: weight loss is possible for anyone willing to make a few small changes to their environment, without need for strict diets or intense exercise.

When Siğirci started working with him, she was assigned to analyze a data set from an experiment that had been carried out at an Italian restaurant. Some customers paid $8 for the buffet, others half price. Afterward they all filled out a questionnaire about who they were and how they felt about what they'd eaten.

Somewhere in those survey results, the professor was convinced, there *had* to be a meaningful relationship between the discount and the diners. But he wasn't satisfied by Siğirci's initial review of the data.

"I don't think I've ever done an interesting study where the data 'came out' the first time I looked at it," he told her over email.

More than three years later, Wansink would publicly praise Siğirci for being "the grad student who never said 'no.'" The unpaid visiting scholar from Turkey was dogged, Wansink wrote on his blog in November 2016. Initially given a "failed study" with "null results," Siğirci analyzed the data over and over until she began "discovering solutions that held up," he wrote. Her tenacity ultimately turned the buffet experiment into four published studies about pizza-eating, all cowritten with Wansink and widely covered in the press.

2013/7/23 Sandra R. Cuellar [redacted]
Hello Ozge,
I am forwarding you a message that Brian sent this morning to my email address to be sent to you. FYI, he is in Taiwan with his family at the moment and he probably didn't find your address in his mailbox there. When you reply please do so to his two addresses: [redacted] and [redacted].
Best,
Sandra

Hi Ozge,
Glad you had a chance to take an initial look at the data.
I don't think I've ever done an interesting study where the data "came out" the first time I looked at it. The interesting stories come from seeing when things—like the 1/2 price buffet—works and when it doesn't.
I would like you to really dig into this to find a number of situations or people for which this relationship does hold—that is where the 1/2 price buffet did result in a difference.
Here's some things to do.
First, look to see if there are weird outliers (in terms of how much they ate). If there seems to be a reason they are different, pull them out but specially note why you did so, so that this can be described in the method.
Second, think of all the different ways you can cut the data and analyze subsets of it to see when this relationship holds. For instance, if it works on men but not women, we have a moderator. Here are some groups you'll want to break out separately:

Males
Females
Lunch goers
Dinner goers

People sitting alone
People eating with groups of 2
People eating in groups of 2+
People who order alcohol
People who order soft drinks
People who sit close to buffet
People who sit far away
and so on . . .

Third, look at a bunch of different DVs. These might include

\# pieces of pizza
\# trips
Fill level of plate
Did they get dessert
Did they order a drink
and so on . . .

This is really important to try and find as many things here as possible *before* you come. First, it will make a good impression on people and helps you stand out a bit. Second, it would be the highest likelihood of you getting something publishable out of your visit.

Work hard, squeeze some blood out of this rock, and we'll see you soon.

Best,

Brian

On July 25, 2013, at 1:30 AM, Özge Siğirci wrote:

Hello Brian,

Thank you very much for your message, I will try to dig out the data in the way you described.

But, actually I have a point to mention. I think the questions in the survey you have sent to me and the data set are not in the same order. So, I could not be exactly sure what some of the variable names refer to, like "Much3", "Amountcm4", "Saladcm5", "Slices7". Is there a way to be sure about what they refer to?

Thank you,

Ozge

From: Brian Wansink
To: Mitsuru Shimizu; Aner Tal; Drew (Andrew) Stephen Hanks; Collin Payne; David Just
Cc: Özge Siğirci; Brian Wansink
Subject: Re: Please Send this note to Ozge
Date: Friday, July 26, 2013 5:28:18 AM

Hi Guys,

There's a new visitor from Turkey arriving this Fall, and I've given her that data we collected a while back from the all-you-can-eat restaurant in Whitney Point. Do any of you remember the specifics about what she's asking? If so, email her and cc me. Thanks much.

Best,

Brian

But that's not how science is supposed to work. Ideally, statisticians say, researchers should set out to prove a specific hypothesis before a study begins. Wansink, in contrast, was retroactively creating hypotheses to fit data patterns that emerged after an experiment was over.

Wansink couldn't have known that his blog post would ignite a firestorm of criticism that now threatens the future of his three-decade career. Over the last fourteen months, critics the world over have pored through more than fifty of his old studies and compiled "the Wansink Dossier," a list of errors and inconsistencies that suggests he aggressively manipulated data. Cornell, after initially clearing him of misconduct, has opened an investigation. And he's had five papers retracted and fourteen corrected, the latest just this month.

Now interviews with a former lab member and a trove of previously undisclosed emails show that year after year, Wansink and his collaborators at the Cornell Food and Brand Lab have turned shoddy data into headline-friendly eating lessons that they could feed to the masses.

In correspondence between 2008 and 2016, the renowned Cornell scientist and his team discussed and even joked about exhaustively mining data sets for impressive-looking results. They strategized how to publish subpar studies, sometimes targeting journals with low standards. And they often framed their findings in the hopes of stirring up media coverage to, as Wansink once put it, "go virally big time."

The correspondence shows, for example, how Wansink coached Siğirci to knead the pizza data.

First, he wrote, she should break up the diners into all kinds of groups: "males, females, lunch goers, dinner goers, people sitting alone, people eating with groups of 2, people eating in groups of 2+, people who order alcohol, people who order soft drinks, people who sit close to buffet, people who sit far away, and so on . . ."

Then she should dig for statistical relationships between those groups and the rest of the data: "# pieces of pizza, # trips, fill level of plate, did they get dessert, did they order a drink, and so on . . ."

"This is really important to try and find as many things here as possible *before* you come," Wansink wrote to Siğirci. Doing so would not only help her impress the lab, he said, but "it would be the highest likelihood of you getting something publishable out of your visit."

He concluded on an encouraging note: "Work hard, squeeze some blood out of this rock, and we'll see you soon."

Siğirci was game. "I will try to dig out the data in the way you described."

All four of the pizza papers were eventually retracted or corrected. But the newly uncovered emails—obtained through records requests to New Mexico State University, which employs Wansink's longtime collaborator Collin Payne—reveal two published studies that were based on shoddy data and have so far received no public scrutiny.

Still, Wansink defends his work.

"I stand by and am immensely proud of the work done here at the Lab," he told *BuzzFeed News* by email, in response to a detailed list of allegations made in this story. "The Food and Brand Lab does not use 'low-quality data', nor does it seek to publish 'subpar studies.'"

He pointed out that an independent lab confirmed the basic findings of the pizza papers. "That is, even where there has been unintentional error, the conclusions and impacts of the studies have not changed," he wrote.

Siğirci and Payne did not respond to requests to comment for this story.

Wansink's practices are part of a troubling pattern of strategic data-crunching across the entire field of social science. Even so, several independent statisticians and psychology researchers are appalled at the extent of Wansink's data manipulation.

"I am sorry to say that it is difficult to read these emails and avoid a conclusion of research misconduct," Brian Nosek, a psychologist at the University of Virginia, told *BuzzFeed News*. As executive director of the Center for Open Science, Nosek is one of his field's most outspoken reformers and spearheaded a massive project to try to reproduce prominent discoveries.

Based on the emails, Nosek said, "this is not science, it is storytelling."

The so-called replication crisis has punctured some of the world's most famous psychology research, from Amy Cuddy's work suggesting that "power poses" cause hormonal changes associated with feeling powerful, to Diederik Stapel's fabricated claims that messy environments lead to discrimination. In an influential 2015 report, Nosek's team attempted to repeat one hundred psychology experiments and reproduced less than one-half of the original findings.

One reason for the discrepancy is "p-hacking," the taboo practice of slicing and dicing a data set for an impressive-looking pattern. It can take various forms, from tweaking variables to show a desired result to pretending that a finding proves an original hypothesis—in other words, uncovering an answer to a question that was only asked after the fact.

In psychology research, a result is usually considered statistically significant when a calculation called a p-value is less than or equal to 0.05. But excessive data massaging can wind up with a p-value lower than 0.05 just by random chance, making a hypothesis seem valid when it's actually a fluke.

Wansink said his lab's data is "heavily scrutinized," and that's "what exploratory research is all about." But for years Wansink's inbox has been filled with chatter that, according to independent statisticians, is blatant p-hacking.

"Pattern doesn't look good," Payne of New Mexico State wrote to Wansink and David Just, another Cornell professor, in April 2009, after what Payne called a "marathon" data-crunching session for an experiment about eating and TV-watching.

"I also ran—I am not kidding—400 strategic mediation analyses to no avail . . ." Payne wrote. In other words, testing four hundred variables to find one that might explain the relationship between the experiment and the outcomes. "The last thing to try—but I shutter to think of it—is trying to mess around with the mood variables. Ideas . . . suggestions?"

Two days later Payne was back with promising news: by focusing on the relationship between two variables in particular, he wrote, "we get exactly what we need." (The study does not appear to have been published.)

"That's p-hacking on steroids," said Kristin Sainani, an associate professor of health research and policy at Stanford University. "They're running every possible combination of variables, essentially, to see if anything will come up significant."

In a conversation about another study in August 2015, Wansink mentioned a series of experiments that "were chasing interactions that were hard to find." He apparently hoped that they would all arrive at the same conclusion, which is "bad science," said Susan Wei, an assistant professor of biostatistics at the University of Minnesota.

"It does very much seem like this Brian Wansink investigator is a consistent and repeated offender of statistics," Wei added. "He's so brazen about it, I can't tell if he's just bad at statistical thinking or he knows that what he's doing is scientifically unsound but he goes ahead anyway."

In 2012, Wansink, Payne, and Just published one of their most famous studies, which revealed an easy way of nudging kids into healthy eating choices. By decorating apples with stickers of Elmo from *Sesame Street,* they claimed, elementary school students could be swayed to pick the fruit over cookies at lunchtime.

But back in September 2008, when Payne was looking over the data soon after it had been collected, he found no strong apples-and-Elmo link—at least not yet.

"I have attached some initial results of the kid study to this message for your report," Payne wrote to his collaborators. "Do not despair. It looks like stickers on fruit may work (with a bit more wizardry)."

Wansink also acknowledged the paper was weak as he was preparing to submit it to journals. The p-value was 0.06, just shy of the gold-standard cutoff of 0.05. It was a "sticking point," as he put it in a January 7, 2012, email. "It seems to me it should be lower," he wrote, attaching a draft. "Do you want to take a look at it and see what you think. If you can get the data, and it needs some tweeking, it would be good to get that one value below .05."

From: Brian Wansink
To: David Just
Cc: Collin Payne; Sandra Cuellar
Subject: Can Branding Improve School Lunches?

Date: Saturday, January 7, 2012 7:17:42 AM
Attachments: Elmo Icon-AJPH—1-7-12.doc, ATT00001.htm
Hi David,
Here's the Elmo study we are going to spin off and submit.
I think we start with the AJPH as a Brief (80 word abstract and 800 word
paper), and go from there. I'll give Sandra a list of the journals and the
priority order we should consider. Let's consider these two first:
Brief—American Journal of Public Health
Research Letter—Archives of Pediatric and Adolescent Medicine
One sticking point is that although the stickers increase apple selection
by 71%, for some reason this is a p value of .06. It seems to me it should
be lower. Do you want to take a look at it and see what you think. If you
can get the data, and it needs some tweeking, it would be good to get
that one value below .05.
Best,
Brian

Later in 2012 the study appeared in the prestigious *JAMA Pediatrics,* the 0.06 p-value intact. But in September 2017 it was retracted and replaced with a version that listed a p-value of 0.02. And a month later it was retracted yet again for an entirely different reason: Wansink admitted that the experiment had not been done on eight- to eleven-year-olds, as he'd originally claimed, but on preschoolers.

Scientists are under a lot of pressure to attain the 0.05 p-value, said Wei of the University of Minnesota, even though it's an arbitrary cutoff. "It's an unfortunate state of being in the research community, in the publishing world."

Still, the Food and Brand Lab appears to approach science far more flagrantly than most other scientists who face the same pressures, Nosek said.

"It's a cartoon of how someone in the most extreme form might p-hack data," he said of the emails as a whole. "There was the explicit goal of 'Let's just get something out of the data, use the data as a device to find something, anything, that's interesting.'"

Back in March of last year, shortly after his pizza papers were called into question, Wansink was interviewed by the *Chronicle of Higher Education.* He told the outlet that before all the hubbub over his studies, he'd never heard of the term *p-hacking* or the replication crisis. "Science is messy in a lot of ways," he said.

*

The emails reviewed by *BuzzFeed News* point to potential problems with two of Wansink's studies that haven't received any public criticism.

In July 2009, Wansink wrote to collaborators about a study in progress. Mall shoppers had been asked to read a pamphlet that described one of two kinds of walks—one that focused on listening to music and the other on exercising. At the end, researchers offered them salty and sweet snacks as a thank-you and recorded how much participants served themselves.

"What's neat about this is that it shows that just thinking about walking makes people eat more," Wansink wrote. "But we should be able to get much more from this." He added, "I think it would be good to mine it for significance and a good story."

Meanwhile, one of his coauthors, former Cornell visiting scholar Carolina Werle, was trying—in vain—to find a link between how much time the participants spent in the mall and other variables she'd tested. "There is no interaction with the experimental conditions," she wrote, adding that "nothing works in terms of interaction."

Werle did not respond to a request to comment for this story. The study wound up in the journal *Appetite* two years later, claiming that just the act of imagining physical activity prompts people to take more snacks.

In 2013, Werle and Wansink were discussing a different study about whether describing a walk as fun, such as by framing it as a scenic stroll rather than a form of exercise, influenced how much the walkers would want to eat afterward.

The scientists emailed back and forth about two facts that the subsequent paper did not disclose: that the "exercise" group was much smaller than the "fun" group, and that there was some missing data.

"Why are you hiding that? That seems like pretty pertinent information," Sainani of Stanford said.

Wansink himself acknowledged that the data was weak. At one point he told Werle that he didn't think the study was good enough to submit to a prestigious journal. In another message he mentioned that "there's been a lot of data torturing with this cool data set." The journal *Marketing Letters* eventually published the paper in May 2014.

Journals should scrutinize these two papers due to questions raised by the emails, said Nick Brown, an independent graduate student at the University of Groningen in the Netherlands who has spent more than a year dissecting Wansink's work.

The paper that told walkers to think of their exercise as fun, for example, reports p-values of 0.04 and less than 0.05. But by Brown's calculation they appear to have been cut in half using an unjustified statistical method. (Wei said the group's method may have been acceptable.) And one of Werle's emails to Wansink indicated that one of the experiments had forty-seven people, but the paper reports forty-six.

Brown remains befuddled by the breadth of errors that he and other critics have unearthed in the Food and Brand Lab's research, from data impossibilities to sample sizes that don't add up.

"They're doing the p-hacking and they're getting other stuff wrong, badly wrong," he said. "The level of incompetence that would be required for that is just staggering."

These papers are only a fraction of the 250-plus that Wansink has produced since the early 1990s. One of the driving factors behind his prolific output, his emails suggest, is a hard truth that all academic scientists face: the more papers you publish, the more likely you are to be rewarded in promotions, funding, and fame.

In August 2012, Wansink relayed some sad news to more than a dozen colleagues: one of his former grad students had just been denied tenure.

"Whenever I called her, it always seemed like she was working on a ton of stuff," he wrote. Yet he was surprised to see that she'd only published one article in a minor journal in seven years.

This unnamed scholar was working on lots of research that never saw the light of day, Wansink wrote: "Too much inventory; not enough shipments." Ideally, he mused, a science lab would function like a tech company. Tim Cook, for instance, was renowned for getting products out of Apple's warehouses faster and pumping up profits. "As Steve Jobs said, 'Geniuses ship,'" Wansink wrote.

So, he proposed, the lab should adopt a system of strict deadlines for submitting and resubmitting research until it landed somewhere. "A lot of these papers are laying around on each of our desktops and they're like inventory that isn't working for us," he told the team. "We've got so much huge momentum going. This could make our productivity legendary."

Kirsikka Kaipainen knows firsthand how the Food and Brand Lab manages to churn out so many papers. She did research there in 2012 as a graduate student visiting from Finland.

Wansink was "warm and generous and energetic, somebody who would take you in with open arms," she recalled.

Soon after she arrived, Wansink handed her a data set from an online weight-loss program run by the lab. At a brainstorming session he led the charge in proposing a half-dozen or so papers that could come out of the data, Kaipainen said.

But when Kaipainen drilled down, there wasn't enough information to support the conclusions he wanted. "I felt I was a failure," she said. "I realized over time it wasn't my wrongdoing—it was just that there was nothing there to be found."

Kaipainen eventually steered the paper to a place she was comfortable with, a straightforward review of how the program worked. Wansink was fine with it, she said, since it wound up in a notable journal. But even though his name is on it, he had little to do with writing it—and his few contributions made her uneasy, she said.

"Like he hadn't really looked at the results critically and he was trying to make the paper say something that wasn't true," she said. "That's when I started feeling like, this is not the kind of research I want to do." (In 2014, Wansink would cite this paper in a Kickstarter campaign that raised $10,000 for a weight-loss service that never launched.)

As months went by, Kaipainen began to notice that her experience fit into a disturbing pattern in the lab as a whole: collect data first, form hypotheses later. She isn't the only former lab member who felt troubled by how the place was run. Other students have told the *Cornell Daily Sun* that Wansink and his team often chased down findings that were intuitive-sounding yet overly broad and unreliable.

Kaipainen was also troubled by lab members' frequent remarks that a finding "would make a good story or a good article" or "be interesting for media." At one point the lab brainstormed questions for an outside party's market research survey. "That was weird also," she recalled, "to come up with some questions not based on any theory, just 'What would be cool to ask?,' 'What cool headlines could we get if we got some associations?'"

Even when writing manuscript drafts, Wansink was thinking about how to sell his inspirational results to the public.

"We want this to go virally big time," he wrote to Payne, Just, and another Cornell colleague on March 27, 2012, explaining why he wanted to make the chart labels for the Elmo-and-apples study sound "more generalizable." Another time he discussed playing up "the quotable point" of the study.

The study about mall shoppers thinking about exercising, he once wrote, "would make quite a media splash." Another time he proposed: "Let's think of renaming the paper to something more shameless. Maybe something like 'Thinking about exercise makes me hungry.'" (Its published title was "Just thinking about exercise makes me serve more food: physical activity and calorie compensation.")

Wansink told *BuzzFeed News* that attracting media coverage is a core part of the Food and Brand Lab's mission "to be accessible and impactful."

"The reality is that by and large, the public does not have access to academic articles," he said. "Framing our work in a way that can be accessed and used by the public is something all social scientists should consider."

These days Kaipainen leads an online mental health startup. She said she stands by the four papers she wrote with Wansink. And she believes her old boss has good intentions at his core. "He wants to help people eat better. I kind of admire him for it," she said. "But ends don't justify the means."

To Nosek, the relentless pursuit of fawning press is just one element of a backward rewards system in science. When a university is deciding whom to hire or a funding institution is selecting a grantee, it's easy to pick those who are publishing a lot, he said.

"And scientists," Nosek added, "have to do those dysfunctional behaviors—do everything you can to seek an exciting, sexy story, even if it means reducing the credibility of the research."

Scientists often rely on peer reviewers—anonymous experts—to weed out errors in papers before they go to press. But journals didn't, or couldn't, catch every inaccuracy from the Food and Brand Lab.

For example, reviewers were generally positive about what ended up being a controversial 2012 study in *Preventive Medicine*. It reported that schoolchildren ate more vegetables at lunch when they had catchy names like "X-Ray Vision Carrots."

"This is a well-written manuscript that addressed critical questions pertinent to vegetable consumption among school-aged children," one reviewer wrote. Another praised the experiments because they "use real-world data and show changes in actual behavior."

Last fall, Wansink admitted that the lunchtime observation part of the carrots study had actually been done on preschoolers, not the reported eight- to eleven-year-olds (just like the Elmo-and-apples article). The paper was corrected on February 1, shocking critics who had called for a full retraction. In their defense, the researchers noted that a subexperiment mentioned in the study did involve elementary-school children. "These mistakes and omissions do not change the general conclusion of the paper," they wrote.

The scientists who reviewed the Elmo study in *JAMA Pediatrics* didn't seem to raise any red flags either, based on Wansink's responses to them. But the journal correspondence does point to a bizarre new discrepancy.

Originally Wansink made it clear that the researchers had let children pick both apples and cookies if they wanted. "We emphasized why we set up a system that allowed children to a cookie or apple, or both, or neither," he explained to the journal editor in a March 2012 draft letter. But five years later, when the team retracted the study the first time, the researchers publicly contradicted this statement, writing that "children were offered to take either an apple or a cookie (not both)."

Sometimes the team's acceptance into top journals surprised even them. In July 2009, Payne and Just, the Cornell professor, were celebrating a paper that had landed in the *Annals of Behavioral Medicine*.

"Is it me or was this way too easy for a journal ranked 10th out of 101 journals in its category?" Payne wrote. "Usually for a top 10 journal I am trying to reinvent statistics." (Just did not respond to a request for comment.)

When their work was rejected, the members of the Food and Brand Lab would often try increasingly lower-quality journals until they succeeded. This practice is in part responsible for the sheer volume of scientific findings that cannot be replicated.

Even so, Wansink and his colleagues were sometimes frank about their desire to put flawed data in publications with low standards.

In March 2009, Wansink asked Payne to look over a manuscript

about how people shop in foreign countries where they're unfamil-
iar with the brands or language. Wansink had written it with Koert
van Ittersum, a professor at the University of Groningen, who did
not respond to a request for comment.

"There's a paper that Koert and I have had shelfed for about 5
years that needs to see the journal light of day," Wansink said over
email. It was based on experiments that were "insightful, but not
very rigorous."

He continued, "There's a bunch of 2nd-tier journals (or lower)
we could send it to," and added, ". . . we'd kind of like to aim at a
pretty quick acceptance."

Time was crucial. "At this point," Wansink wrote, "we don't want
to redo any studies, just deal with the ones we have and find an editor that says, 'Interesting, and good enough.'" So far, none have.

To Brown, the grad student who may know Wansink's work better than Wansink himself, the lab is like a food-processing company.

"What they're doing is making a very small amount of science go
a very long way when you spread it thinly and you cut it with water
and modified starch," he said. "The product, which is the paper, is
designed and marketed before it's even been built."

He suspects that more of Wansink's papers will be corrected or
even retracted. (Cornell confirmed to *BuzzFeed News* that its investigation into Wansink's research is ongoing but declined to share
any details.)

Brown is less sure, however, whether this saga will lead to any
meaningful changes beyond Wansink's oeuvre. As illuminating as
the emails are—he likens them to security footage of a bank rob-
bery—he also thinks that the behavior is "probably quite typical of
what goes on in a lot of labs."

"Science by volume, science by output, by yardage, that has to
stop," Brown said. "The problem is that it's an awful lot of people's
paychecks and an awful lot of people's business models."

SHANE MITCHELL

Hot Wet Goobers

FROM *Bitter Southerner*

Sitting by the roadside on a summer's day
Chatting with my mess-mates, passing time away
Lying in the shadows underneath the trees
Goodness, how delicious, eating goober peas.
Peas, peas, peas, peas
Eating goober peas
Goodness, how delicious,
Eating goober peas.

> —Civil War folk song, original sheet music published by A. E.
> Blackmar, New Orleans, 1866

"STOP THE CAR," I shouted. "Pull over now. Now!"

We were driving on a county road near the Georgia border. My husband, Bronson, startled, swerved to the shoulder, and I flung open the passenger door to run back to a makeshift stand—two sawhorses, a plank, and a pot—tended by an old man sitting in a lawn chair under a live oak.

Returning to the car, I offered the soggy paper sack.

"What . . . ?"

"Just try them," I said. "Stick one in your mouth."

"They look disgusting. Don't let that drip on the mat."

Bronson is from New Jersey. I watched him cautiously shell and eat his first boiled peanut.

"Oh, my God."

"See?"

That was twenty-five years ago. And we're still married.

The Peanut Belt

The peanut belongs to the New World, but it's a long journey from genesis to a boiled peanut stand in Georgia. Somewhere in the Bolivian Andes, two wild plant ancestors cross-pollinated 10,000 years ago to create the hybrid cultivar *Arachis hypogaea*, a scientific reference to how this weedy member of the legume family grows under the earth. From its center of origin, cultivation spread into Brazil, Argentina, Peru, Mexico, and the Caribbean; when the Portuguese and Spanish arrived, colonists added it to their pantries as well. In 1570 explorer and naturalist Gabriel Soares de Souza noted that cooks in Bahia had begun to exchange peanuts for Old World nuts in recipes "cut and covered with a sugar mixture as confections . . . candied and cured in long thin pieces." Portuguese traders subsequently introduced the peanut to their colony in China, now the world's biggest producer, and also ports in West Africa, where indigenous cousins, especially the Bambara groundnut, or *Vigna subterraneana*, were already a subsistence crop.

And this is where the history of the peanut turns ugly: it was a provision on slave ships plying the Middle Passage, which is how it eventually arrived in the South. Known to Kongo speakers as *nguba* or *mpinda*, these root words evolved into *goober* and *pindar* when enslaved African Americans subsequently planted them in their colonial kitchen allotments. In *Notes on the State of Virginia*, Thomas Jefferson documented the cultivation of peanuts there by 1781 — he planted sixty-five hills of "peendars" and remarked during his presidency that they were very sweet. Henry Wansey, a member of the Bath and West of England Agricultural Society, ate roasted nuts on his tour of America in 1794. He is credited with the first located use of the word *pea-nut*. During the Denmark Vesey Conspiracy of 1822 in Charleston, a conjurer named Gullah Jack was reported to instruct superstitious plotters to eat parched corn and groundnuts and carry a crab claw in their mouths as an amulet for invulnerability. Confederate troops ate them as an emergency ration. Consequently the goober pea song. The sheet music first printed by a

Confederate sympathizer is jokingly credited to A. Pindar (words) and P. Nutt (music).

Peanuts have become an aspect of our intangible cultural heritage, essential to tailgate parties, baseball games, political rallies, school lunches, state fairs, circuses, and even prison commissaries. Roasted, parched, buttered, and raw. Only in the South do we truly love them boiled. Slippery on the outside, chewy in the pod. Those who slurp oysters raw but think "country caviar" tastes like snot? Shame on you. My father loved eating them with a Grape Nehi, but I prefer an ice-cold Coke, with enough throat-choking fizz to kill down the salt. Unlike my husband, I don't recall eating my first boiled peanut, but I haven't forgotten the outrage when vendors first introduced unorthodox flavorings to the brine. Cajun spice? Old Bay? BBQ rub? (More recently Atlanta-based chef Asha Gomez, who wrote *My Two Souths,* posted about adding turmeric and Serrano peppers to the brine, and I can't stop thinking about it.) Boiled peanuts always seemed within reach during my childhood summers, at the height of the harvest, when stands spontaneously popped up on the two-lane highways of the Peanut Belt.

"It's serendipitous," said Matt Lee, of the Lee Bros. Boiled Peanut Catalogue. "Never know when you'll come across a good one."

Big Peanut

When a horse-man passes, the soldiers have a rule
To cry out their loudest, "Mister here's your mule!"
But another custom, enchanting-er than these
Is wearing out your grinders, eating goober peas.

Just before the battle, the General hears a row
He says "The Yanks are coming, I hear their rifles now."
He turns around in wonder, and what d'ya think he sees?
The Georgia Militia, eating goober peas.

Alex Hardy remembered his grandfather plowing fields with a mule. A rawboned man in his late sixties, he surveyed row after row of peanut vines as a harvester churned past, uprooting the late-season crop with a little shimmy to shake off the sandy Georgia soil. A tractor followed, pulling a combine that threshed the nuts and spewed out chaff. The swirling dust was ballet-slipper pink.

Hardy's wife, Jacque, a retired studio photographer, picked up a handful of green nuts left on the ground and cracked them open.

"At one time, Alex's granddaddy had a stable of thirty-eight mules," she said.

"They were a prized possession," he said, nodding. "Couldn't do without them. My daddy had a mule for a year or two but quickly switched to tractors once he got out the war."

Hardy's ancestors migrated to Pulaski County, Georgia, in the late eighteenth century and for generations have farmed at the tail end of the Atlantic Coastal Fall Line, the geologic boundary where the outwash plain of the upper continental shelf deposited sandy, loamy soil, which happens to be paradise for raising peanuts, give or take a bankrupting drought. The lesser roads in this part of the state are lined with pecan groves and loblolly pine. Before forced onto the Trail of Tears, the Creek Confederacy had its capital here; Sherman's March to the Sea passed to the north. And the extended Hardy family currently owns one of the larger peanut operations in south Georgia, which includes an oil-roasting plant and a packing warehouse. They also farm 1,000 acres of peanuts. More than half are green nuts selected for boiling.

"Our first year we planted three acres," said Hardy. "That yielded ten thousand pounds. Sold them in gallon buckets and trash bags. Now we're up to a million pounds."

We climbed back into Hardy's pickup and drove to the warehouse, a red-trimmed, metal-sided facility on U.S. Highway 341, close by the family farmhouse and an artificial lake where the grandchildren fished until an alligator interloped. Nuts from the field wagons were being loaded into bulk containers, then passed through a cleaning system and tumbled along conveyor belts as contract workers processed them, picking out stray stems and imperfect pods. (Seasonal employees are bused in daily from Americus, an hour and a half away. The break room has signs in English and Spanish.) Forklifts moved pallets of bushel bags into cold storage. Most of the green harvest would be shipped to southern supermarket chains like Kroger and Winn-Dixie or picked up by wholesale distributors with customers farther north.

"We send one or two semi loads a day to New York, and it all winds up in Chinatown," said Hardy. "Chinese, Africans, Indians. They might not cook them the way we do, but it's a good market. A guy originally from Gambia buys them for Minnesota. We also pack out a one-ounce size; you know, the kind on airplanes, for colleges and farm organizations. And a two-ounce size, believe it or not, for the prison system."

Peanuts are a singularly southern crop because they need 140 frost-free days to mature. They are historically grown in fields from Virginia to Texas and more recently are expanding into Arkansas and southern Missouri. Seedsman John Coykendall is even spreading the gospel of Bambara groundnuts in Tennessee. But Georgia remains the epicenter of peanut farming.

Hardy explained that the four commercial cultivars are Spanish, Valencia, Runner, and Virginia. (He grows Jumbo Georgia Runners.) "We've got twenty-five roadside stands and sell the Runners there. They are the preferred flavor for the connoisseurs and those who have the palate and know the difference. We've tried the Virginias, but customers will turn around and walk off."

We passed through plastic curtains into the boiling room, where his nephew Ken Hardy supervised the steam kettles. Measuring bowls brimmed with spice mix. Brining salt was piled against the wall. Ken boiled them at home too. Adding ham hocks to the brine for flavor was his next day-off project.

"A peanut will not take in the salt until the heat's turned off," he said. "I've wanted to try this with ham hocks at home, but I need pantyhose to put them in, and my wife won't give me a pair."

His uncle smiled.

"In 1991 we decided to add on value to the crops we were growing," Hardy said. "We couldn't get boiled peanuts the way we liked them, fresh out of the field. The green peanut is bright and pretty and has sweetness to it. They're harvested before full maturity and still at the tender stage."

"When do you eat boiled peanuts, and what do you drink with them?" I asked.

"Usually watching the game," he said. "Best to me? Beer. Otherwise, Coke."

Since I was driving deeper into Georgia that night, we went into nearby Hawkinsville for lunch at a cafeteria opposite the train tracks. The Hardys greeted neighbors at other tables and then heaped their plates with fried chicken, stewed tomatoes, and collards from the buffet. Dessert was yellow sheet cake with peanut butter–caramel icing. A waitress brought over a pitcher of sweet tea. Hardy removed his AgGeorgia Farm Credit gimme cap and placed a paper napkin on his lap.

"Peanuts, to me, that's the perfect food," he said. "They say with water and a piece of bread and peanut butter you can live."

Jacque refilled my tea glass.

"Like every southern town, you never go the ball game of any sort that you don't see peanut hulls everywhere," she said. "And yesterday, in the next county, we went down there with a little wagon and gave away peanuts at a fundraiser boil for Lieutenant Governor Casey Cagle."

Hardy walked over to the cash register to pay for lunch. I asked how he felt about the season ending.

"More glad than sad. I'm ready for a break. It's so demanding."

Jacque chimed in.

"We have a little boy at church, he's probably five, you never see him but he says, 'When are the peanuts going to be gone? I hate to see them leave. Tell me they're going to be around for a bit longer.'"

We headed back to their farmhouse. Jacque tapped me on the shoulder and pointed out the truck window to an unexceptional meadow surrounded by oaks.

"As we're passing, see that monument in the yard? Confederate president Jefferson Davis camped right there the night before he was captured by northern soldiers."

Will Work for Peanuts

> Remember when Jimmy Carter had to sell his peanut farm?
> —Internet meme, 2016

Actually, he still owns it.

Plains is even smaller than Hawkinsville, with a population of 683, including the two who require a permanent Secret Service detail posted outside their white clapboard house. On the outskirts of town, a grain silo complex, cotton warehouse, and transfer station for peanut wagons are clustered. Main Street consists of two commercial blocks and is bisected by a rail line, which passes next to the whistle-stop depot that served as the thirty-ninth president's campaign headquarters.

Every September, Plains celebrates the peanut harvest with parade floats and a road race. A peanut princess is crowned. Concession stands sell funnel cakes and shaved ice. The Carters sign books at the antique store. In the account of his childhood, *An Hour Before Daylight*, Carter writes:

> I began selling boiled peanuts on the streets of Plains when I was five years old. This was my first acquaintance with the outside world. As soon as the nuts began to mature on the vines, I would take my little wagon into one of the fields nearest our house, pull a load of peanut vines out of the ground, carry them home, pick the peanuts off the vines, wash them, and soak them in salty water overnight. The next morning, as early as possible, I boiled the peanuts for a half-hour or so until they were cooked but still firm, filled about twenty half-pound paper sacks (forty on Saturdays), and carried them to town in a basket, either walking down the railroad tracks or riding on my bike.

By the time I arrived, one morning after eating green nuts in the Hardys' fields, the parade was long over and the Nobel Prize laureate away from home. I bought a bag of boiled Georgia Runners and a used copy of *The Carter Family Favorites Cookbook* (1977) in a gift shop. A chapter is devoted to peanut recipes: peanut butter brownies, peanut praline cakes, bacon and peanut butter cornbread, peanut vegetable loaf, peanut butter fondue. The high school Jimmy Carter and his wife, Rosalynn, attended has been converted to a museum and contains memorabilia from their childhood and political campaigns. The grinning peanut logo—based on Carter's own generous smile—is singularly weird. On display in a hall are peanut drawings by schoolchildren who have visited the National Historic Site.

More compelling is the Jimmy Carter Boyhood Farm, a few miles outside of town in the rural community of Archery, named for a nineteenth-century relief organization of the African Methodist Episcopal Church. Originally the modest house lacked running water and electricity, and the family cook prepared meals on a wood-fired stove. The dining room table was set with plastic replicas of fried chicken, deviled eggs, iced tea—a homespun reminder of how the Carters would eventually entertain in a bigger white house. The kitchen garden supplied the family with vegetables, and a dry-goods store on the property operated by Carter's father supplied the neighbors, predominantly black farmers and railroad employees. Walking around the quiet yard gave me a better sense of how growing up on the farm shaped the president's commitment to service, starting with early-morning chores and his first commercial venture as a boiled-peanut vendor.

While Carter served in the Oval Office, he placed the family businesses into a blind trust to avoid conflict of interest. (How times have changed.) An Atlanta lawyer named Charles Kirbo was appointed financial trustee. Suffice to say, he did not do well by Jimmy Carter. After three years of drought and mismanagement, the plain-speaking president left the White House over $1 million in debt and dangerously close to losing the family farm.

Carter saved the fields with a book deal and the sale of his family's processing plant. His life in public service extended beyond his term as president, most notably with the founding of the Carter Center, whose peace and health initiatives extend around the world. Even in his early nineties, he continues to volunteer with Habitat for Humanity, which has its headquarters in nearby Americus. But in 2013 the former leader of the free world admitted, "I'm a peanut farmer at heart, still grow peanuts on my farm in Georgia."

Tough Nuts

> But now we are in prison and likely long to stay,
> The Yankees they are guarding us, no hope to get away;
> Our rations they are scanty, 'tis cold enough to freeze,
> I wish I was in Georgia, eating goober peas.
> Peas, peas, peas, peas,
> Eating goober peas;
> I wish I was in Georgia, eating goober peas.
>
> —stanza of a prison song

The Reverend Wayland Fuller Dunaway recorded a rare stanza of the goober pea song when confined at the Union prison on Johnson's Island, Ohio, during the latter half of the Civil War. Dunaway was serving as a captain in Company I of the 40th Virginia Infantry when captured during the Battle of Falling Waters in July 1863. W. H. Shelton, an officer with the First New York Artillery, was incarcerated in 1864 but escaped from a Confederate prison camp in Columbia, South Carolina. As he fled toward Union lines, emancipated blacks offered him goobers to eat. In the account of his escape, he noted he was regularly provided "boiled peanuts, which was a favorite way of cooking when the bean was too green to bake." And in March of 1865, two months from surrender, Robert E. Lee was quoted as saying to his son, G. W. Custis Lee, "I have been up to see the Congress and they do not seem to be able to do anything except to eat peanuts and chew tobacco, while my army is starving."

Peanuts keep showing up in dire circumstances, whether on slave ships or in war zones, because they are packed with protein and insanely nourishing. Bob Parker, president of the National Peanut Board, told me, "It's the number-one food requested by food banks. When there is a natural disaster, we send peanut butter to those areas." Parker cited Project Peanut Butter, of St. Louis, which produces and distributes RUTF [ready-to-use therapeutic food] peanut paste to combat child malnutrition in Ghana, Malawi, and Sierra Leone. He also referenced MANA, another peanut paste produced in Georgia, distributed by UNICEF and other aid organizations.

"A one-ounce bag of peanuts will carry you a long time," he said. "And peanut butter is in ninety-four percent of American pantries."

George Washington Carver did not invent peanut butter. That's one of those conflated facts taught in grade school, much like everyone still believing the earth was flat in the fifteenth century when Columbus discovered America. Actual first honors go to a Canadian, Marcellus Gilmore Edson, who was issued U.S. Patent No. 306727 for his "flavoring paste" to be used in the manufacture of "peanut-candy" on October 21, 1894. (Pre-Columbian Aztecs also pounded peanuts into a paste, so nothing is really new in the New World.) But Carver's botanical research at the Tuskegee Institute contributed greatly to peanut butter's rise in popularity. In 1916 he published a bulletin titled "How to Grow the Peanut & 105 Ways of Preparing It for Human Consumption," which included his recipes for soup, cookies, fudge, and mock chicken. He also recommended peanuts for shampoo, mayonnaise, paint, massage oil, and flour. The Carvoline cosmetics company of Birmingham manufactured peanut hair pomade with his endorsement.

It is unlikely Carver would have imagined the use devised more recently by twelve inmates at Walker County Jail in Jasper, Alabama, on a Sunday evening last July. They saved peanut butter from their sandwiches and molded it like clay to alter a number above a door leading outside, then tricked a rookie guard into opening it. (The employee thought he was letting them back into the cells.) The prisoners ditched their orange jumpsuits, flung blankets over the razor-wire fence, and busted out. Most didn't get far—two were captured at the Flying J truck stop in town. At a news conference the next day, county sheriff James E. Underwood said, "Changing some numbers on the door with peanut butter—that may sound crazy, but these people are crazy like a fox."

When I reached Jasper mayor Paul Liollio for comment, he wrote back: "This wasn't Jasper's finest hour."

Little Peanut

> I think my song has lasted almost long enough.
> The subject's interesting, but the rhymes are mighty tough.
> I wish the war was over, so free from rags and fleas
> We'd kiss our wives and sweethearts, and gobble goober peas.
> Peas, peas, peas, peas
> Eating goober peas
> Goodness, how delicious,
> Eating goober peas.

Nat Bradford tipped a pail of Carolina African Runners into the blast path of an industrial fan, scattering chaff and dust and twigs on his driveway. His farm also lies near the Fall Line, in Sumter, South Carolina, about 275 miles northeast from the Hardys' spread in Hawkinsville. Here the loamy soil is military tan, the fields of soy and cotton are fronted by evangelical churches, and small white crosses marking traffic accidents sprout next to kudzu-smothered fire hydrants. Thunderclouds were stacked in the distance, promising relief from the scorching upcountry heat, but the swarming gnats were relentless whenever Bradford shut off the fan to inspect the odd little nuts piling up in a plastic tub.

"It's an old, persnickety heirloom," he said, adjusting his tiger-orange Clemson University visor. An eighth-generation farmer, the forty-three-year-old landscape architect specializes in growing persnickety crops on 10 acres. For the past two years he has battled drought stress, late spring frosts, thrips, weed competition, and tomato spotted virus to grow this bijou peanut organically. (It's one-quarter the size of a Virginia Jumbo.) Now he is experimenting with threshing and winnowing techniques to prevent losing a huge percentage of his yield.

"The last time this nut was harvested? It was done by hand in the 1920s. It's not suited to modern-day, mechanized farming," he said, waving toward the scant bag at his feet. "But I'd rather have all my peanuts here than scattered on the field. Last year I was out there with a rake and a leaf blower, figuring out how to get them. And when you turn those peanuts over and the deer find them, they'll put a hurt on them, so you don't want them to sit long."

Bradford is one of the seedsmen working to revive *Arachis hypogea v. carolina african*. Listed in the Slow Food Ark of Taste, this foundation variety is thought to have arrived by slave ship at the end of the seventeenth century and been raised by enslaved Africans in the West Indies and the South, essentially returning full circle a landrace cultivar to native soil. According to the entry, "Its original culinary uses were greatly inflected by West African practices: The nuts were boiled, ground into meal for fritters, candied, mashed and decocted into a hot beverage, roasted, and pressed into oil."

These were likely the goober peas of song and story.

One of my favorite narratives about the Carolina African Runner involves the "maumas" of Charleston, free black women who peddled a peanut-and-molasses candy known as groundnut cake. Sold for a penny, it was a humble treat that transitioned from the street to grander kitchens on the peninsula. Sarah Rutledge listed two recipes in *The Carolina Housewife* (1847), one of which has a close resemblance to the candy observed by Soares de Souza in colonial Brazil more than two centuries earlier. In her influential Reconstruction-era recipe collection, *Mrs. Hill's New Cook Book* (1872), Annabella P. Hill, who lived through the Civil War in LaGrange, Georgia, not too far north of Plains, has a recipe for ground pea candy that resembles taffy, with additions of coconut and almonds. Earlier versions included egg whites, brandy, and lemon peel.

Few in living memory recall what groundnut cake tastes like, as the Charleston vendors were shut down before the Depression and the Carolina African Runner nearly vanished as larger cultivars prevailed. Until five years ago a remaining handful of stock sat dormant in a seed bank at North Carolina State University. Its come-back is credited to the persistence of horticultural preservationists at Clemson's Coastal Research Center. Reviving groundnut cake is the present and parallel task of culinary historians like Gullah chef Benjamin "BJ" Dennis, who sat with me at a picnic table outside Rodney Scott's BBQ in North Charleston before I drove upcountry to Sumter.

"We've still got the same palate as our ancestors," he said. "True Gullah Geechee food is really more related to what you see in West Africa. Those candies were molasses-based, that was the dominant sweetener, fresh ground from the sugarcane. But it can overwhelm. You want to *taste* that peanut. Those are the characteristics we're still trying to recreate."

Dennis's roots research took him to the southernmost Caribbean.

"The story got deeper when I went to Trinidad and saw toolum, monkey meat, and groundnut cake candies being sold there," he said. "It was interesting talking to people in the West Indies and looking back at desserts from West Africa. It seemed like a typical dessert of the diaspora."

"How do you eat boiled peanuts?" I asked.

"I treat my peanuts like a bean, not cooked to mush, gotta have a little bite, salt, and chili flake. If I dump them over the sink into a strainer, I don't usually leave the sink. They don't last long."

Talking with Dennis reminded me of another cultural link buried in the chapter on Brazil in Vertamae Smart-Grosvenor's *Vibration Cooking or the Travel Notes of a Geechee Girl:* "Bahia lies one thousand miles north of Rio and thirteen degrees south of the equator . . . Everything was everything I had dreamed of and more. Bahia felt like home. It was South Carolina and Africa."

When Bradford finished winnowing, the two of us went back out in the field. We stopped at a drying shed where several wagons parked. He had me climb up the side and stick my nose in the one containing his Carolina African Runners. The aroma nearly knocked me to the ground. It smelled like childhood.

"It's the tastiest peanut I've eaten," said Bradford.

"This is your whole crop?"

"We may get thirty-two hundred pounds if everything is firing on all cylinders, but we're already a foot in the hole because

plants don't even want to look at processing less than several eigh-
teen-wheelers at a time. Might take a while to crack that nut."

Bradford scooped out several more bushel bags.

"If we can scale it up, I think this nut has a really good chance of
getting out of the niche market. That's my dream, to have a wagon
full one day. Not the bottom of a wagon."

"What's your favorite way to eat peanuts?"

"Boiled. If you can harvest them young, they are juicy and the
shells are so thin you can eat the whole peanut. I like mine to be
a little spicy, Cajun style. And I'm definitely a beer person. Really
start to hanker for those dark beers, porters and stouts, this time of
year. Oh, my word."

Bradford's oldest son needed a ride to a football game, an hour
away, and I was mindful of driving back to Charleston with late-season thunderheads in my way. He gave me a bag of nuts to carry
away.

"How many kids?" I asked.

"Got five kids," he said. "That's four generations in a row with
four boys and a girl. Think maybe it's terroir. If it has an effect on
food and plants, why wouldn't it have an effect on us?"

Nuts to You

> Formerly these groundnut cakes were sold by our Maumas on
> street corners or on the Battery on July 4th and other special
> occasions. The Maumas were picturesque, with their turbaned
> heads, waving a short fly brush made of dried grasses."
>
> — *Charleston Receipts* (1950), headnote for groundnut cakes
> recipe by Miss Ellen Parker

"Could you please stop making a big mess?"

My husband surveyed our kitchen with dismay. A dozen cookbooks lay open, peanut shells scattered, a precious cup of Bradford's Carolina African Runners parched in a cast-iron skillet. The
groundnut candy recipe in *The Carolina Housewife* requires boiling the mixture over a slow fire. How to interpret that? And the
parched nuts: skins on or off? Mindful of the conversation with
Benjamin Dennis, I substituted Sapelo Purple Ribbon cane syrup

for harsher molasses. (It has a parallel history to the Carolina African Runner, but more about that another time.) Dennis is right to want this precious nut dominant.

"Want to try one?" I asked, offering a plate of the cooled candies.

"I don't want to loosen my fillings," Bronson replied.

"Oh, come on."

My Jersey boy bit into one cautiously. I waited.

"Well, so what does it taste like?"

"Peanuts."

Bison Bars Were Supposed to Restore Native Communities and Grass-based Ranches. Then Came Epic Provisions.

FROM *New Food Economy*

To HEAR THE processed-food industry tell it, the bison bar—the trendy, protein-dense snack now ubiquitous at high-end grocery stores across the country—has a clear, undisputed origin story. It was invented in 2011 by Katie Forrest and Taylor Collins, vegan endurance athletes who turned to meat to power their punishing training regimen. They got hooked on grass-fed bison, started making unusual bars from meat, dried fruit, and seeds out of their home kitchen, and quickly incorporated their obsession into a business. As cofounders of their new company, Epic Provisions, Forrest and Collins were smart and idealistic and naive in all the right ways. Demand grew so quickly it's almost as if they stumbled onto their defining moment: an acquisition by General Mills, to the tune of $100 million, that would launch countless imitators and have major implications for the American bison market.

The temptation to elide history in this way is understandable. The consumer packaged-goods industry needs this story to make sense of itself. Perhaps more than any other product, bison bars illuminate the state of American processed food, and Epic exists at the intersection of several trends that food manufacturers are convinced are the key to their survival. There's "snackification," a fixation with convenience rooted in the suspicion that we're all too busy to eat sit-down meals. There's "wellness," which includes a new category of functional superfoods marketed as though they have medication-grade power to give us stronger and better bodies. And there's "clean label," the increased insistence that packaged foods contain just a few familiar ingredients you might find in your pantry.

Perhaps most importantly, there's the narrative that big food companies cannot save themselves, the idea that they must bring on outside help if they are to survive. By acquiring natural and organic food startups—helmed by mostly young, mostly college-educated, mostly white cofounders—multinational food conglomerates can buy their way to success and offset the flagging sales of aging marqee brands. The food industry is too old, too set in its ways, to change. But maybe it can be a benevolent master to the next generation of food companies, who are trying to offer America something new and truly different—or so the story goes.

That newness is what's emphasized again and again as food media tell Epic's story. The takeaway is that Taylor and Forrest invented something no one else had ever thought of and that General Mills never would have tried in a million years. "At the time, no protein bar of this kind existed," wrote *Inc.*'s Tom Foster in a breathless profile published last month. "Forrest and Collins had hit on a powerful formula for new food brands. It was a novel product concept that fused two hot categories, protein bars and meat snacks like jerky. There was their mission for a larger purpose— sustainable sourcing—and, of course, the couple's own compelling story. It all added up to exactly the kind of authenticity that legacy companies only wish they could create on their own."

But there's a problem with the insistence, central to Epic's own marketing and repeated endlessly in the press, that Forrest and Collins invented something that didn't exist before: It isn't true.

In 2006, almost a decade before General Mills acquired Epic, social entrepreneurs Mark Tilsen and Karlene Hunter started making the Tanka Bar, the first commercial meat and fruit bison bar, on the Pine Ridge Reservation in South Dakota. The goal was to create a product sourced from and produced by Native people who would help reduce the reservation's unemployment rate, which hovers around 65 percent. The second goal was cultural. The cofounders hoped demand could be the economic driver that would restore the buffalo's place in the lives of the Oglala Lakota people.

Tanka may have been a community-minded enterprise, but it wasn't a niche product. Sold in more than 6,500 retail locations across all fifty states, it's been a bona fide commercial success in its own right. But Tanka's role in popularizing the bison bar has been largely ignored by food media and rarely mentioned in Epic's glowing coverage. It matters because both companies, in their own ways, are making the claim that they better the world through food. But though the two products have superficial similarities, they couldn't be more different. Their two divergent fates—an underdog struggling mightily to correct intractable social issues on its own terms, and a media-beloved startup trying to change a leading food multinational from within—do much to illuminate the challenges of making "good" food today.

While Tanka has had modest financial success, the company has sometimes struggled to attract funding and media attention, and its goal of making life better for a specific community has had both triumphs and setbacks. Epic, on the other hand, has been rewarded with admiring coverage and nearly bottomless investment—even though there are signs the company hasn't lived up to the sweeping claims made in its marketing materials. Though Collins and Forrest insist they're remaking America's entire bison supply chain for the better—helping the planet and our bodies while they're at it—the truth is more nuanced. Epic's efforts have been viewed by producers and others in the bison business with, at best, mixed reviews. Questions about whether the company lives up to its promises are far from settled. And the broadly accepted narrative that Epic has been a force for good in the industry—and a transformational influence on its parent company—is worth revisiting.

In 2006 a group of Lakota bison producers approached Tilsen and Hunter for help. The duo had a successful record of establishing community projects on the Pine Ridge Reservation, a poverty-stricken place with rampant unemployment and attendant social ills like diabetes and suicide. With no background in the food business, the duo decided to develop a value-added product to give the producers a market for their meat: Tanka Bar, the first meat and fruit snack bar. "In our naiveté we didn't even realize we were disrupting an industry and were creating a new [retail] category," says Tilsen.

The formula for their bars was based on *wasna* ("wash-NAH"), a traditional meat and berry food eaten in the Great Plains for hundreds of years. Tilsen calls it the first packaged meat because it was meant to travel long distances for months at a time without spoiling. Grandmothers still teach their daughters to make it by drying the meat and berries, adding buffalo fat, and pounding the mix together in a stone bowl, a key step that binds the acid in the berries with the proteins in the meat to prevent spoilage. When the people were nomadic, the resulting meat patties were sealed back in the bison stomach, where they would provide sustenance through the lean season.

Making a modern version of *wasna* for commercial sale without the use of chemical preservatives was a high hurdle to overcome. But in late 2006, Tilsen met Jon Frohling, a fifth-generation South Dakota butcher and nationally recognized maker of award-winning preserved meats. Within hours they had their first test batches going at Frohling's plant. Tilsen credits Frohling with the success of their formula. "The truth is, the reason Tanka Bar is better than every other bar on the market is because of Jon," he says. "While we didn't have the expertise, we met these incredible people along the way who really loved what we were doing."

While Frohling was developing the bars, Tilsen and Hunter undertook community outreach to create their brand. In Lakota society the buffalo is sacred, and the duo wanted to seek input on how their company might best exalt the bond between the animal and the Lakota Nation while restoring the buffalo to the land, lives, and economy of the Lakota people. They surveyed almost eight hundred community members, including youth, elders, and tribal leaders, to learn the proper way to honor—and not exploit—the buffalo with their product. The result was a document they call their branding shield, and it spells out the values behind Native American Natural Foods (NANF), Tanka Bar's parent company. To this day every employee is expected to not only sign the document but live by it.

It took about ten months from the night those first batches went into the smoker to the launch of the bars at the 2007 Black Hills Powwow. Frohling packaged 10,000 small sample bars, which the company gave away to attendees. When the local TV weatherman opened one and ate it on air, Tanka Bar became a national sensation, ending up a few days later on the front page of the *New York*

Times food section. "The story from the *New York Times* got picked up worldwide and literally melted our server to the ground," says Tilsen. "We were totally unprepared for real production." He and Hunter own a marketing company, and so, unable to find an investor who understood what they were trying to do, they leveraged all of their assets and borrowed $1 million to ramp up production.

The company prospered in its early days, with sales growing by double digits every month. But then, as in most of America, business stalled with the Great Recession of 2008. Still, NANF persevered, and Tanka Bar sales eventually started to grow again. But after thirty quarters of strong growth, the competition changed. Other small meat companies popped up and tried to compete, but they lacked the production values and the backstory that made Tanka Bar so popular. Then multinational corporations started jumping into the meat snack space. In 2015, Hershey acquired Krave, a California jerky company, for more than $300 million. A year later, General Mills bought Epic Provisions, maker of the Epic Bar, for a reported $100 million.

Though a global recession couldn't stop Tanka's growth, a flood of new imitators did. By 2017 the company was turning to the public for financial support, raising $125,000 from the equity crowdfunding site Wefunder.

"I really misunderstood who my competition was," says Tilsen. "I thought I was competing against other little meat companies who were trying to figure it out. I'm still surprised by the magnitude of that capital."

While Tilsen and Hunter were building Tanka Bar into a national brand, two young entrepreneurs in Austin, Texas, were creating vegan protein bars for endurance athletes. Taylor Collins and Katie Forrest were tired of fueling their athletic endeavors with the traditional soy-based, sugar-laden protein gels and bars and instead started experimenting with whole plant foods. Their Thunderbird Energetica line of bars launched in 2011 with an assortment of flavors that included fruit and nuts while eschewing GMO ingredients, wheat, soy, dairy, and refined sugars. The bars were a hit, and in 2012 the pair scored a local producer loan from Whole Foods to expand the business.

But when Forrest started suffering unexplained knee pain, the pair decided to kick veganism and try a Paleo diet. "Within a few months, Katie and I were stronger, faster, and leaner than we had ever been," Collins would write later on his company's website. In 2013 they debuted the Epic Bar, an offering with striking similarities to Tanka's hit product. The main ingredients? Grass-fed bison and cranberry, like a spin on traditional *wasna.*

Cameron Smith, an angel investor, fell in love with the idea —and with a $750,000 infusion, Epic Provisions became a stand-alone company. With the subsequent help of an Austin business accelerator and a $3 million investment led by the Boulder Brands Fund, Epic Provisions expanded its product offerings from the original bison bar to include other meat, fruit, and nut bars as well as bone broth and tallow. But the grass-fed bison bar has always remained at the center of its marketing efforts.

Epic Bars have been a big hit with the clean-eating Paleo crowd, and that's no accident. The company's explicit pitch to customers is that Epic provides a way to "eat like our ancestors ate." Its website is littered with references to evolutionary biology, indigenous cultures, and hunter-gatherer lifestyles, suggesting that to bite into an Epic Bar is to perform a kind of time travel—going back to an era before modern processing technologies distanced us from the sources of our food. Each bar features an illustration of the animal that supplies the main ingredient—grass-fed bison, grass-fed cattle, wild-caught salmon, wild boar—rendered as if by a nineteenth-century naturalist painter. The company slogan is "Live wild, eat wild." It calls its office staff and customer base its "tribe."

But though Epic's brand relies on a nostalgic vision of Stone Age eating, its purported mission goes far beyond that. The company's reason for being, according to its marketing, is to change American animal agriculture over to pasture-based systems. Over and over again in its marketing and on its blog, Epic has spelled out in exacting detail its commitment to a nose-to-tail, whole-animal model where little is wasted, along with its efforts to scale the grass-fed bison supply chain, bringing new bison ranchers into the grass-fed fold. This goal of providing financial support for ranchers who want to get into the business of pastured meat is central. As Collins put it in a 2016 blog post, Epic's model means "grow[ing] supply chains of grass fed bison by financially incentivizing ranchers to do the 'right thing.'"

But that's where things get complicated.

After General Mills acquired Epic Provisions, many in the natural-foods world questioned whether a company trying to spread the gospel of grass-based, minimally processed proteins could partner successfully with a multinational conglomerate specializing in grain-heavy snack foods. Still, a year after the sale, Epic reported that things were going well. "We still operate EPIC independently at our World Headquarters in Austin, TX, wear flip flops to anything important, curse like ranchers, and seize any opportunity to be outdoors," Collins wrote in a blog post commemorating the acquisition's one-year anniversary. To hear him tell it, selling out hadn't changed Epic, it had only increased the company's positive impact.

"From the beginning, it was our intention to utilize all the best parts of General Mills to accelerate our mission of large-scale grassland restoration and to create supply chains of pastured, grass-fed, and antibiotic free animals," Collins wrote. "With General Mills adding muscle to the brand, EPIC accomplished over 10x the impact we could have accomplished independently ... Within the last year EPIC has sourced over 250,000 pounds of regenerative protein, [impacting] millions of acres of grasslands."

But it's not clear that Epic's impact has in fact been a net positive, and the company's efforts have been divisive in the bison community. Many producers and others in the business were hesitant to talk on the record about Epic for this story, citing their relationships with Collins and Forrest, or their fear that their businesses and the grass-fed bison niche in general could suffer if they aired criticisms in the press.

Still, the main point of contention—the 2,000-pound animal in the room—is clear. General Mills bought Epic pledging to build the grass-fed bison supply chain, quickly reneged on its promise, and left a generation of suppliers in the lurch.

When Epic decided to source grass-fed bison for its original bars, it hit up against serious supply-chain limitations. As a result the company had to supplement its grass-fed supply with grain-fed bison; those bars are labeled "natural" rather than "grass-fed." Epic still has not overcome that supply bottleneck. Collins says that today about half the bars are labeled "grass-fed," an improvement from past years, when only 10 percent of the bars were grass-fed.

Collins and Forrest hoped that General Mills would be able to help them build their grass-fed bison supply chain. At first it seemed like their ambitious regenerative model would come to fruition. General Mills committed $3 million to a program to buy grass-fed bison in partnership with Northstar Bison, a family-owned operation based in Cameron, Wisconsin. The plan was that Northstar would buy the bison and contract with other graziers to feed them on grass until they were ready for harvest in three years.

"We were up front with them from the beginning," says Lee Graese, the founder and owner of Northstar. "We told them it was going to be very expensive because of the cost of infrastructure, land, and animals."

That's where the culture clash seems to have started. General Mills owns brands that primarily produce processed, grain-based products—cereals, baking products, snack bars—and frozen fruits and vegetables. The company's buyers are used to driving hard deals with distributors for the best prices on massive amounts of grain and produce over a single growing season. But meat, especially pasture-raised meat, works on a very different timetable. Everyone I talked with felt that General Mills didn't understand bison or how to build a meat supply chain. (No one from General Mills would comment for this story. After the article was published, the General Mills public relations department contacted us to dispute the fact that they canceled the program but did admit to changing it. Whether it was canceled or changed, producers and other affiliated businesses suffered.)

Graese says General Mills' buyers expected that any cost savings would be passed along to General Mills. When it became obvious there wouldn't be any savings, the company canceled what was supposed to be a five-year program after just a few months. Collins says that initial batch of 1,200 animals, now close to harvest, will end up costing Epic more than it would have spent buying meat wholesale.

Northstar still has a contract for 2019 with General Mills, but at a lower negotiated price. Graese says the company asked him how low he could go, and he gave them a price, "but I told them they don't get the regenerative story with it." Many of the small graziers and other businesses that jumped at the chance to be a part of the Epic Bar story and scaled up to handle the demand are now suffering because the anticipated business didn't materialize.

"We took the leap and went all in, but the rug got pulled out from under us," one producer, who asked not to be identified by name, told me. "We really did bet the farm. We still need money coming in to run the place."

With the supply of grass-fed bison stretched so thin, what exactly is going into Epic's bars? While the company claims to "use over 80% of the cattle and bison we source," the suggestion that Epic is buying whole carcasses appears not to be true. On the bison side, the company is buying trim, a blend of the meat and fat left after the more salable parts like steaks and roasts are fabricated. At Northstar—a company Epic has cited extensively in its marketing materials as a kind of archetypal supplier—the high-end cuts remain with the ranch, which sells them independently. "That's our end of the deal where we make the profit," says Graese. Only the trim is sold to Epic. The company claims it's using 80 percent of the animal, but however much it uses, it's really buying only what's left over after the more desirable cuts are parceled out.

Collins says Epic also uses bones and fat in its bone broth and tallow. But it doesn't buy whole carcasses or offal, as would be the norm in a true whole-animal, nose-to-tail operation—despite using the term *whole animal* prominently in its marketing.

You might think that buying trim would help bison ranchers somewhat. But even that marginal effort has been made in a way that doesn't reinvest in the supply chain.

Currently, Collins says, much of the trim Epic buys comes from culls—mature cows at the end of their reproductive life—or animals from ranches where herd sizes need to be reduced because of drought or other management issues. While there's a benefit to not wasting old or unwanted animals, especially when the end result is a processed meat bar, relying on culls isn't building a sustainable supply chain or regenerating the land, as Epic purportedly wants to do. It's economically unfeasible to invest in the enormous amount of land needed to raise bison entirely on grass, the fencing and other infrastructure necessary to keep the animals safe and healthy, and the cost of building a herd without a buyer willing to pay for prime animals rather than culls. For most new bison ranchers, the numbers don't add up.

Many of the other marketing claims Epic makes are also aspirational rather than real. Collins says the company is excited that first-generation bison ranchers are joining the business. "We oversaw the first generation of people who want to get into ranching.

It's exciting to see fresh blood. We're demystifying ranching, making it cool and desirable again," he tells me. But he cites only two of those ranches. One is ROAM Ranch in Texas, purchased by Collins and Forrest after the General Mills buyout. The other, Wisconsin-based Grand View Bison Ranch, left the Epic program when the General Mills deal fell apart.

Where does that leave Epic and grass-fed bison? Almost everyone I spoke with agreed that the increased consumer awareness of bison as a protein option has been a positive for the bison business. But to a person they all felt that Epic got too big too fast without understanding how to build a sustainable grass-fed bison supply chain. That's because in order for the economics to work, the capital investment has to be a long-term one, and buyers have to be willing to pay more for grass-fed bison.

So far, General Mills and Epic have not managed to do either.

As the influx of corporate money rushed into the meat bar business, Tanka suffered. Tilsen says he's had to lay people off in the past couple of years, which is especially painful. "When you lay off folks in a community like this, it isn't like there's another job. It almost feels like it's taking their dreams," he says.

Still, as a mission-driven company, NANF is taking the long view and refocusing. Tilsen and Hunter established the Tanka Fund, a nonprofit that provides grants for infrastructure projects for producers, as well as Tanka Resilient Agriculture, a producer co-op that will offer Native ranchers guaranteed contracts so more of them will be able to transition to raising grass-fed bison with sustainable wild-pasture management standards, the original regenerative agriculture. Right now Tanka Bars don't carry a grass-fed label because, while Native ranchers don't feed grain, the company also sources from non-Native producers who do. The goal is to eventually have a 100 percent Native supply chain.

While capital has been hard to come by, Tanka Bar has been successful in other ways. The Tanka Fund has provided money for fencing and solar wells and helped a producer build a small slaughter plant on the reservation. In one example, a geological formation called Buffalo Ridge in Minnesota had become home to wind generators, but the Tanka Fund was able to bring animals back to the land, supporting one of its ranchers to open up springs on the ridge and construct fencing.

"That allowed us to put buffalo on top of Buffalo Ridge for the first time in one hundred and fifty years. And the day they opened the gate and the buffalo went up there, in all honesty, the buffalo danced on the grass," says Tilsen. "It made you think, 'We're doing the right thing.' All the bureaucratic stuff and all the stuff we do, this is what success smells like. Just the buffalo back on the grass where they came from."

While Tilsen admits NANF isn't an attractive takeover or acquisition target, he believes success will continue. "I'm not that naive to believe we're going to return to a buffalo-based economy. But I am idealistic enough to believe that we can recreate a regenerative economy," he says. "There's no reason for forty thousand people on 2.9 million acres, living in a protein factory, to be protein starved and have the second highest diabetes rate in the country because they have no food system."

Big in Japan

FROM *The New York Times Magazine*

THE SEVEN-STORY DON Quijote megastore in the Shibuya district of Tokyo is open twenty-four hours a day, but it's hard to say when it's rush hour, because there's always a rush. A labyrinth of aisles leads to one soaring, psychedelic display after another presided over by cartoon mascots, including the mascot of Don Quijote itself: an enthusiastic blue penguin named Donpen who points shoppers toward toy sushi kits and face masks soaked with snail excretions and rainbow gel pens and split-toe socks. The candy section is vast, with cookies and cakes printed with Gudetama, Sanrio's lazy egg character, and shiny packages of dehydrated, caramelized squid. It's one of the few places where an extensive array of Japan's many Kit Kat flavors are for sale. Though the chocolate bar is sold in more than one hundred countries, including China, Thailand, India, Russia, and the United States, it's one of Japan's best-selling chocolate brands and has achieved such a distinctive place in the market that several people in Tokyo told me they thought the Kit Kat was a Japanese product.

A Kit Kat is composed of three layers of wafer and two layers of flavored cream filling, enrobed in chocolate to look like a long, skinny ingot. It connects to identical skinny ingots, and you can snap these apart from one another intact, using very little pressure, making practically no crumbs. The Kit Kat is a sweet, cheap, delicately crunchy artifact of the twentieth century's industrial chocolate conglomerate. In the United States, where it has been distributed by Hershey since 1970, it is drugstore candy. In Japan you might find the Kit Kat at a drugstore, but here the Kit Kat has levels. The Kit Kat has range. It's found in department stores and luxurious Kit Kat–devoted boutiques that resemble high-end shoe stores, a single ingot to a silky peel-away sheath, stacked in slim boxes and tucked inside ultra-smooth-opening drawers, which a well-dressed, multilingual salesclerk slides open for you as you browse. The Kit Kat in Japan pushes at every limit of its form: it is multicolored and multiflavored and sometimes as hard to find as a golden ticket in your foil wrapper. Flavors change constantly, with many appearing as limited-edition runs. They can be esoteric and so carefully tailored for a Japanese audience as to seem untranslatable to a global mass market, but the bars have fans all over the world. Kit Kat fixers buy up boxes and carry them back to devotees in the United States and Europe. All this helps the Kit Kat maintain a singular, cultlike status.

The Kit Kat first came to Japan in 1973, but the first 100 percent, truly on-brand Japanese Kit Kat arrived at the turn of the millennium, when the marketing department of Nestlé Japan, the manufacturer of Kit Kats in the country, decided to experiment with new flavors, sweetness levels, and types of packaging in an effort to increase sales. Strawberry! A pinkish, fruity Kit Kat would have been a gamble almost anywhere else in the world, but in Japan strawberry-flavored sweets were established beyond the status of novelties. The strawberry Kit Kat was covered in milk chocolate tinted by the addition of a finely ground powder of dehydrated strawberry juice. It was first introduced in Hokkaido—coincidentally and serendipitously—at the start of strawberry season. Since then the company has released almost four hundred more flavors, some of them available only in particular regions of the country, which tends to encourage a sense of rareness and collectibility. Bars flavored like Okinawan sweet potatoes, the starchy, deep-purple Japanese tubers, are available in Kyushu and Okinawa. The adzuki bean sandwich bars are associated with the city of Nagoya, where the sweet, toasted snack originated in a tea shop at the turn of the twentieth century and slowly made its way to café menus in the area. Shizuoka, where gnarly rhizomes with heart-shaped leaves have been cultivated for centuries on the Pacific Ocean, is known for its wasabi-flavored bars.

The most popular kind of Kit Kat in Japan is the mini—a bite-sized package of two ingots—and Nestlé estimates that it sells about 4 million of these each day. In any given year there are about forty flavors available, including the core flavors—plain milk chocolate, strawberry, sake, wasabi, matcha, Tokyo Banana, and a dark-chocolate variety called "sweetness for adults"—plus twenty to thirty rotating new ones. In August, Nestlé was preparing to release a *shingen mochi* Kit Kat, based on a traditional sweet made by the Japanese company Kikyouya, which involves three bite-sized pieces of soft, squishy *mochi* packed with roasted soybean powder and a bottle of brown-sugar syrup, all assembled to taste. It seemed almost presumptuous for Nestlé to flavor a chocolate bar like *shingen mochi,* which is rooted in traditional Japanese confectionary, then stamp its brand on it and produce it en masse.

A salesclerk was restocking the Kit Kat display in Don Quijote when I asked her which were the most popular flavors. She shook her head. "They're all popular," she said. She gestured at the empty tunnels of matcha-, grape-, and strawberry-flavored Kit Kats that she was filling as a small group of Chinese tourists carried armloads of glossy snack bags and boxes back to their shopping carts, undoing her work. An Australian father and son rushed by in a panic, their cart heaped with gifts to take back home. "Which one, Dad? Which one?" the child asked desperately, pointing to all the varieties. "It doesn't matter," the father shouted, as if the timer on a bomb were running out. "Just take one!"

The Kit Kat was first produced as a crisp, four-finger chocolate wafer bar in the 1930s, in Britain, by the chocolate manufacturer Rowntree's. The company was named for Henry Isaac Rowntree, who bought a small grocery store in York that also operated a cocoa foundry. In the 1860s the foundry was known for its finely ground rock cocoa, but the business grew quickly into candy- and chocolate-making. From the beginning the Kit Kat was self-consciously packaged as a kind of workingman's chocolate—as if the break of the bar could be aligned with the break the working class deserved from the monotony of their day. The Kit Kat was meant to be plain, unpretentious, cheerful. The stars of its commercials were often construction workers, cops, or commuters taking five hard-earned minutes to enjoy a moment of sweetness in an otherwise bleak day.

In Japan, Kit Kats were first licensed by the Japanese sweets company Fujiya, which capitalized on the chocolate's general association with Britain and the West. Early Japanese TV commercials for the candy drew on the chocolate bar's British roots to promote it as a foreign product, depicting British soldiers breaking for a treat. But in 1988, Nestlé acquired Rowntree's and took over manufacturing and sales in Japan, eventually changing strategies. Since 2010 sales in Japan have increased by about 50 percent. Japanese Kit Kats are now produced in two Nestlé-owned factories in Himeji and Kasumigaura.

There are three ways for a new Japanese Kit Kat flavor to make its way into the world. The classically trained pastry chef Yasumasa Takagi, a kind of Kit Kat maestro, was brought in by Nestlé as a collaborator in 2003, after the success of the strawberry Kit Kat. He may decide he wants to make a special bar and propose the new flavor to Nestlé—his first was passion fruit, in 2005. The marketing team may also build a partnership with a brand, like Tokyo Banana, the locally famous cream-filled cakes on which the Kit Kat flavor is based, then ask a product-development team to experiment so they can bring a sample bar to the pitch meeting. Or the product-development teams themselves may feel inspired on a late night in the test kitchen after one too many cups of green tea and vending-machine sweets.

Only the fanciest bars are devised by Takagi, made with higher-grade chocolates and other ingredients, like dehydrated seasonal fruits, and sold in Kit Kat Chocolatory stores, the boutique-like shops for luxury versions of the bar. In some cases they are decorated like plated desserts at a fine-dining restaurant, the Kit Kat logo entirely hidden by tiny, delicate, colorful crunchies, or individually wrapped like a gift—a single Kit Kat finger in a crinkly plastic wrapper, tucked inside a box. After Kohzoh Takaoka, now chief executive of Nestlé Japan, persuaded Takagi to work with the company, Takagi decided he wanted to make the bars more sophisticated, to play with the form and sweetness levels. He wanted, as he put it, to make Kit Kats for grownups, like the Chocolatory Sublime Bitter, a long, cigarillo-like bar of 66 percent dark chocolate, packaged in black and gold. (The marketing team uses the word *premiumization* to describe this part of Kit Kat's strategy.) Now Takagi runs the brand's Japanese Chocolatory shops, including the one where I met him, in a particularly posh part of the Ginza neighborhood in Tokyo.

"Japan is number one in terms of sales and profits, compared with Nestlé's other markets," said Ryoji Maki, Nestlé Japan's marketing manager at the time, who was dressed in a beautifully tailored suit and eating a tiny pudding cup. Nestlé did a market test after its strawberry flavor caught on in Hokkaido in 2000, to see how much production would be required for sales to go national. What it found was that the strawberry Kit Kat was especially popular among tourists, both Japanese tourists and those from abroad. Subsequent market tests suggested that Kit Kat had potential not just as a candy but as a kind of Japanese souvenir. The company looked to Kobe, Tokyo, Kyoto, and other cities and wondered how to develop a chocolate for each that consumers might associate with the places themselves. Now Nestlé's most recent flavors focus on regional Japanese products—maple-leaf-shaped cookies, plum wine, roasted tea.

There are also carefully chosen collaborations that capitalize on Japan's culture of *omiyage,* which can be loosely defined as returning from travels with gifts for friends, family, and colleagues. The Kikyou *shingen mochi* Kit Kat, which would go on sale in mid-October, would be sold right alongside the real Kikyou *shingen mochi* at souvenir shops and in service areas along the Chuo Expressway, a major four-lane road more than 200 miles long that passes through the mountainous regions of several prefectures, connecting Tokyo to Nagoya. With any luck, people would associate the Kit Kat with the traditional sweet and snap it up as a souvenir. But for this to be a success, for Kit Kat to expand into the souvenir market, consumers would have to believe that Kit Kat, originally a British product, was Japanese, and that although it was manufactured in a factory far away, it somehow represented the very essence of a region.

Before I could enter the Kasumigaura factory, northeast of Tokyo, I had to zip up an all-white coverall and place a white plastic skullcap under a hard white helmet, tucking in all of my hair. I had to wrap the exposed skin of my neck in a white scarf. I had to change out of my sneakers into the provided white slip-ons and take a fully clothed air shower with Takeshi Iwai, the factory's production manager, in a sealed room the size of a linen closet. Afterward, side by side, we sticky-rolled our entire bodies for dust and lint and eyelashes and any other invisible debris that might still have been clinging to our clothes, to avoid contaminating the chocolate.

It smelled strongly of cocoa and toasted almonds on the other side of the doors. Iwai assured me that this scent changed daily, often more than once a day, according to what was being made. He also warned me not to run, because I might slip in my new shoes. Iwai studied microbiology at university and has been working for Nestlé since 2001; he has managed the Kasumigaura factory for the last three years. Wafers were the beginning of the line, the beginning of every single Kit Kat.

I stood mesmerized for a few minutes under an archway of uncut wafers, like edible golden windowpanes, which were being cooled by ambient air before they reached an actual cooler. I heard almost nothing Iwai said over the sharp clanging and drone of the machinery. The factory is large and open, loud and clean, its production lines totally transparent. But the wafers had been baked out of sight, most likely between engraved, molded plates. Now they looked like thin, delicate altar breads floating above us. They formed a continuously moving line, the sheets traveling up and curving toward pumps of cream in the distance.

What makes a Kit Kat a Kit Kat? A Nestlé executive told me it was the shape of the connected pieces: those long, skinny ingots with their recognizable, ridgelike feet of chocolate surrounding each base. A few people said it was the logo itself, in big blocky letters, embossed on the top of each bar. But when I spoke with Takagi, the pastry chef, he didn't hesitate. "The wafer," he said. "The wafer!"

Wafers are an art form within the food industry. And although plenty of companies make decent wafers, there is something about the Nestlé wafer, Takagi said, that is quite extraordinary. Not that he knew exactly what it was. The wafer was the corporate secret, the heavily guarded soul of the Kit Kat. But like many lightweight, low-fat industrial wafers, the Kit Kat wafer is very likely mostly air and gelatinized wheat flour. It is crisp but not brittle. Crunchy but not dense. It is fragile but still satisfying to bite into. It is totally and alarmingly dry to the touch, like packing material. But after it has been touched with a little saliva, it doesn't even need to be chewed, and you can swallow it with no effort. Plain, the wafer is almost but not entirely tasteless. It has a very gentle sort of toastiness, barely there, but with an almost bready flavor. A sort of toast ghost. Not that it matters. A wafer's highest purpose is the nuance of its crunch.

When a wafer doesn't meet standards—when it is cracked, broken, improperly embossed—it is tossed into a tall plastic bin next to the factory line. The company recycles these substandard wafers as local animal feed. "This is the countryside, so we have farms," Iwai said with a shrug. The good wafers—smooth, intact, deeply and evenly embossed—move along the line. They are covered with cream, then sandwiched with another wafer and more cream. The arms of a huge, gentle machine with extraordinary fine-tuned motor functions do all the work of building the Kit Kat, smoothing the cream and pressing the wafer on top of it, then pass the large, sheet-cake-sized sandwiches along a slow conveyor belt through a massive cooler. After they're cut, four sheets at a time, the Kit Kats begin to look familiar, like ladyfingers.

On the molding line, the chocolate depositor fills empty Kit Kat molds with tempered chocolate, and the fingers are dropped in and covered with more chocolate. A scraper removes excess chocolate and smooths the surface. When the chocolate is cooled, the bars are popped out and whipped through a wrapping machine. On my visit the mostly automated factory was making several types of Kit Kat, including chestnut—a seasonal flavor for the fall—made with white chocolate and a mix of chestnut purées from Europe and Japan. The production line was a barely interrupted blur of white, like dotted lines rushing by on the highway, becoming indistinguishable from one another.

I learned that Kit Kats were slightly, subtly different all over the world. In Britain, Nestlé uses milk crumb, a sweetened, dehydrated milk product, to make the bars. In the United States, Hershey uses nonfat milk and milk fat, while in Japan the factories work with whole-milk powder. In Japan, Nestlé buys most of its cacao beans from West Africa. In the United States, a mix of beans from West Africa and Latin America is favored.

Almost everything changes, but the wafers? The wafers never change. The wafers have a fixed standard that needs to be maintained, and deviations are not acceptable. Standing beneath the fresh, moving wafers, I asked Iwai if I could hold one, as if it were a newborn, and I did not expect him to let me. But he reached into the line and pulled one out, passing it toward me with two hands. The breeze created by his movements seemed to curve the wafer inward with pressure, but it didn't break. What I wanted to know was if this wafer, the one in my hands, would pass Nestlé's standards, but Iwai wouldn't share many details about that. All I knew was that the wafer was huge, golden, marked with square cups, and totally weightless. That if it hadn't been still warm from the oven,

I wouldn't have known it was there. That if this was the soul of a Kit Kat, then holding the soul of a Kit Kat was like holding nothing at all.

Kikyouya, originally a small, family-run sweet shop that specialized in *kintsuba,* a Japanese sweet filled with red-bean paste, has been making *shingen mochi* since the late 1960s. A single package of Kikyou *shingen mochi* is complex, but it's also small—small enough to fit in your palm—and contained in a flexible plastic box that's wrapped in a soft sheet of pretty, floral-printed plastic and sealed with a topknot. It's messy to eat, or at least it can be, but the clever packaging considers this: the wrapping itself doubles as a tiny tablecloth to prevent stains and spills. Before I knew this, I ate *shingen mochi* in my hotel room, as Tokyo was being soaked by the outermost edges of a passing typhoon. With my first bite I sent a little cloud of roasted soybean powder into the air and coughed with surprise. The rice cakes were soft, chewy, delicious. And where the brown-sugar syrup trapped the powder, it turned into a gorgeous caramel sludge. I couldn't quite imagine how a sweet like this, one defined by such varied textures, and by such a distinct form, could ever be transformed into a chocolate bar.

Tomoko Ohashi was the lead developer on the Kikyou *shingen mochi* Kit Kat. Ohashi, a soft-spoken woman from Mito in Ibaraki Prefecture, ate *shingen mochi* when someone brought it for her as a souvenir from Yamanashi, the prefecture where it's still made today, and she knew how beloved it was. What she didn't know was how the *mochi* texture could translate into a chocolate bar. "I was also very worried about replicating the flavor," she said, standing in the test kitchen of the factory in Kasumigaura, wearing the factory's all-white uniform with its white hoodie pulled tightly across her hairline.

The kitchen didn't look like a lab. It was more like a real pastry kitchen, full of dehydrated fruit powders and matcha organized in tubs, chocolate molds and serrated knives and a marble counter for tempering chocolate. The challenge with *shingen mochi,* Ohashi said, was finding the balance between the soybean powder and the syrup. Because the sweet is so adaptable, everyone who eats it calibrates it obsessively, adjusting the ingredients so it tastes the way they like.

Ohashi started work on the new flavor last September, and she finished it in May. In tests she would make about fifty pieces of four to five different versions by hand, tempering chocolate on the marble table, and then taste them side by side, looking for the right balance of soybean powder to sugar syrup. The rice was the *shingen mochi* itself, but it couldn't play such a big part in the chocolate bar. "There's no device or machine for putting a rice cake in a Kit Kat," Ohashi said sadly. She knew from the start that it wouldn't be possible to replicate the texture of fresh *mochi*—tender, almost slippery in the mouth—in a chocolate bar. She did, to be true to the *mochi*, end up putting sticky rice in the Kit Kat's cream filling. Did the sticky rice in the Kit Kat help to mimic the *mochi* texture? "No," Ohashi said, bursting into laughter because she had made an uncomfortable kind of peace with what she could and could not do within the boundaries of her form. "Actually not at all."

After all the testing, Ohashi concentrated all the flavorings in the cream filling: the sticky rice as well as soybean powder and brown-sugar syrup. The bars went on sale on October 15, with packages of nine selling for 780 yen, or about $7. Standing in the test kitchen, I unwrapped the new flavored Kit Kat and broke into it with a crack. The bar was a mini, two tiny connected ingots. They were ivory, eggshell, the off-white color of a rich lady's kitchen, and the fine cream filling inside appeared a light brown.

Just a few days earlier I had made a pilgrimage to Kikyouya's factory in Yamanashi, where workers wrapped thousands of pieces of fresh *shingen mochi* by hand each day, to see exactly what Nestlé was trying to capture. On my way I stopped for lunch at a small noodle restaurant and sat by the window, eating a pile of salted plums. I could see busloads of tourists filing out in the parking lot, their floppy hats secured with strings, their shirts wet with sweat. They were fruit hunters. Yamanashi is green, dense with red pine and white oak forest and beautifully kept orchards that cut deep into its slopes. Fruit hunters pay to eat as much ripe, seasonal fruit as they like in a short span of time. Say, thirty minutes of thin-skinned peaches, or fat pink grapes, or strawberries, warmed from the sun, dipped into pools of sweetened condensed milk.

Unlike apple-picking in the fall in the United States, the fruit doesn't really function as a souvenir, carried home in baskets to commemorate an idyllic, well-documented visit to the countryside. Fruit hunters travel to eat the fruit on site, right off the trees, in their allotted time. When the concept was explained to me, I thought the time limit seemed embarrassing. But seeing the fruit hunters of Yamanashi, I realized that it wasn't embarrassing at all. It was practical, it was beautiful, and it acknowledged that souvenirs were, like memories, at best only approximations of the moments they represented. That it was in fact completely impossible to remove a taste from its origin without changing it in the process.

"How is it?" Ohashi wanted to know. The Kikyou *shingen mochi* Kit Kat was smooth to the touch, shiny. It had a brilliant, crumbless snap, which gave way to a pure white chocolate and caramel flavor and a lightly savory note. It was sweet, it was good. It was in balance. And it recalled fresh Kikyou *shingen mochi*, vaguely, like a memory gone soft around the edges.

HELEN ROSNER

Anthony Bourdain and the Power of Telling the Truth

FROM *The New Yorker*

I HAVE LONG maintained a theory that Anthony Bourdain—who died on Friday, at the age of sixty-one, of an apparent suicide—was the best-known celebrity in America. There are, I realize, actual ways to measure this sort of thing, but the intimacy that Bourdain cultivated with his fans was of a sort that transcended Q scores and approval polls. His show brought in millions of viewers, his books found millions of readers, and—especially for people outside of the food world, and to his own great irritation—he seemed to be everyone's first idea of the "celebrity chef," even though he hadn't worked in a restaurant kitchen in years. (At best, he said, he could be described as a "cook.")

Bourdain's fame wasn't the distant, lacquered type of an actor or a musician, bundled and sold with a lifestyle newsletter. Bourdain felt like your brother, your rad uncle, your impossibly cool dad— your realest, smartest friend, who wandered outside after beers at the local one night and ended up in front of some TV cameras and decided to stay there. As a writer himself, he was always looking out for other writers, always saying yes, always available for interviews and comments. You had to fight through a wall of skeptical PR to get to someone like Guy Fieri, but Bourdain was right there, for everyone, in equal measure. He remembered names. He took every question seriously. He was twenty minutes early to every appointment, to the minute. Every newspaper, every magazine, every website that asked got its Bourdain quotes—and good ones too! Not prescribed pablum but potent missiles of cultural commentary—bombastic wisdom, grand pronouncements, eviscerations of celebrities, flagrantly named names.

Another way of putting it is that Anthony Bourdain built his career on the telling of truth. The son of a French father and an American mother (Gladys Bourdain, writing as G. S. Bourdain, was a writer and a copyeditor at the *Times*), he was a novelist before he became an essayist, but even in the realm of fiction—as in his series of sardonic crime thrillers, including the novels *Bone in the Throat* and *Gone Bamboo*—he evinced a fascination with how people lived within and around their ill behaviors. "Guys who wake up every morning, brush their teeth, shower, shave, then go to work at the serious business of committing felonies," he wrote in "A Life of Crime," an essay in his collection *Medium Raw*. "These are the characters who continue to dominate my reverie." In crime there's not just transgression, there's clarity: being in the conspiracy, knowing the inner workings of the machine, seeing what's really going on. This was the engine that powered "Don't Eat Before Reading This," Bourdain's 1999 *New Yorker* story, which stripped the elegant window dressing from the world of high-end restaurants—the article that in short order evolved into his blockbuster 2000 memoir, *Kitchen Confidential*.

This attraction to the secrets behind the façade—the frantic, shadowed stage-managing happening in the wings—is perhaps the singular theme threading through all of Bourdain's work. He was a relentless reader, looking not only for knowledge and diversion but for tools of the craft. He was less a television star than a television creator: an obsessive film buff, he crafted each episode of *Parts Unknown* like a feature film, plotting every shot, every musical cue, every visual flourish. When I interviewed him for a podcast, in 2016, we talked about how he used those tools of storytelling as a way to bring members of his audience to him, to get them to a place where they could receive what he was giving. "You want them to feel how you felt at the time, if you're telling something that you experienced," he said. "Or you want to drive them to a certain opinion or way of looking at things."

As Bourdain's career grew, the truths he was positioned to tell grew too. He was never able to shake off his association with the now pedestrian revelations of *Kitchen Confidential*—the cook's antipathy toward brunch, the daily special as a dumping ground for leftover ingredients, the questionable integrity of Monday's fish.

But his Food Network show, *A Cook's Tour,* his Travel Channel show, *No Reservations,* and his CNN show, *Parts Unknown* (which remains in production; at the time of his death, Bourdain was filming in France for the show's twelfth season), allowed him to acknowledge that the point of his journeys—and of sharing them with his massive, ever-growing audience—was not a gastronomic fluency but a broader cultural one. In what is likely the most famous episode of *Parts Unknown,* Bourdain sat on low plastic stools at an unadorned noodle shop in Hanoi, Vietnam, eating *bún chả* with Barack Obama —at the time a sitting president. The meeting, which Patrick Radden Keefe chronicled in a Profile for the magazine, was momentous for both men—both had grown up in the shadow of the Vietnam War, and that conflict, its long shadow, and its human costs suffused the hour-long episode. Bourdain ended the episode on a brutal note, with an infamous quote from William Westmoreland, the commander of U.S. forces in Vietnam, a reminder of America's racist dehumanization of the culture we at home had just spent an hour celebrating.

Bourdain effectively created the "bad-boy chef" persona, but over time he began to see its ill effects on the restaurant industry. With *Medium Raw,* his 2010 follow-up to *Kitchen Confidential,* he tried to retell his story from a place of greater wisdom: the drugs, the sex, the cocky asshole posturing—they were not a blueprint but a cautionary tale. Ever resistant to take on the label of chef, he published a book of home recipes in 2016, inspired by the cooking he did for his daughter. Despite its chaotic cover illustration, by Ralph Steadman—and its prurient title, *Appetites*—the book, which was cowritten with his longtime collaborator, the writer Laurie Woolever, is a tender memoir of fatherhood, an ode to food as a vehicle for care.

Beneath the vivaciousness and the swagger, Bourdain was still a man whose life was marked by darkness. His memoirs, in *Kitchen Confidential* and elsewhere, tell of an early life spent struggling with anger, hard-drug use, and other self-destructive behaviors. His parents' marriage ended when he was young, leaving a lasting scar; Bourdain's own first marriage, to his high school girlfriend, Nancy Putkoski, lasted for twenty years, ending in 2005, shortly after his ascent to fame. When the dissolution of his second marriage, to Ottavia Busia, the mother of his daughter, was announced in the tabloids, Bourdain seemed profoundly disturbed by the evidence of public interest in his private life. In a 2016 episode of *Parts Unknown*, set in Buenos Aires, he held an on-camera therapy session. "I will find myself in an airport, for instance, and I'll order an airport hamburger," he says, lying on a leather couch. "It's an insignificant thing, it's a small thing, it's a hamburger, but it's not a good one. Suddenly I look at the hamburger and I find myself in a spiral of depression that can last for days."

In other moments, particularly when he wasn't the one controlling the narrative, Bourdain could be slippery about personal matters—the critic Maria Bustillos, in a 2017 piece analyzing his literary œuvre, observed his tendency toward "a gentle drawing of the curtain over private moments." A year and a half ago, just after the presidential election, I interviewed Bourdain for a profile in *Eater*, where I was an editor at the time. We sat for a few hours at a yakitori restaurant in midtown, eating chicken hearts and drinking beer. The Rome episode of *Parts Unknown* had just aired, and as we settled into our conversation, I jokingly mentioned his obvious crush on the Italian actor and filmmaker Asia Argento, who had been featured in the episode. At the mention of her name, Bourdain's large, tanned hand swept over the microphone of the recorder. "What do you mean, my crush on Asia?" he said, and I laughed, telling him his puppy-dog eyes were in every frame—not to mention his Twitter posts about the episode, which fairly breathed with infatuation. He took his phone out and scrolled through his recent tweets, asking me to point out specific evidence. "We're trying to keep it under wraps," he said.

Toward the end of that conversation—which had jumped around from the global rise of the far right to the responsibilities of celebrity to the frustrating futility of protest—I asked him point-blank if he considered himself a feminist. His answer was long and circuitous, what I'd come to think of as classic Bourdain: more of a story than a statement, eminently quotable, never quite landing on the reveal. He talked about his sympathy for the plight of women and gay men, his formative years as a student at Vassar, his forceful resentment of the "bro food" movement, with which he remained entwined, and his unwavering support for reproductive rights. "I don't know if that makes me a feminist," he said. "It makes me a New Yorker. Doesn't it?"

In October of that year, Ronan Farrow published a story in *The New Yorker* detailing multiple women's allegations of sexual harassment and assault by Harvey Weinstein. Asia Argento was a central figure in that story, detailing the effect that Weinstein's predation had on her creative and personal life. Bourdain, whose public identity had been built for decades on a focused, auteurish individualism, seemed to find in his relationship with Argento a transformative creative and political partnership. She consulted on *Parts Unknown* and stepped in to direct a recent episode set in Hong Kong. In turn, Bourdain's sterling credentials as a man's man and a taker of no guff served as a bolster of the #MeToo movement at large. His unwavering support of Argento—as well as his ardent rejection of so much as a quantum of sympathy for famous chefs accused of transgression—brought him a new sort of celebrity as an activist, a revered elder statesman, an overt and uncompromising figure of moral authority.

The last time I saw Bourdain was a few months ago, at a party in New York for one of the books released by his imprint at the publishing house Ecco—of his many projects, his late-career role as a media rainmaker was one he assumed with an almost boyish delight. At the bar, where I'd just picked up my drink, he came up and clapped me on the shoulder. "Remember when you asked me if I was a feminist, and I was afraid to say yes?" he said, in that growling, companionable voice. "Write this down: I'm a fuckin' feminist."

Food Fight

FROM *The New Yorker*

IN SOUTH-CENTRAL UTAH, where the topography is spectacular, desolate, and extreme, the pessimistic tradition in place-names runs strong. Head south from Poverty Flat and you'll end up in Death Hollow. Head east from Dead Mare Wash and you'll end up on Deadman Ridge, looking out toward Last Chance Creek and down into Carcass Canyon. During the Great Depression, when the whole state turned into a kind of Poverty Flat, the Civilian Conservation Corps sent a group of men to the region to carve a byway out of a virtually impassable landscape of cliffs and chasms. The men nicknamed the project Poison Road: so steep that a single drop would kill them. Midway up, the ridge they were following gaped open and plunged 1,500 feet to the canyon floor. They laid a span across it and called it Hell's Backbone Bridge.

Today the entire route built by those men is known as Hell's Backbone Road. Still largely unpaved, still treacherous in bad weather, it connects the town of Escalante to the tiny hamlet of Boulder, long reputed to be one of the most remote settlements in the continental United States. As late as 1940 the mail there was delivered via an eight-hour trek by mule team; the first lights did not flicker on until Christmas Eve 1947. Until the 1970s locals had to spend up to forty-eight hours in transit to obtain any number of essential goods and services: a new pair of socks, medical care, anything beyond an eighth-grade education.

Eventually the county paved a different road into town, the two-lane Highway 12; as a result, assuming that you are already in Utah, getting to Boulder is no longer particularly difficult. Yet by contemporary standards the town remains strikingly out of the way. Its population hovers around 250 people, many of whom bear the same last names as the earliest westerners to settle the area: to the extent that Boulder is full at all, it is full of Kings and Roundys, Lymans and Ormonds and LeFevres. Most of those families came to Utah because they were Mormon and came to Boulder to pasture their cattle, and the twin influences of the Latter-day Saints and ranching still dominate today. Boulder is the kind of place where those who aren't related by blood are related by marriage, and those who aren't related by either are effectively kin by proximity—the kind of place, in short, where everyone knows everyone else's children, parents, politics, struggles, scandals, and cattle brands.

Despite its small population, Boulder is geographically large— 21 square miles, about the size of Manhattan. Most of that space is occupied by farms and ranches; there is no bank in town, no ATM, no grocery store, no fast food, no medical clinic, no pharmacy. For that matter, there is no town in town—no business district, no Main Street, not even a traffic light. Instead, scattered along or just off Highway 12, there is a post office, an elementary school, a town hall, and a state park. There is a ten-room motel, a three-room motel, a convenience store, a church, and a gift shop. And down at the end of town, just before the road starts climbing steeply back into the wilderness, there is a hotel called the Boulder Mountain Lodge, and on its grounds a restaurant called Hell's Backbone Grill.

Actually the restaurant is the second Hell's Backbone Grill. The first one opened in 1996, closed in 1999, and sat empty until it was acquired, for three thousand borrowed dollars, by two women who had never attended culinary school or started a restaurant or lived in Utah. Nonetheless, in 2000 they moved to Boulder, reopened Hell's Backbone Grill, and in short order changed everything about it except the name. In the years since then it has gained a reputation as one of the best restaurants in the Southwest, and also the most improbable. It is an all-organic, sourcing-obsessed, vegetarian-friendly venture in the middle of a traditional ranching community; a part-hippie, part-hipster, Buddhist-influenced culinary retreat in conservative Mormon country; a farm-to-table operation in a landscape not exactly known for its agricultural bounty; and a high-end, foodie-magnet restaurant that is four hours on a good day from the nearest major metropolitan area.

Yet somehow, despite its unlikely vision and inhospitable location, Hell's Backbone Grill has managed to flourish. Last year, though, the restaurant faced an existential threat—to itself and to Boulder, but also to a place, and an idea, much larger than both. Which is why, in addition to serving apple-poblano pork chops and garlic-scape pesto and elk posole with cotija cheese seven days a week, the owners of Hell's Backbone Grill have become entangled in an epic battle with the president of the United States.

Jennifer Castle and Blake Spalding, the co-owners of Hell's Backbone Grill, met in 1997, while working as cooks for rafting trips in the Grand Canyon. In contemporary American life, there are few circumstances less conducive to preparing decent food. The two worked for different outfits, but the routine was basically the same: before each trip, everything they needed, from the salt to the stove, was sealed into waterproof containers and trekked to the bottom of the canyon, where it was loaded onto boats and transformed into meals at portable kitchens reconstituted daily on the banks of the Colorado River. Some days sand got into everything. Occasionally a boat would flip and the dairy cooler would vanish downstream. Once, Spalding got into a fight with a ring-tailed cat that sank its teeth into 2 pounds of roast beef.

Still, it was wild and beautiful and, as jobs in food go, much better than those which had marked the two women's earliest working years. Both Spalding and Castle came from financially strapped families, started cooking young, and did stints at, respectively, Bob's Big Boy and McDonald's. Spalding was raised in New Hampshire and Arizona, by former beatniks who expected their three children to fend for themselves. As the oldest, she was responsible, by age eleven, for getting food on the table several days a week; by twelve she took her first cooking job, picking lobsters and frying clams at a local seafood shack. Later she put herself through Northern Arizona University by tending bar and, in the 1990s, started her own catering company.

Castle, who was raised by a single mother in New Mexico, learned to cook young because it was a way to help at home, and learned "to cook big," because her mother was one of thirteen and the extended family ate together regularly. At eighteen she started college in Flagstaff, found it hugely expensive and minimally useful, dropped out, and began working at a café there instead. She stayed for seven years, clocking in at 2 a.m., clocking out at nine, then going straight to the public library to pore over cookbooks, jotting down recipes and refining her own. Eventually she arranged her schedule so that she could work in the Grand Canyon as well, which is where she met Spalding.

By then Spalding's catering career had taken an unexpected turn. One day out on the river, another boat caught up with hers in order to deliver a fax: she'd been offered a job cooking for the cast and crew of MTV's *The Real World* on an island in the Exuma Cays. She accepted the job, followed by others in reality television that took her everywhere from North Carolina to Suriname. Then the Discovery Channel invited her to cater a show in the Pacific Northwest and asked if she knew anyone who could help.

The timing was propitious; Castle had just broken up with a boyfriend and was looking to get away. For the next month she and Spalding lived in a tent, cooking constantly, barely sleeping, and discovering that they worked together exceptionally well. That was partly because, like many successful collaborators, they are strikingly different. Spalding, who is older by eight years, is an extrovert and a risk-taker, qualities that, combined with her placid cheeriness and thoroughgoing sincerity, make her seem something like a good witch: formidable yet benevolent. Castle, by contrast, is a pragmatist and a worrier: systematic, detail-oriented, inclined to lie awake at night contemplating the optimal texture of cake. What they have in common is an intense work ethic, an ability to laugh even in extremis, and an abiding admiration for each other. "I'm just me and she's just her," Spalding says, "but between us we're six people."

Although Castle loved the Discovery Channel gig, she finished it feeling "done with smelling like garlic and coffee" and decided to quit cooking. Spalding, however, had other plans. After the job ended, she visited Boulder and found Hell's Backbone Grill sitting empty; back in Arizona, she asked Castle to help start a restaurant in a remote Utah town. "I was like, 'What? No. That's crazy. And besides, I don't want to cook anymore,'" Castle said. Spalding, persuasive as ever, pointed out that at least she wouldn't have to go to work at two in the morning or sleep in a tent. Moreover, unlike many of the places they had cooked, Hell's Backbone Grill had electricity. It had running water. It had a roof. How hard could it be?

*

In 1996, four years before Spalding and Castle plated their first meal at Hell's Backbone Grill, President Bill Clinton announced the creation of Grand Staircase-Escalante National Monument: 1.7 million acres of Utah wilderness, later expanded by Congress to 1.9 million, to be protected in perpetuity.

Clinton drew his authority to do so from the 1906 Antiquities Act, an influential piece of legislation that permits presidents to unilaterally designate as national monuments any federal lands they deem culturally, historically, or scientifically significant. It was signed into law during the second term of Theodore Roosevelt, who then used it eighteen times in three years, to protect everything from Devils Tower, in Wyoming—the first national monument—to the Grand Canyon. With the exceptions of Richard Nixon, Ronald Reagan, and George H. W. Bush, every subsequent president has made use of the Antiquities Act. Collectively they have designated 155 monuments, from the African Burial Ground, in New York City, to the Gates of the Arctic, in Alaska.

Before Grand Staircase-Escalante joined those ranks, very few people outside Utah knew anything about the lands within it. Even the new monument's name reflected, on both sides of its hyphen, a certain confusion. The Franciscan friar Silvestre Vélez de Escalante did explore parts of Utah, but he never set foot in the region that now bears his name. The eponymous Grand Staircase, meanwhile, stretches far beyond the monument's boundaries. That's because it is not a single geological feature, like the arches at Arches or the bend at Big Bend, but a metaphor for a series of cliffs and plateaus that work their way upward from the Grand Canyon in Arizona to Utah's Aquarius Plateau, the highest tableland in North America, which runs for 100 miles along the monument's northern edge.

Although Native Americans lived in what would become Grand Staircase for 12,000 years, early European Americans avoided the area assiduously; so daunting was its terrain that for centuries it deflected the otherwise unstoppable force of Manifest Destiny. As late as 1868, a U.S. War Department map of the western United States contained an enormous blank spot where the monument would one day be. In 1871, when the explorers of the second Powell expedition arrived at the edge of that blank spot, their leader looked out on the "multitude of chasms before us" and declared that "no animal without wings" could cross it. When they crossed it anyway, they encountered both the last river and the last mountains in the Lower Forty-eight to be named and mapped.

Under Clinton, all that land was reborn as the largest national monument in the continental United States. It straddles two counties, Kane and Garfield, which have a combined population of 12,000 people, most of whom live in towns on the monument's perimeter. The smallest of these is Boulder, which sits almost 7,000 feet above sea level, in the shadow of the Aquarius Plateau. Although the town's fate, like that of the rest of the region, has always been tied to the wilderness at its front door, the monument designation reversed the terms of that relationship: suddenly the same remoteness that had always deterred outsiders began attracting them instead.

That shift reflected a trend that was already well under way throughout western rural areas: the transition from the Old West, with an economy based on farming, ranching, and resource extraction, to the New West, with an economy based on technology, tourism, and recreation. Like many changes, that one was divisive. Some people welcomed it while others mourned it. Some people benefited from it greatly, others not at all. And some people, wittingly or otherwise, embodied it.

The early years of Hell's Backbone Grill, which were also the early years of Grand Staircase-Escalante National Monument, were not particularly easy ones for either entity. Bill Clinton was hanged in effigy and flags were lowered to half mast in nearby towns. Local officials encouraged illegal all-terrain-vehicle activity in the monument and ran bulldozers through its ostensibly protected land. The commissioners of Garfield County turned down $100,000 in federal planning funds, deriding it as "blood money," then spent many times that unsuccessfully suing the U.S. government. Even those in the region who were disinclined to spectacle, litigation, or lawlessness worried about the new monument's potential impact on the regional economy.

All told, it both was and was not an auspicious moment to open a restaurant in a gateway town. On the one hand, Spalding and Castle could count on revenue from tourists who stopped for a meal on their way through Grand Staircase. "We never would have moved here if the monument hadn't been declared," Spalding said. "We're crazy, but not that crazy."

On the other hand, it wasn't an ideal time to settle in Boulder, which even under the best of circumstances is wary of interlopers. Nor was the town initially enthusiastic about the new restaurant in its midst. The issue wasn't expense, exactly; although Hell's Backbone Grill charges big-city prices, it offered residents a 50 percent discount in the early years, bringing the bill for, say, a $10 pancake breakfast down to what it would cost at an IHOP. (These days the discount is 20 percent.) The bigger problem had to do with identity: food typically contains almost as many cultural markers as calories, and the kind that Spalding and Castle serve was at first utterly foreign to many of their neighbors.

Spalding had long believed that cooking was a moral and political act, one capable of either contributing to or ameliorating environmental and health issues. Castle came later to food ethics (when she met Spalding, she said, "I thought Alice Waters was Alice Walker. I was like, 'I loved *The Temple of My Familiar*'"), but by the time they bought Hell's Backbone Grill they shared a vision of local, organic, responsibly sourced meals made from scratch. That vision was not shared, however, by most of America in 2000. Organic restaurants were still scarce, the farm-to-table movement was barely getting started, and the word *locavore* had yet to be coined. According to the *Salt Lake Magazine* editor and food writer Mary Brown Malouf, the culinary culture of Utah at the time consisted chiefly of whatever the Sysco truck delivered.

In that context, what some Boulder residents found off-putting about Hell's Backbone Grill wasn't its prices but its dishes: slow-cooked things, grass-fed things, sage-smashed potato pancakes, seared duck with rose-hip cream sauce. A curious feature of the local-food movement is that it is sometimes alienating to actual locals; the people most likely to recognize prickly pears or tumbleweeds in the wild may be the ones least inclined to pay for the pleasure of eating them.

Along with their different ideas about food, Spalding and Castle parted ways with most of Boulder on religion. The town was predominantly Mormon, while Castle was raised Catholic and Spalding has been a practicing Buddhist for twenty-five years; Hell's Backbone Grill features a statue of Buddha in the garden and prayer flags on the patio. Socially both women were respectful of the prevailing religion—Spalding, who has a cheerfully foul mouth, learned to curb it in a place where people routinely say

"Shut the front door" and "Oh my heck"—but professionally it presented a problem. For restaurants, alcohol sales can be the difference between survival and insolvency, but observant Mormons do not drink, and Utah, known officially as the Beehive State and unofficially as the Behave State, has the strictest liquor laws in the nation. Just before Castle and Spalding bought Hell's Backbone Grill, the Utah Supreme Court had affirmed the right of Boulder's town council to prevent its previous owners from so much as applying for a liquor license.

In short, almost everything seemed to be working against Spalding and Castle at first, including the fact that no one wanted to work *for* them. Their initial HELP WANTED sign attracted zero interest, until finally the local postmistress took pity and told her teenage daughter to go on down and apply. The rest of the staff was assembled in similar catch-as-catch-can fashion. At one point Spalding persuaded her sister to move to town and help out, and when they were particularly shorthanded neither she nor Castle was above begging a pliable-seeming customer to stick around and work in exchange for meals. (Two years ago a customer named Tim decided to stay for a different reason. He and Spalding now live together in Boulder, with a three-legged cat, a four-legged cat, two dogs, and seven goats.)

If hiring staff was challenging, acquiring ingredients was almost as difficult—chiefly because in 2005, to make good on their commitment to local food, Spalding and Castle bought 6 acres of overgrazed horse pasture and started a farm. This was, as Spalding later put it, "a monumental pain in the ass." Snow fell in June. Freak hailstorms wiped out whole crops. The wind blew away two consecutive greenhouses, inverted a third like an umbrella, whipped a field of peppers around until they effectively strangled themselves, and blew squash plants clean out of the ground. Mountain lions proved fond of honey and destroyed expensive bee boxes to obtain it. Worst of all was the soil, which consisted almost entirely of nutrient-free sand. As a result, the main thing that the Hell's Backbone farmers had to learn to grow was dirt.

And yet it was this same demanding land that drew Spalding and Castle to Boulder in the first place. On a clear day—and clear days are abundant in this part of Utah, which boasts some of the driest air and lowest pollution levels in the world—they could climb almost any rise outside their restaurant and look out over 100 miles in all directions. From most places within Grand Staircase, there is, in all that distance, no visible or audible sign of human existence: no roads, no cars, no power lines, no cell towers, no buildings. At night there are no artificial lights. Overhead, the sky goes dense and dimensional with stars; below, the land is so dark that you can spot a single hiker with a headlamp 15 miles away.

Filling up all that immensity is some of the most spectacularly wild terrain left on earth. There are the sheer cliffs and forested highlands of the Aquarius Plateau. There are, in shades of cream and copper and flame, the unlikely geometries of eroded sandstone: narrow gorges, strange whorls, sudden holes in the ground. There are California condors and desert tortoises and bighorn sheep and panthers. There are hanging gardens, slot canyons, vegetation that has lingered since the Pleistocene. There are astonishing quantities of 200-million-year-old fossils, and the relics of multithousand-year-old cultures, and the world's most continuous record of 4 billion years of geology.

For Spalding and Castle, what was so captivating about Grand Staircase was its vastness of scale, both spatial and temporal. Nowhere else in the country, outside of Alaska, was so large a tract of land so relatively unspoiled—so ecologically close to the condition it had been in before Europeans arrived in North America. Paradoxically, that is a large part of why President Clinton had protected it: because for millennia it had done such an excellent job of protecting itself.

Like many things, although not all things, life at the restaurant got better. On their first Fourth of July in town, Castle and Spalding threw an ice cream social, complete with gallons of homemade toppings, then sat around worrying that no one would show up. Instead, most of the town materialized. The two women gradually befriended some of their neighbors and over time employed many of them, including two identical-twin Mormon ranchers, a former cook at the elementary school plus her three children and two grandkids, a thirty-year-old business manager who began on the prep line as a teen, and seven of the fourteen children of a sixth-generation Boulder ranching family.

Eventually, when goodwill toward the restaurant had increased but its bottom line had not, Spalding and Castle approached the town council to ask permission to apply for a liquor license. Mindful of the pitched battles fought there over alcohol before, they kept their case to a single fact: a drinks menu would help keep their doors open. To the surprise of pretty much everyone, the council voted to let them apply. They did, and the state subsequently granted them a liquor license, the first in the history of Boulder.

Sixteen years later, the bar at Hell's Backbone Grill is full, and from when it opens, in March, until it closes, just after Thanksgiving, the restaurant almost always is too. Its dining room, which seats sixty-five, looks like a WPA lodge if Martha Stewart had been around to do the decorating: warm and unshowy, with exposed beams, deep-red walls, and light fixtures fashioned from colanders that Spalding bought at thrift shops and spray-painted copper. Because some guests still stumble in by chance while others make reservations months ahead, the clientele is notably eclectic: bow hunters and backpackers, Paul Simon and Scarlett Johansson and Jamaica Kincaid. Some arrive in evening wear, some in flannel, some looking as if they forgot to wipe the grime and sunscreen off their faces. In the spring and the fall, cycling tours bring clients in weekly; one recent night eight of them were seated next to a table full of the other kind of bikers—Mexican motorcyclists, midway through a Southwest circuit. Nearby, three generations of a family, in from Salt Lake to celebrate an engagement, were on their fifth meal at the restaurant in two days.

As the crowds suggest, Hell's Backbone Grill is now thriving. The staff has stabilized at around fifty people, many of them returning for the twelfth or the sixteenth season, while the farm now yields some 23,000 pounds of organic produce every year. Virtually all of that winds up on the menu, served up in what Castle and Spalding call "Four Corners Cuisine": an updated combination of cowboy classics, Mormon recipes, and traditional southwestern fare. With Spalding's sister Lavinia, a travel writer and a former Hell's Backbone employee, Castle and Spalding have also produced two cookbooks, *With a Measure of Grace,* in 2004, and *This Immeasurable Place,* in 2017, which feature profiles of Boulder residents and the restaurant's staff as centrally as recipes.

Yet it is those recipes which have made Hell's Backbone Grill so beloved. The restaurant has received accolades from Fodor's, Zagat, the *New York Times,* the James Beard Foundation, and a governor of Utah. *Salt Lake Magazine* gave it seven consecutive annual awards, then put it in the publication's hall of fame. In 2013 a food critic for the *Salt Lake City Weekly* came to the restaurant reluctantly, then had what Spalding called "a *Ratatouille* moment, where he literally wept into his posole." He wrote up a column calling Hell's Backbone Grill "Utah's Chez Panisse" and named it the restaurant of the year.

As Hell's Backbone Grill has grown more famous beyond Boulder, it has also grown more central within it. The ice cream social has become an annual ritual; this Independence Day, Spalding and Castle gave away more than four hundred sundaes. Former employees have started other food-related ventures nearby, including a food truck that serves tacos and burritos in the parking lot of the state park. At Spalding's invitation, a group of monks from the Drepung Loseling monastery, in South India, have spent a week in Boulder almost every year for eighteen years, and their visits are now as much a part of the town's calendar as the school graduation and the Memorial Day parade.

Although their business runs more smoothly than it did in the early years, Castle and Spalding still work just as hard. When I was in town, they were gearing up for a wedding for seventy, followed by a benefit dinner for five hundred, on top of all the usual restaurant obligations. But these days, at least, they have a day off each week, plus a manageable division of labor: Castle takes the early shift and works mostly in the back of the house, while Spalding takes the evening shift and handles the front of the house. Inside the restaurant as well as out, she is the public face of Hell's Backbone Grill.

Which lately has become a much bigger job. Last year, not long after President Donald Trump took office, he ordered the Department of the Interior to review twenty-seven national monuments, from Katahdin Woods, in Maine, to Giant Sequoia, in California. Seven months later, on December 4, 2017, he issued proclamations dramatically reducing the size of two of them, both in Utah. One was Bears Ears, 1.35 million acres in the southeastern part of the state, protected by President Obama, which Trump reduced by 85 percent. Partly because a historic coalition of Native American tribes had successfully fought for its establishment just a year earlier, Bears Ears attracted most of the news coverage about the monument decisions. But that same day, to considerably less national attention, Grand Staircase was cut almost in half.

*

As a rule, national monuments are created to end controversies, not start them. Their roots often lie in some public-lands conflict so enduring and intractable that a president finally steps in, Antiquities Act in hand. Tempers flare, for a while the fuss gets worse, then it begins to settle down. Soon the monument is accepted; eventually it is beloved. Sometimes Congress goes on to turn it into a national park. Zion, Bryce, Acadia, Death Valley, Joshua Tree, the Grand Tetons, the Grand Canyon: all these and many more were originally national monuments.

That is the general trajectory Grand Staircase was following until President Trump issued his proclamation and, as he has in so many arenas, rekindled old animosities. Support for the monument was broad and bipartisan; among Utah citizens who submitted public comments during the Department of the Interior's review process, almost nine out of ten wanted it left intact, while a conservative pollster found that two out of three Utahans approved of Grand Staircase. But the commissioners of Kane and Garfield Counties opposed it, as did the governor, the majority of the state legislature, and the entire Utah congressional delegation, all of whom had long despised the whole idea of public lands.

That sentiment is common throughout the West, where it is the most notable regional instantiation of the grand American tradition of disliking the federal government. The Sagebrush Rebellion of the 1980s and the Wise Use movement of the 1990s both sought to diminish national land ownership and management, and both enjoyed strong support, from Texas up to Washington, Idaho, and Montana. But there is a reason that Trump cut monuments only in Utah. Among other western politicians, shifting economies and demographics have begun to change attitudes toward public lands, but Utah's governing class remains intensely hostile to federal authority.

That hostility stems in part from a long history of conflict between the U.S. government and the Mormon Church. Driven steadily westward by religious persecution, the early Mormons arrived in Utah in the mid-nineteenth century and began trying to establish an autonomous theocracy. When the federal government declined to tolerate either that or the practice of polygamy, church leaders found themselves in a bind. They were acutely aware of the benefits of joining the Union and petitioned to do so constantly over the course of forty years; at the same time they were, as the apostle Orson Pratt wrote in 1845, "determined to get out of this evil nation." The former impulse finally won out in 1896, when the Mormon leadership agreed, to the enduring dismay of some of the faithful, to abandon both polygamy and theocracy in exchange for statehood.

Upon joining the Evil Nation, Utahans also found themselves surrounded by it: the United States owns two-thirds of Utah, a higher percentage than anywhere except Nevada. (By contrast, it owns 0.6 percent of New York.) The federal government compensates states for lost property taxes on those lands and shoulders the hefty cost of managing them, while the states reap the financial benefits of tourism. Critics nonetheless talk about that arrangement as if the feds had seized the state's most precious assets, but historically the opposite has been true: for most of its existence, the U.S. government was in the business of transferring land *to* the states, generally by giving it away for free, through land grants and the Homestead Acts. Most of what it kept for itself was terrain that no right-minded settler wanted—including those millions of acres which so daunted the Powell expedition.

Because all that acreage already belonged to the United States, the creation of Grand Staircase didn't increase the total amount of public land in Utah. Indeed, by law national monuments can be made only from land the federal government already owns. Clinton's designation did, however, change what activities were permitted inside the monument's boundaries: mining and drilling were prohibited, while ranching was allowed to continue. But many locals mistrusted Clinton (he lost the 1992 presidential election in Utah not only to George Bush but also to Ross Perot), and despite the grazing provision, many ranchers were convinced that the monument would destroy the cattle industry.

That fear resonated deeply in a region settled by ranchers, and once Trump took office politicians seized on it to make the case for cutting Grand Staircase. The Garfield County commission chairperson, Leland Pollock, claimed that the monument had "eliminated most grazing," while Representative Chris Stewart said it had "kicked ranchers off the range." A resolution passed by the Utah legislature and signed by the governor asserted that Grand Staircase "had a negative impact on the prosperity, development, economy, custom, culture, heritage, educational opportunities, health, and well-being of local communities."

*

Criticisms like these drive monument supporters batty, for the straightforward reason that almost none of them are true. Prior to 1996, Garfield County had an unemployment rate of more than 12 percent, the highest in Utah, while its per-capita income was 14 percent below the state average. Since the monument was established, though, per-capita income in the region has grown by 17 percent, higher than the Utah average, and employment has grown by 24 percent, with Grand Staircase supporting some 1,600 new private-sector jobs. Many of those are at locally owned businesses, and not all are in tourism; finance, health care, and construction jobs are also on the rise, and a building boom in Boulder and Escalante has left contractors with multiyear waiting lists. In Escalante a hardware store opened recently, as did a movie theater that had been shuttered since the 1960s; the medical clinic got its first X-ray machine, opened a pharmacy, and began offering dental services.

These gains did not come at the expense of local ranchers, none of whom were "kicked off the range." Throughout the monument's existence, almost 97 percent of it was actively and legally grazed; as a 2017 Bureau of Land Management report noted, "no reductions in permitted grazing have been made as a result of the Monument designation." The price of a permit remained the same, and the fee for grazing on federal lands is, on average, a tenth or less of the price on private and state property. What hurt ranchers around Grand Staircase was the rise of factory farming, plus other market forces that made everything from fuel to feed more expensive while the price of beef failed to keep pace—factors that long predate the creation of the monument.

No changes to the status of Grand Staircase could reverse those trends, and, except rhetorically, the decision to redraw its boundaries had nothing to do with the cattle industry. It did, however, have to do with other industries. In addition to removing almost 900,000 acres from protection, Trump's proclamation carved the remaining land into three separate units: Grand Staircase, Kaiparowits, and Escalante Canyons. The logic governing those boundaries became clear this summer, when the Department of the Interior accidentally released a report that contained extensive information —redacted in a subsequent version—on the whereabouts, within the original monument, of oil, gas, coal, tar sands, copper, cobalt,

uranium, and other natural resources. The location of those resources made plain that the restructuring amounted to a kind of
environmental gerrymandering: Grand Staircase had been carved
up to maximize access for extractive industries.

Proponents of that change argue that it will strengthen the regional economy, but that assertion is doubtful. Take coal: there is
an enormous amount of it within the monument, but virtually zero
demand for it. In a report on the impending closure of a mine just
outside Grand Staircase, the Institute for Energy Economics and
Financial Analysis noted, "The overall coal sector, which includes
coal plants and mines, is in structural decline. There is no market
for the power from the plant or for coal from the mine." Other resources remain lucrative, but not necessarily for locals: most energy
and mining companies are national or multinational operations
that bring in many of their own employees, and the industry as a
whole is subject to boom-and-bust cycles that can devastate on-site
communities both culturally and financially.

In reality, the most lucrative thing about Grand Staircase is the
landscape itself. As of 2016 the outdoor-recreation industry in the
United States brought in $370 billion, more than twice the value of
the oil-and-gas industry. Twelve billion of those recreation dollars
currently fuel Utah's economy, but they will dry up around Grand
Staircase if it is opened to resource extraction. Any mines or wells
in the area would require an enormous amount of new infrastructure—roads, processing plants, storage facilities, pipelines—and
industrial pollutants would contaminate air and water alike. All this
would affect even ostensibly protected lands, because under the
new plan Grand Staircase no longer abuts Capitol Reef and Bryce
Canyon, leaving those national parks exposed to downstream effects. Indeed, two of the three new mini-monuments don't even
abut each other, eliminating not only ecological buffer zones but
also wildlife corridors.

In shrinking Grand Staircase, Trump parroted critics who claim
that they don't object to the monument per se, only to its size.
But ecologists have known for decades that in the long run, one
of the single most devastating things you can do to an ecosystem is
make it smaller. Put a road through Grand Staircase and you don't
just bisect it; as the science writer David Quammen once observed,
you tear it in half, like fabric, and the natural world on both sides
begins to unravel. In Grand Staircase that logic extends to the hu-

man world as well. Whole communities and careers and lives have grown up around the monument; now, with its protections gone, those are threatening to come apart as well.

Shortly after the 2016 election, Spalding and Castle sat down to talk about their future. They knew that Grand Staircase would soon be in Trump's crosshairs—and given how high emotions were running, they knew that coming to its defense could land their restaurant in trouble. But they also knew that any major changes to the monument could likewise imperil their livelihood. It didn't take them long to decide what to do. In the Grand Canyon, they had been taught that if the boat tips and you fall into the river, you don't panic and look around for someone to save you. "You get your bearings and swim like hell," Spalding said. "You participate in your own rescue."

One virtue of life in a small town is that getting your bearings is relatively easy. At most, Spalding and Castle were a degree or two removed from everyone in the region, and they began reaching out to others who cared about the monument. They met with business owners who depended on it for income, conservationists who valued it as wilderness, and scientists who regarded it as one of the planet's greatest fieldwork locations. (With less than 7 percent of it surveyed, the monument has already yielded some six thousand archeological sites and forty-five new paleontological species, including twelve previously unknown dinosaurs.) They joined Grand Staircase Escalante Partners, the official friends group for the monument, and got to know its executive director, Nicole Croft. Between rejiggering the menu and replacing the fan in the walk-in freezer, they began speaking out—to neighbors, customers, politicians, the press—about their devotion to the monument.

This change was not entirely easy for either woman. Spalding has always cared about politics and long been an evangelist for ethical food—she is happy to explain to customers for the umpteenth time why they shouldn't want to see salmon on the menu in Utah—but she also possesses enough empathy and business savvy that she was mindful of potentially alienating neighbors or customers. Castle, meanwhile, is "by nature a behind-the-scenes worker" who would rather be in the relative privacy of the Hell's Backbone kitchen than onstage for a land-use panel. On top of that, neither of them was in the market for a longer to-do list. After nearly twenty years, life at the restaurant had achieved a more reasonable rhythm, and spending what little free time they had on political organizing was not part of the plan.

It was, however, part of a phenomenon. For some left-leaning Americans, many of them middle-class white women whose prior political frustrations were tempered by a buffer of distance and privilege, life under the Trump Administration has produced an entirely new experience: the disbelief, impotence, and rage of being unable to prevent immoral or unlawful actions. The shock of that experience has galvanized some of those women, sending self-described little old ladies to their first protests, motivating suburban moms who couldn't previously name their political representatives to start calling them daily, and inspiring twentysomethings to run for office. Taken as a whole, such women are neither exceptionally driven nor exceptionally radical; other activists have been at it far longer, and for more progressive causes. But of all demographic groups in America, the Harvard sociologist Theda Skocpol and the University of Pittsburgh historian Lara Putnam observed in a study earlier this year, it is these women whose "political practices have most changed under Trump."

For Spalding and Castle, as for many others, that change began with trying to get their representatives to represent them, an experience that was reliably frustrating. They got up before dawn to drive two and a half hours to a county commission meeting to voice support for the monument, only to have the commissioners unanimously pass a resolution in favor of shrinking it. Together with all fifty-three members of the Escalante and Boulder Chamber of Commerce, they tried to tell interior secretary Ryan Zinke how much Grand Staircase meant to their business—first in letters, which got no response, then in person when he visited Utah for a "listening tour," during which he met only with monument critics, and finally by sending a delegation to Washington, D.C., where he likewise refused to see them. "I called his office daily," Spalding said, "saying, 'I'm Blake Spalding, I'm the largest employer in the north end of this county, we pay nearly a million dollars a year in payroll, I want to talk to you about what the monument has meant for our business.' No one ever called me back."

When public pressure didn't work, Spalding and Castle started looking for other options. One of these walked into their restaurant last year, in the form of Garett Rose, an attorney with the international law firm Covington & Burling. Rose (who now works at the Natural Resources Defense Council) had flown to Utah to meet with Grand Staircase Escalante Partners, and at Nicole Croft's suggestion came by Hell's Backbone Grill to discuss possible legal remedies if the monument was altered. Over the course of two days and several meals, he outlined what the firm had in mind: suing the president of the United States.

As with so many of Trump's actions, the decision to shrink national monuments was so unusual as to raise the question of whether it was also illegal. In the 112-year history of the Antiquities Act, presidents had expanded their predecessors' monuments frequently but contracted them in any significant measure only four times. (Minor reductions in acreage were common, and one president, William Howard Taft, reduced his *own* monument significantly.) None of those major reductions were ever litigated, leaving a constitutional question unanswered: does the authority to reverse a monument designation lie with Congress or with the president?

To Covington & Burling, the answer was clear: it lay with Congress, and if Trump arrogated that power to himself, the firm was prepared to take on a lawsuit pro bono. At the lawyers' request, Spalding and Castle drew up an affidavit describing what would happen to their restaurant if the designation changed. On December 4, 2017, the day the proclamations became public, Covington & Burling, acting on behalf of Grand Staircase Escalante Partners and two other nonprofit organizations, sued Ryan Zinke and Donald Trump.

That lawsuit was one of five filed that day against the president. Two of the suits concerned Grand Staircase and three concerned Bears Ears; they have since been consolidated, so that the cases about each monument will be heard together. In the meantime, Covington & Burling has filed a motion for summary judgment, while the Department of Justice has requested a venue change, from Washington, D.C., to Utah, a move that all the plaintiffs oppose. Those requests are presently awaiting rulings by the U.S. District Court for the District of Columbia. Since the monument cases raise a previously unlitigated question concerning the separation of powers, they are in all likelihood headed for the Supreme Court. But lawsuits tend to move slowly, and by the time *Grand Staircase Escalante Partners et al. v. Donald J. Trump et al.* gets litigated at the district level and then, inevitably, appealed, we will be past 2018, past 2019, probably even past 2020. A new president may or may not be in the White House; a new ethos may or may not prevail about public lands.

Disinclined to sit around in the interim, Spalding and Castle, like many of their fellow activists, have increasingly turned their attention to electoral politics. They still speak out about Grand Staircase, and they still bring allies over for strategizing and dinner. But, mindful that only political change will protect the monument in the long term, they have begun campaigning for Marsha Holland and Shireen Ghorbani, pro-conservation candidates running for, respectively, the Utah and U.S. House of Representatives, and they have thrown their weight behind Better Boundaries, a bipartisan organization with an anti-gerrymandering measure on the ballot in Utah this fall.

Neither Spalding nor Castle has any illusions about the magnitude of the battle they are fighting: they live in one of the most conservative regions of one of the most conservative states in the nation. Still, as the owners of a successful farm-to-table restaurant in rural Utah, they are perhaps less daunted than most of us by long odds. More to the point, they can't imagine any other course of action. "I made a deal with myself when I saw the writing on the wall," Spalding said. "I would say yes to everything I could to save the monument. When all this is over, whatever the outcome, I want to be able to say that I did everything I could."

In the meantime, there are black-powder biscuits on the breakfast menu at Hell's Backbone Grill, and a Backbone BLT for lunch, and braised beef with green-chile polenta for dinner. There is a SAVE GRAND STAIRCASE sign out by the Buddha in the garden and at the hostess station a stack of fact sheets about the monument, complete with contact information for Congress members.

Spalding, manning the late shift, still offers a buss on the cheek to old friends, a how's-your-meal to new arrivals, a complimentary bottle of organic soda to a customer reluctant to try it. But beneath her unfailingly warm and calm demeanor, she says, "I'm in a rage, to be quite honest. I'm nice to the monument opponents I know, but I do not hesitate to tell people when they get here that they have arrived at a remote outpost of the resistance."

Out of other restaurants come celebrity chefs; at Hell's Backbone Grill, Spalding and Castle have become activist chefs instead.

In doing so, they have learned the lesson of countless other outspoken citizens before them: when you stand up, you stick out. They do their best to brush off vicious Facebook comments and hostile visitors and bad-faith bad reviews ("People write us shitty Trip Advisors and I'm like, 'You didn't even eat here,' but whatever," Spalding says), and they've learned that denatured alcohol and sandpaper will remove graffiti written in permanent marker. ("Liberals are the new Nazis," someone scrawled this month in both of the restaurant's bathrooms.) Other things, however, are harder to ignore. Last summer Spalding, speaking at a major pro-monument rally in Salt Lake City, criticized Utah's government for not defending public lands. Not long afterward she and Castle were notified that Hell's Backbone Grill had been selected for a comprehensive four-year audit by the state. The only other two vocally pro-monument businesses in Boulder were also audited. Whether or not the move was punitive, they worry about other forms of retaliation and find themselves increasingly embattled. "There's not a day that goes by that I don't feel like we're doing some kind of hand-to-hand combat," Spalding said. "The effect it's had on us and our staff is extremely destabilizing."

It remains to be seen what other effects the shrinking of Grand Staircase will have on Hell's Backbone Grill. Boulder is still a gateway town, only to a much smaller monument with a different name, Escalante Canyons. It is also now the gateway town to the first industrial incursion since Trump's proclamation. In June a Canadian mining company acquired cobalt and copper claims on land that was previously part of the monument. Those will likely be rendered void if the Trump administration loses in court, but in the meantime—and the meantime could last a long time—the company has announced plans to begin surface exploration soon and drilling shortly afterward.

If those and other developments proceed, Spalding and Castle know that their days at Hell's Backbone Grill could be numbered. People seldom make reservations months in advance to eat at restaurants in mining towns, or plan sightseeing vacations or cycling tours near trucking routes and pit mines. What took two entrepreneurs twenty years to build could be gone in a fraction of that time, together with things that took nature 20,000 centuries.

That kind of rapid destruction has happened in the region before. When the first ranchers arrived in Boulder, they encountered nearly ideal rangeland: dense with bluegrass and bunchgrass and wild oats, veined with natural troughs to channel the rain. In the words of Nethella Woolsey, the daughter of the rancher John King, who arrived in time to enjoy the bounty, those were the "good old days": there was nothing to do but turn your livestock out on the range, and no fees to pay in order to do so. Word soon spread, and men began bringing in cattle and sheep by the thousands.

The good old days lasted ten years. By 1905, Woolsey wrote, "the rich meadows on the mountain plateau had turned to dust." Cows died by the hundreds. The bloated bodies of sheep washed into streambeds, poisoning the drinking water. Overgrazing so denuded and compacted the hillsides that they couldn't absorb rainfall or snowmelt. Instead water poured off them in floods, eroding the ground as rapidly as in a time lapse. That pattern, repeated all over the West—the famous tragedy of the commons—is why the federal government finally stepped in, determining how much livestock the land could sustain and issuing permits accordingly. The ranchers, in the main, were not grateful.

A century later, however, with that same land facing a different threat, the rest of us could learn a lesson from their mistakes. It is terrifying how quickly something can be destroyed, how fragile a seemingly robust system can turn out to be. Institutions that appear solid can crack, protections can decay, democratic norms can erode faster than riverbanks. A nation can seem as durable yet be as vulnerable as its physical terrain. One of the most beautiful things about being in Grand Staircase is that out in the deep middle of it, with all of prehistory underfoot and 12-billion-year-old starlight overhead, the world feels enduring and eternal. But that is, of course, an illusion. All things change. The only question is whether they change for the better.

The Gay Man Who Brought Tapas to America

FROM *Taste*

IT WAS 1982 when James Beard learned that Felipe Rojas-Lombardi, a man four decades his junior who had once been his assistant at his cooking school, wanted to open a tapas bar called the Ballroom in New York's Chelsea neighborhood. Beard didn't understand.

"Topless bar?" Beard said, befuddled, before he let out a sigh and shrugged. "Well, if that's what he wants."

Rojas-Lombardi—a tiny, handsome, scruffy man with hair the color of squid ink—was used to the confusion. Back then the word *tapas* elicited puzzled glances from most New Yorkers. The traditional Spanish style of serving small plates like the kind Rojas-Lombardi served at the Ballroom struck many as alien. These were tapas of tender roasted eggplants drizzled with lime juice, garlic, hot pepper, salt, pepper, coriander, and olive oil, and tapas of red beans tossed with parsley and caracoles (snails) that'd been cooked in a brew of garlic, onions, olive oil, white wine, flour, paprika, cloves, cayenne, and beef stock. Some of his dishes, like bowls of a Peruvian stew called *altamada,* even had chewy little pearls that looked like tadpoles (it was called quinoa), virtually unknown to many Americans at the time.

The Ballroom was a noisy cabaret-restaurant hybrid where fading legends like Blossom Dearie and Peggy Lee performed and sausages and pheasant carcasses dangled from the ceiling as decorative props. The performances were as much of a draw as the food. The entertainment made the Ballroom a destination for the city's theater crowd, a place where people would flock to see the great divas of the past in the twilight of their careers and have a good time ("rated no. 1 in *NY Magazine*'s 'Great Places to Have a Party,'" read ads plastered in the pages of *New York* magazine through the late 1980s).

It became one of Beard's favorite haunts too. Rojas-Lombardi and Beard, both gay men, were kindred spirits, though Rojas-Lombardi was born and raised in Lima and Beard in Portland, Oregon.

They kept in close touch until Beard's death in 1985 at the age of eighty-one. Just six years later Rojas-Lombardi died too. He was forty-six.

Somewhere along the way, Rojas-Lombardi's name fell through history's cracks. In the decades since his death, Rojas-Lombardi has drifted in and out of public consciousness, though he was included in 2014's "Celebrity Chefs Forever" stamp collection from the United States Postal Service, along with Beard, Julia Child, Edna Lewis, and Joyce Chen. But unlike many of those lauded chefs, Rojas-Lombardi is barely a household name.

When the USPS asked food writer Ana Sofia Peláez to write a short promotional biography of Rojas-Lombardi, she hadn't even heard his name. "He wasn't somebody I was familiar with," Peláez says. "But when I read more about him, it made perfect sense."

As Peláez dug through archives and microfiches of newspaper stories, she discovered just how trailblazing Rojas-Lombardi was: He parlayed his stint working at the James Beard School into a role as executive chef at *New York* magazine's test kitchen. He published a cookbook for kids, 1972's *A to Z No-Cook Cookbook* ("It is a gay and light-hearted collection of assembly foods," Julia Child wrote in the *New York Times*). He authored "the world's first talking cookbook," consisting of two forty-minute cassettes, in 1973.

He was the founding chef of Dean & Deluca in 1977, where he became known for some of the earliest pasta salads America had seen—and the mere act of serving pastas cold and in salad form constituted a culinary revolution for the era. He got to the Ballroom in the early 1980s, when journalists credited him with introducing tapas to America through his work at the restaurant: there he made tapas of chicken escabeche, skinny slices of Serrano ham, fried calamari, grilled blood sausage.

He also wrote two straightforward cookbooks, 1985's *Soup, Beau-*

tiful Soup and 1991's *The Art of South American Cooking*. Perhaps it's no wonder that the *New York Times*'s Craig Claiborne, in his foreword to the former book, feted Rojas-Lombardi as "without question one of the most creative chefs in this country."

Rojas-Lombardi rose to prominence well before the Internet era, in a time when food television was just embryonic, and it's tempting to wonder whether Rojas-Lombardi would've been more famous had he been around in an era when the medium was more robust. In fact, both his *New York Times* obituary and Peláez's USPS biography credited Rojas-Lombardi's one-off 1985 appearance on an episode of the PBS series *New York's Master Chefs*, where he cooked a fish-and-Swiss-chard pie and a bay-leaf-flavored caramel custard, with spawning a number of copycats of his tapas in restaurants across the country.

"Only a few people, even in the food world, writers and chefs alike, know about Felipe, despite the fact that he was quite a figure in New York back in the eighties," Peruvian journalist Diego Salazar, who's been at work on a book about Rojas-Lombardi for the past few years, says. "My guess is he died too soon, and he passed away before chefs truly became big stars."

Born Edward Rojas-Lombardi in Lima in 1946 to an Italian mother and a Chilean father whose ancestral roots were in Spain and Germany, Rojas-Lombardi was the eldest of six siblings. He was different from kids his age. The other kids idolized Superman, but as Rojas-Lombardi told Gael Greene in 1975, he worshipped chefs. The other boys played sports, kicking around soccer balls in their backyards; he was more attracted to his grandmother's cavernous kitchen.

Rojas-Lombardi briefly attended law school in Peru, as his father wished, before committing his life to cooking. He departed for Europe and spent his time in restaurant kitchens in Spain, Italy, and France, where he cooked with Richard Olney, the gay American food writer who spent the majority of his life in rural France. In 1967, when Rojas-Lombardi was eighteen, he moved to New York. There he served as Beard's protégé for five years. Theirs was a mutually beneficial (and platonic) friendship, according to John Birdsall, the author of an upcoming biography of Beard.

"James actually relied on younger cooks to learn about new foods, new techniques," Birdsall says. "Someone like Felipe would bring new ingredients, new styles of cooking, new flavors, and the energy James lacked." The fact that Rojas-Lombardi was gay "also made him family, in James's mind."

Today I see Rojas-Lombardi's food as reflecting a queer sensibility in its own right, magnificent and opulent in its presentation, unconcerned with rules that governed what was within culinary bounds at the time. This was a man who put veal kidneys on skewers made of rosemary sprigs. His food was intimidatingly exacting and technique-driven, but motivated too by a subtle disregard for convention.

To me, this is fundamentally queer. To borrow a page from Birdsall's own reading of queer food in *Lucky Peach,* queer food is "food that takes pleasure seriously, as an end in itself," bulging with energy and messy feeling, electric without sacrificing technical excellence. In an otherwise only marginally charitable one-star review for the *Times* in 1983, Bryan Miller wrote of the "stunning array of strange and wonderful foods" that greeted patrons when they entered the Ballroom, identifying Rojas-Lombardi as the "conscientious chef who strives for authenticity," one who "does things the right way, with no short cuts." Rojas-Lombardi's food was colorful and unapologetically playful, and he married this sense of culinary whimsy to a dazzling, careful aesthetic. He'd developed a style entirely his own: Beard once told famed food writer Barbara Kafka that Rojas-Lombardi "had the best eye for arranging food of anyone I have ever met," adding that he "could make anything look beautiful."

But the matter of Rojas-Lombardi's sexuality, at least in public, was unspoken. Even his lifelong romantic partner, Tim Johnson (who died in 1997), was referred to as Rojas-Lombardi's "business partner" in obituaries. The silence surrounding sexuality was a condition of cultural attitudes at the time.

"Nobody thought about their personal lives," Caroline Stuart, who worked under Beard in the late 1970s, says of both Beard and Rojas-Lombardi. "They were just thought of as chefs."

According to Stuart, Beard visited the Ballroom often after it opened; Rojas-Lombardi treated him like a king. "When Jim would go, they would just bring him everything they could fit on the table," she says. Beard and Rojas-Lombardi talked on the phone regularly until Beard's death in 1985.

"He liked Felipe a lot," Stuart says, mentioning that Beard kept a framed portrait of Rojas-Lombardi in his dining room. "Everybody liked Felipe." Rojas-Lombardi dedicated his first cookbook, 1985's *Soup, Beautiful Soup,* to the memory of Beard.

It was 1983 when chef, food historian, and cookbook author Maricel Presilla met Rojas-Lombardi. Back then she was a doctoral student finishing a dissertation on medieval Spanish history at New York University; she never thought she'd work in food. The course of Presilla's life changed when she wandered into the kitchen of the Ballroom to visit a chef friend and Rojas-Lombardi approached her.

"He said, 'Why don't you wear an apron and start cooking?'" Presilla recalls. Presilla was confused, but she put on an apron and made flan. Rojas-Lombardi loved it and decided to sell it at the restaurant.

"Felipe and I immediately established a rapport, both being from Latin America," Presilla, a native of Cuba, remembered. She agreed to work at the kitchen of the Ballroom once a week, and she stayed there for years.

Through it all, Rojas-Lombardi's vibrant culinary personality and playful, precise aesthetic attracted patrons. "That was before the Health Department got into people's lives and made life awful for everybody," Presilla says, laughing. "Today he wouldn't be able to have those dead ducks and turkeys and codfish hanging from the bar. It looked like one of those Renaissance feasts."

Things changed in 1989, when Rojas-Lombardi got sick with degenerative osteoporosis. He had recently begun working on a cookbook and enlisted Presilla's help in writing recipes. The book that resulted from this, *The Art of South American Cooking,* is ambitious and expansive in scope, over five hundred pages long, aspiring to be a definitive volume on a whole continent's foodways.

The book came out in the fall of 1991, just after his death in September. Presilla took a proof of the book to the Cabrini Center in the East Village, where Rojas-Lombardi was staying, the night before he died.

"His death was a blow to us," Presilla says. The Ballroom just wasn't the same without him, she says; it closed its doors for good in 1995. "They tried to keep things the way Felipe had them, but it just did not work."

It's been decades since Rojas-Lombardi died, but Presilla still feels his spirit. He lurks as a textual presence within Presilla's writing; in the acknowledgments of last year's *Peppers of the Americas*, she mentions her "dear late friend chef Felipe Rojas-Lombardi." She inherited his semimonstrous cookbook collection and revisits these cookbooks often. She remembers her days in the kitchen of the Ballroom clearly. The chocolate tart he once made her for her birthday, topped with candied violets and gilded gold leaves. The way he moved, the way he looked.

"He was small, very beautiful, but he had this larger-than-life persona," Presilla says. "He was a giant."

KHUSHBU SHAH

The Vegan Race Wars: How the Mainstream Ignores Vegans of Color

FROM *Thrillist*

SEARCH THE PHRASE *vegan person* on Shutterstock, and it will return 486 pages of results that would insinuate all vegans live a life among lavish spreads of ripe fruits and crisp vegetables, eating bowls of perfectly dressed salad and basking their lithe bodies under an abundance of sunlight while donning perfectly bleached smiles. Spend a few more minutes scrolling and you realize that something a little more questionable is afoot: it takes until the bottom of page 3 until you see a single face of color in an image.

Shutterstock, as a proprietor of easily digestible slices of curated reality, is a strange crystal ball that can reveal uncomfortable truths about mainstream narratives if you stop to think about it. There is a clear divide within the world of veganism that is quite literally black and white. Mainstream veganism, which advocacy sites like Vegan Voices of Color define as "white veganism," tends to overlook vegans of color by excluding them from the dominant discourse. The result is two very distinct and separate vegan cultures often at odds with each other.

Veganism as most people think of it today didn't emerge as a concept until 1944, when British woodworker Donald Watson coined the term to separate vegetarians who ate animal products from those who did not. Watson, lauded by many as the father of mainstream veganism, went on to found the Vegan Society, which helped solidify veganism's place as a lifestyle. But these ideologies and traditions had flourished in communities of color for centuries prior, if not longer. Eastern religions like Hinduism, Jainism, and Buddhism all advocate eschewing animals and animal products in some format because of the belief systems centered around nonviolence.

Cruelty-free eating is also a strong thread in Rastafarianism, where followers, who reject unhealthy manners of living, engage in a way of eating know as Ital, stemming from the word *vital*. The diet, encouraging plant-based unprocessed meals, was developed in the 1930s in Jamaica and is believed to have evolved from Hindu traditions brought over with indentured Indian servants, according to the *Miami New Times*. The Black Hebrew Israelite community, which was established in the late nineteenth century, also adheres to a strict vegan diet, believing it to be the secret to eternal life.

"My dad grew up in the Hebrew Israelite community, so I've always known a lot of black vegans," says Jenné Claiborne, a vegan food blogger and the author of the upcoming cookbook *Sweet Potato Soul*. "In Atlanta, where I was raised, there are a few black-owned vegan restaurants that have been around for decades. It's nothing new."

Zachary Toliver, a producer at PETA, seconds this. "Black vegans aren't a new thing," he says. "Vegan restaurants have been around for decades in black communities. There's a vegan Jamaican spot here in Tacoma [Washington] that's been around as long as I've been alive. White vegans didn't invent cruelty-free living. It didn't start with them, and it won't end with them either."

Do a quick Google search and it's easy to see why mainstream veganism is largely considered to be a white movement worldwide. Lists of "25 Vegan Celebrities" typically include only a handful of black and brown faces among a glut of white entertainers. Each entry of the *Independent*'s "9 Best Vegan Cookbooks" is written by a white author and employs a strikingly similar minimalist aesthetic that would sell well to the Goop set of people who are slender, white, and wealthy enough to afford $30 plates of kelp-noodle *cacio e pepe* to go with their $13 turmeric elixirs. Spoon University's list of "10 Vegans to Follow on Instagram" compiles image after image of healthy bowls made by white vegans specifically to play well on Instagram. The majority of high-profile vegan restaurants—ones that land in the pages of publications like *Food & Wine* and *Bon Appétit*—are also run by white chefs.

See a pattern?

Due to this misrepresentation about the true scope of veganism, it's not unusual for many vegans of color to think that they are alone. "I can't tell you how many people come up to me at events and tell me that it's so good to see someone who looks like me speaking," says Lauren Ornelas, the founder of the Food Empowerment Project and a self-described "proud Mexican American." Emiko Badillo, the founder of Portland's first all-vegan grocery store, credits the same acute visibility problem to why she decided to start the Portland Vegans of Color group. "I started becoming disenfranchised with the vegan community in Portland when I realized how white-dominated veganism was," Badillo explains. "I put a call out to see who might be interested in forming a vegans of color group, and the responses showed me how much of a need there was for [one]."

Vegans of color have inadvertently developed their own language that they use to talk about their veganism. "When you are a marginalized group within a marginalized group, it only makes sense for this to form," says Badillo. "It is a survival instinct." Books proudly display terms like *soul, afro, sistah,* and many other phrases especially popular in the African American vernacular. "It's very important to have this language," adds Claiborne. "The words have different meanings to different groups of people. It's almost like a code. It's a signal that this book is for vegans of color."

The community is vibrant, filled with large food festivals and support groups like Black Vegans Rock and Badillo's Portland Vegans of Color that aim to empower, educate, and celebrate the contributions of vegans of color. Activist Aph Ko was so fed up with the idea that "veganism is white" that in 2015 she decided to compile a list of prominent black vegans to show that many people were out there. Her efforts resulted in a list of one hundred people, ranging from the civil rights activist Coretta Scott King to cookbook authors like Afya Ibomu, which was widely circulated. It was the first time someone had compiled undeniable proof that veganism was thriving in communities of color. It was a turning point, says Claiborne: "I thought I lived in a bubble, that black vegans only existed in big cities, but then I realized that we are everywhere."

In the handful of years since Ko's list, the community has continued to expand rapidly, with some members managing to break into the mainstream. The year 2017 saw the release of black vegan chef Bryant Terry's popular cookbook *Afro-Vegan,* which saw an incredible amount of success, selling 50,000 copies since it was released.

"We are happy with the sales of this book and it is doing very well in a crowded market. Ten Speed is also doing a second book with Bryant Terry that should publish next year," says Erin Welke, a senior publicist at the publishing house. Alongside Terry, a handful of vegan cookbooks written by vegans of color (including Claiborne) will be released by big-name publishing houses like Random House this year as well. POC-owned vegan restaurants are now more common than ever, and continue to open across the country. And more black celebrities are publicly jumping on the vegan train, including RZA, Venus Williams, and Beyoncé, with the launch of her twenty-two-day vegan diet plan.

Even with that much star power, mainstream veganism still manages to elbow out vegans of color as it's convenient. In the most striking example, foods most associated with vegan meals—crumbly blocks of tofu, fluffy quinoa, pots of chia pudding, wraps made from collard greens instead of tortillas, pulled-pork sandwiches made from jackfruit—originated in communities of color who had been eating these items for hundreds of years before they were plucked and reclothed as "superfoods" or clever meat alternatives, stripping of them of their identities. "They borrow from so many different cultures, for sure," says Claiborne with an exasperated laugh. When anything gets sucked up into the current of what's trendy, the price goes up, making it harder for the communities that have long depended on these ingredients to afford them. "When a thin white vegan lady says something is cool, tons of people listen," says Badillo.

In addition to lifting ingredients from cultures of color and calling them their own, mainstream vegans are frequently "veganizing" cuisines that never needed it. "It's as if they think that communities of color are unable to turn their own food into something that's vegan," says Claiborne. It was something that she feared as she was writing her upcoming soul food cookbook—one that is inspired by her grandmother's cooking and her upbringing in the American South. "I was thinking to myself, 'Please don't let any white people come in and make a vegan soul food cookbook before I get around to it, because that is just going to be crazy,'" Claiborne admits. Her fears are well founded: there are cookbooks presenting vegan Mexican, Chinese, and Thai food out there written by white authors.

Perhaps the most egregious example of appropriation is *Thug Kitchen,* the ultra-popular vegan cooking blog that eventually spun off multiple *New York Times* best-selling cookbooks that have sold millions of copies collectively. *Thug Kitchen* built a name for itself writing voicey, expletive-laced directions for its vegan recipes. The tongue-in-cheek style borrowed heavily from African American culture (the name alone suggests as much), leading most people to believe that the anonymous author was someone like "a calorie-conscious, gangly young black man who's particularly vehement about clean eating," as writer Akeya Dickson described in *The Root*. Instead it came out that the blog was actually run by a white man and white woman, both in their late twenties. "It's deceptive and feels a lot like the latest iteration of nouveau blackface," Dickson continued in the same post. Claiborne, Ornelas, and Badillo all shared the same negative, indignant reaction to the question of *Thug Kitchen*. "That's not the kind of veganism I choose to follow," says Ornelas.

Like most things, the divide in the vegan world boils down to money. Brands are failing to capitalize on the buying power of vegans of color, often advertising for their snacks and beauty products with a noticeable drought of nonwhite faces. "I see this all the time, that these big vegan brands, they seem to be marketing only to white people," says Claiborne. The Instagram accounts of brands like Ripple, a popular plant-based milk alternative, and Sweet Earth Foods, which makes frozen vegan meals, are streams of naturally lit photos with few brown hands or faces. Claiborne finds it extremely frustrating when these brands sell in major stores like Whole Foods and Sprouts and fail to acknowledge that vegans of color shop there too. "I don't know the numbers, but I'm sure a big chunk of their consumers, people spending money, are not white people," she says.

"It's really unfortunate," says Toliver. "You have vegan businesses that are breaking into new markets, but [instead of advertising to vegans of color], they're going after the money, and start with the bougie crowds."

It's an issue that arises in funding organizations created for vegans of color. Ornelas faces this issue constantly with her work with the Food Empowerment Project, which she describes as a vegan food justice group. She and her team focus on promoting ethical veganism, but they also work to support farmworkers and correct food access and inequality in communities of color and low-income communities (though these frequently overlap). "We are entering our eleventh year, but we still don't get the big bucks," explains Ornelas. While major vegan donors are willing to pony up plenty of cash to put toward their cause, Ornelas explains that they don't see the Food Empowerment Project as a vegan organization. "They look at our work and they say this isn't really just focused on veganism," she says, so they don't donate. It's a tough reality to swallow when there is a strong stream of cash being put toward vegan causes: PETA, by and large a mainstream organization (albeit a controversial one), received over $65 million in contributions in 2016 alone.

Ornelas believes that prevailing veganism doesn't always recognize that helping people to get access to more fruits and vegetables "is a form of working on veganism." It's just one that doesn't look like the veganism that most of them are used to seeing, she says, adding that "there are issues that interconnect, and that is not a distraction." Ornelas offers up a historical example of two interconnected issues: when Frederick Douglass was talking about abolitionism, he would also talk about women's right to vote. "They were seen as linked, not as distractions from one another."

This is where vegans of color feel the largest rift: that veganism is not a single-issue cause but an intersectional one. Which is not to say that all mainstream vegans do not believe that veganism is a complex, multifaceted issue. (*Thrillist* reached out to several mainstream vegan voices for a comment and didn't hear back.) But the prevailing focus on the suffering of animals only doesn't leave much room to focus on the human elements core to the vegan mission either. "Veganism is not just about animals," states Claiborne. "It's not only for one group either. If you care about animals—and humans are animals—then it should be inclusive. All factions of veganism, in my opinion, should be about empathy toward every person." Ornelas puts it plainly: "You can be vegan and not cruelty-free."

To Ornelas, solving food inequality in communities of color is a crucial step toward spreading holistic veganism. "People should be able to eat according to their ethics," she says. "They should be able to eat healthy and have access to fruits and vegetables, and options. A grave injustice is taking place that communities that do not have the same access to healthy foods that everybody else does."

Many people of color are also now heavily dependent upon the sources of food that are available to them—cheap cuts of meat and dairy products. These products were frequently introduced to these communities through European colonialism, even though many, especially people of color, are lactose intolerant. "Colonization is what brought these animals to our lands," says Ornelas. "We can't digest their milk. So we like to call it 'lactose normal' instead of 'lactose intolerant,' because intolerance makes it sound like there's something wrong with us when there's not."

"So many people, including a number who are Mexican, don't recognize how much of our food wasn't really dependent upon cheese and animal products," says Ornelas. While "Mexican food" may conjure images of porky tacos and cheese-slathered enchiladas, it's a far cry from indigenous Mexican cooking, in which meat was used sparingly, dairy was nonexistent, and meals were constructed mainly from beans, wild greens, seeds, and squash. This inspired her to start the site VeganMexicanFood.com as a way to prove how vegan-friendly Mexican cuisine really is. It is a way to course-correct, to decolonize Mexican food and reclaim the heritage, centuries after Spanish colonists settled in Mexico in the 1500s who introduced meat and dairy products, changing the cuisine forever.

This is true for the African American community as well, says Claiborne. Before being brought over to the United States, the foodways of slaves were not heavily dependent upon animal products. Neither was the food they ate in the American South—which was mostly plant-based. But during the Great Migration, when many blacks moved from the South to the North and West, they moved off family farms where they were growing their own food, explains Claiborne. "They moved to these big cities with no outdoor space, so that took a lot of that plant-based culture. It was too expensive to buy vegetables all of a sudden, because they couldn't grow them themselves," she adds. In many ways, poverty forced them to find different food sources. These black communities soon became heavily reliant upon highly processed foods from fast-food chains and convenience stores as their access to fresh fruits and vegetables became deeply limited.

For vegans of color, the movement is also about health—not just personal health but that of their communities, while changing stereotypes in the process. "Communities of color can especially benefit from ditching animal parts," says Toliver. "Black Americans, we are disproportionately affected by obesity, more likely to have diabetes than white people. We're nearly twice as likely as whites to die from heart disease or stroke," he adds.

Though the battle against institutionalized problems within our food system is an uphill one, Claiborne is hopeful that one day there won't be a divide between mainstream veganism and vegans of color. "I see organizations trying to expand to not include just the same old healthy American white people stuff," she says. Until then, vegans of color refuse to sit around waiting for mainstream veganism to become more inclusive. As their identities and communities are threatened across other facets of society, diet choice has become an important avenue for vegans of color to express, reclaim, and protect their identities. "I've heard other black vegans talk about living this way as a revolutionary act, and I totally agree," says Toliver. "It takes courage to unlearn these destructive habits that have been taught by both our families and centuries of oppression. There's something powerful about taking back one's health and consciousness."

Sugartime

FROM *Eater*

IN A ROMANTIC oil painting by Will Cotton, Katy Perry lies naked on a cotton candy cloud, a whisper of pink spun sugar draped over her butt. The landscape bulges and billows with emphatic softness, dominating the painting except for a hint of blue sky. Perry offers a look both languid and post-orgasmic, lips parted, her hair nostalgically curled like a 1950s pinup. When the painting made its debut on the cover of Perry's 2010 album *Teenage Dream,* it sat somewhere between commercial pop and high-art comment on all of the above. The uncomfortable excess of Cotton's work was used to sell uncomfortable excess. And it all hinged on sugar.

Sugar is sprinkled everywhere in our language. When children are good and happy, they are cutie pies. Cool stuff can be "sweet, man." Our crush is a sweetheart, and our sweetheart might be our honey. "A spoonful of sugar," as Mary Poppins croons, is a bribe, something to help "the medicine go down." Sugar is leisure and celebration—what British birthday would be complete without the stickiness of cake frosting on fingers? It is, according to Roland Barthes, an attitude—as integral to the concept of Americanness as wine is to Frenchness. In the 1958 hit song "Sugartime," to which Barthes was referring, the sunny, smiling McGuire Sisters harmonize sweetly, filling their mouths with honey: "Be my little sugar / And love me all the time."

And like anything pleasurable, sugar is often characterized as a vice. The flood of industrial sugar into packaged food has real public health consequences, but predictably, the backlash has taken on a puritanical zeal far beyond reasonable concerns. Sugar is "America's Drug of Choice," one headline claimed. "Is Sugar the World's Most Popular Drug?" wondered another. Even those selling sugary food winkingly parrot the language of addiction—consider Milk Bar's notoriously sticky, seductively sweet Crack Pie. A drug that decimated predominantly poor black American communities is now a punchline for middle-class white indulgence.

For black Americans, sweetness was an essential ingredient in Jim Crow–era stereotypes designed to keep newly emancipated people from their rights. Those stereotypes persist—and even generate profit—today. The racist trope of watermelon-eating African Americans, popularized in this era, framed black people as simpletons and children craving nothing beyond a sweet slice of melon. Aunt Jemima, a character derived from minstrel shows, is the apotheosis of the happy, nurturing "mammy" stereotype, empty and filled with sweet syrup, her smile used to sell sugar for Pep-siCo. "The shelf on which i sit," reads Lucille Clifton's poem "Aunt Jemima," "between the flour and cornmeal / is thick with dreams."

And sugar's history is brutal. The artist Kara Walker tackled a profoundly different collision of femininity and sweetness than Katy Perry on a candy cloud when she conceived of a 35-foot sugar sphinx inside the former Domino Sugar Refinery in 2014. Titled *A Subtlety, or the Marvelous Sugar Baby,* Walker's sculpture was the single largest piece of public art ever shown in New York City. A crouching black woman made from 40 tons of glistening white sugar, surrounded by life-sized figurines of black boys carrying bananas or baskets, she hunched forward on her toes, knees, and forearms, her lips, breasts, butt, and labia swelling round in cartoonish extravagance—an uneasy reflection of the fetishization of black women's bodies and the commodification of their flesh. The sugar sphinx, the artist wrote in the work's full title, was "an Homage to the unpaid and overworked Artisans who have refined our Sweet tastes from the cane fields to the Kitchens of the New World on the Occasion of the demolition of the Domino Sugar Refining Plant."

Sugar is survival. It is a respite for palates swept clean of childish joy for too long. It is sexual desire and pleasure, and also temptation and sin. And it is a commodity, one historically produced with some of the most brutal labor practices on the planet. In the Western imagination sugar is pleasure, temptation, and vice—and in modern history it is original sin.

*

Sweetness is a primal pleasure, like warmth or softness. Our desire to find, taste, and consume it is profoundly natural, but our quest to make more of it, to cook, bake, caramelize, and fry our way to sweet—that is profoundly human. Our love of sugar is shaped when we're gummy infants and follows us through adulthood into gummy old age. One study found that when sweet solutions were injected into the womb, fetuses, whose nutritional needs are entirely met by the umbilical cord, swallowed more amniotic fluid. When bitter solutions were injected, less was swallowed. Another study found that anencephalic infants—babies born with much of their brain mass missing, who rarely live longer than a few hours —reacted positively when a sweet substance was placed on their lips and grimaced when given something bitter, even though they lacked the part of the brain typically responsible for taste.

In the current age of abundant, industrial food, this sweet tooth is considered hedonistic. But our love of sugar is about survival: where food was scarce, sweetness offered a clue that it contained a large number of much-needed calories, just as an aversion to bitterness kept us away from many toxic plants. Even the breast milk that humans produce is sweet.

In nature, sweetness often accompanies ripeness, in just-picked peapods and baby corncobs as well as melon slices and punnets of late-season cherries. As chef and author Samin Nosrat explained to me, "At the farmer's market . . . one of the highest compliments is to say that something is very sweet." Unlike the sledgehammer thwack of candy, natural sweetness is in constant flux, according to Nosrat, receding from the moment the fruit or vegetable is picked. "Peas," she said, "can taste totally different from one day to the next."

Cooking unlocks sweetness in wondrous ways, and we've become experts in harnessing that power: red bell peppers are sweet when they're roasted, and onions yield to a sticky, caramelized tangle if cooked slowly. Entire meal courses are devoted to candies, chocolate, cakes, ice cream, and pie. These foods—from sticky slabs of ginger cake to root beer floats—are joy that unfurls across the tongue. Molecules responsible for sweetness fit with protein receptors on the taste buds like pieces of some honeyed jigsaw puzzle.

It is also a pleasure contained in its own little box. For American and western European palates, sweetness occupies its own lonely niche in our cooking, sequestered and scrutinized. We have steaks and lobster rolls and quiche and potatoes and pizza . . . and then dessert separately, afterward. We eat vegetables and milk and bread . . . and then ice cream as a treat. Sugar is craved one moment and controlled the next.

We've not always had such polarized tastes. Capon (a type of castrated cockerel, bred for eating), blanched almonds, rice, lard, salt, and sugar were the cornerstones of a medieval blancmange, or *blank mang*, as it was written in the fourteenth-century *The Forme of Cury*, one of the earliest known collections of English cookery writing. The blancmange Brits are familiar with today is a sweet milk custard, set like a jelly, often in a decorative mold. The medieval version is a jarring admixture of sugar alongside meat. And this was in no way an unusual dish. Sweet courses were interspersed throughout a meal, and dishes such as *frytour of erbes*, or honeyed herb fritters, whose recipe is also archived in *The Forme of Cury*, straddled the sweet-savory divide. With such a strikingly different culinary grammar, the idea of a monolithic, wondrous, dreadful sugar would hardly have made sense to medieval cooks. Sweetness was not a behemoth category in itself but a seasoning, no different than salt or a pinch of spice.

In many cultures this sugar-salt symphony is still foundational. "The food I grew up eating every night—that is to say, Persian home cooking—is all about balancing the plate with sweet and sour, salty and rich, crisp and soft," says Nosrat. "Fresh and dried fruits—pomegranates, sour cherries, dates, raisins—all regularly found their way onto our dinner plates. So I have always been drawn to a little sweetness in my food."

Food writer Yemisi Aribisala explained to me that Nigerian tastes demand sweet with an acidic counterbalance: "There won't be any kind of dessert accompanying meals in most homes. People will snack on star apples (which are very tart) or cashew fruits, almond fruits, or guavas. I can't even bring to mind one common fruit that is like the European apple, with considerably more sweetness than tartness."

Some vestiges of this approach to flavor remain in Western cooking—sugar coaxes out flavor in everything from ketchup to honey-glazed ham—but these happy harmonies are largely erased by rigid taxonomies. In a 2016 article in the *Charlotte Observer*, Kathleen Purvis documented the disdain that white southerners

often hold for their black neighbors' cornbread: light, cakey, and
sweetened with sugar, compared to the paler, more savory corn-
breads that cater to white tastes. Food writer Ronni Lundy once
commented that "if God had meant cornbread to have sugar, he
would have made it cake." Rather than finding value in the million
ways that good taste can manifest, we are drawn into a polarized
debate, where blackness is sweetness and excess and whiteness is
tasteful restraint.

How has sweetness—something we are evolutionarily programmed
to like, for survival—come to stand in for sex and escapism and
hedonism? Humans are metaphor machines, and our mouths are
liminal places where food and words mingle, where hot dogs, ta-
gliatelle, and Nigerian puff puff meet *my name is,* memory, and *I.*
True synesthesia—the blurring between one sense and another—
is relatively rare, but its logic pervades our language, so that trum-
pets might sound hot, or sadness taste sour. One study found that
honeycomb toffee tastes less sweet when eaten while listening to
a "bitter" soundtrack than when eaten while listening to a "sweet"
soundtrack. And our senses don't just crisscross randomly—"How
come silence is sweet but sweetness isn't silent?" one paper asked.

No sugared association is stronger than that between sweetness
and femininity. Girls are made of sugar and spice and everything
nice. Women are honey, sweetheart, cupcake, candy girl, honey-
bunch—or they're tarts. In the Bible, "The lips of an adulterous
woman drip honey" (Proverbs 5:3). Meanwhile, black women have
been "caramel," "brown sugar," "mocha latte," "chocolate," and
"molasses"—both desired and diminished. Making sweet foods is
considered women's work—and eating them is too. Girls receive
an Easy-Bake Oven; cake mixes are marketed exclusively to women;
home bakers are overwhelmingly female. Candy and chocolate are
so heavily feminized that a Yorkie bar in the U.K.—normal chocolate, massive chunks—until recently stood out by marketing itself
as "not for girls."

It's not just in American and European food cultures that this
holds true. I spoke to food writer and journalist Mayukh Sen
about the gendering of foods within Bengali cuisine. "Sweetness
is very much gendered female in Bengali cooking," he explained.
"There's a word, *mishti,* that stands for both Bengali sweets and
is also used to describe someone, usually a woman, who is 'sweet'

(pleasant, youthful, and nonthreatening/demure)." In Japan, *amato* and *karato* refer to those who love sweets and those who prefer salty, savory, and spicy foods, respectively, and yet these labels loosely trace the dividing line between men and women. Jon D. Holtzman writes that a Kyoto-based confectioner—by all accounts a man who loved his sweets—assured him that he was more a *karato* kind of guy: "strong, energetic, and ambitious."

The collision of women and sex and sugar reaches a metaphorical and not-so-metaphorical climax in Katy Perry's *Teenage Dream,* with those sumptuous cotton-candy clouds and Perry's nakedness. The same aesthetic runs through the "California Gurls" video—a project that Cotton also consulted on—as Perry sweeps through a world of candy canes and gummy bears in a cupcake bra. Perry continues to use food as part of her brand's visual language, last year premiering the video for her single "Bon Appétit," in which she is kneaded, picked over, sliced, and cooked by celebrity chef Roy Choi.

Will Cotton's art has, since the late 1990s, been obsessed, and stickily engaged, with sugar. Beginning with 1998 paintings of eerie candy trailers and housing projects—recalling the fairytale gingerbread cottage—Cotton painted a series of ever-more-excessive and surreal candy landscapes. Women begin to populate these landscapes in the early 2000s, with sultry nudes bathing in hot chocolate or reclining on sugar sands. In one, a topless young woman looks intently through the edge of the canvas, a many-tiered cake perched atop her head like a crown. In another, a nude woman sits astride a sea creature—a seething, swelling ice cream thing rising from tumbling waves, spume, and spray. Every inch of these scenes is saturated with sugar and sex, where a time-old narrative unfolds: about all the temptations your mother warned you about, about lust, greed, instant gratification, and tooth-rotting candy.

Cotton takes the culture's ready metaphors—the cotton-candy cloud and the perky butt; a landscape of erect candy canes; a macaron-clad woman, good enough to eat—and magnifies them to the point of absurdity. And yet there's no sense of subversion in this surrealness: in fact Cotton plays directly and uncritically into the sexist tropes he portrays. The women in his artworks are nonthreatening, limp, and inviting (albeit in an unsettling way), and despite the omnipresence of food in the scenes, the women occupying these landscapes never eat: they are there not to consume but to be consumed. In a review of Cotton's 2011 show at the Kohn Gallery in Los Angeles, Leah Ollman wrote: "Exhausting familiar sexist correspondences between women and fantasy, desire, indulgence and consumption, the work exploits a single gimmick to the point of sugar shock." What's more, the young, white, limber women draped over Cotton's candy clouds raise an important question: in a world where sweetness is innocence and innocence is whiteness, who is allowed to be sweet?

If Cotton's oeuvre is populated by an almost entirely white parade of female hedonists, Kara Walker's sugar sphinx is physical, imposing, and powerful. Like so many conversations about femininity, bringing race into the picture of sweetness upends and complicates familiar narratives—and forces the viewers to confront truths they might not want to see.

"When we arrived in Barbados," wrote Olaudah Equiano in his 1789 autobiography, "many merchants and planters came on board and examined us. We were then taken to the merchant's yard, where we were all pent up together like sheep in a fold. On a signal the buyers rushed forward and chose those slaves they liked best." Having already suffered the brutality of the Middle Passage —the journey from the west coast of Africa to the Americas, during which up to 20 percent of people considered "cargo" would die— these auctions marked the beginning of a new, nightmarish chapter in the lives of enslaved people like Equiano. They were branded and given new names, stripped of every vestige of their freedom, language, and identity, dehumanized by the people who bought them. From the planting of the cane to the boiling of the syrup, sugar plantations ran on the blood and sweat of enslaved African laborers. "When [English people] go to the West Indies they forget God and all feelings of shame, I think, since they can see and do such things," wrote Mary Prince in 1831. "They tie up slaves like hogs—moor them up like cattle, and they lick them, so as hogs, or cattle, or horses never were flogged."

The brutality of sugar's history is often erased beneath a parade of craving, cake, and metaphor, and Walker's sphinx confronts and shames this forgetting in an extraordinary way. To my mind, it is a paradox: its crouch is both submissive and the precursor to a deadly pounce; in all those tons of pure white sugar is a grandeur at odds with the meek honeys, sugars, and sweethearts we're used to. It refuses the ahistorical fantasy narratives that sugar has so long been used to invoke and instead plants its feet firmly in the context of a brutal, racist exploitation. By creating a monumental black body—specifically a black woman's body—from sugar in this place where it was once refined into whiteness that was built on blood, Walker inverted the hierarchy of worth: blackness was now a precious, extraordinary thing, and pure, white, sugar mere material.

Unlike Cotton's saccharine dreamscape, this setting was confrontational physicality, anchored in the earth and inseparable from the histories of slave labor that forged it. The factory "stank of molasses," Walker explained to Doreen St. Félix in *Vulture*. "The history would not dry."

Walker's childhood was one of contrasts between the integration and acceptance she'd found in Stockton, California, and the racism leveled at her during her high school years in Stone Mountain, Georgia; between the whiteness that molded the institutions she studied within and the defiant blackness she channeled through her work. After earning an MFA from the Rhode Island School of Design in 1994, she immediately found global recognition with her murals: stories of race, sex, violence, and gender told through cut-paper silhouettes. In one of her most famous— *Gone: An Historical Romance of a Civil War as It Occurred b'tween the Dusky Thighs of One Young Negress and Her Heart*—caricatured figures dance across the walls in a story of sex and slavery. Walker's art is an uneasy juxtaposition: black paper on white walls; racist stereotypes replayed and reconfigured in a black woman's art; the brutality of slavery playing out against dreamy antebellum landscapes. This curdling of opposites is the artistic context from which Walker's sugar sphinx arose: historic ruins and an urgent, unlikely sweetness.

Stuart Hall alluded to this shared history of blackness and sugar when he famously wrote, "I am the sugar at the bottom of the English cup of tea." A black, Jamaican-born theorist living and working in London, Hall could feel—even taste—the legacy of the enslaved black people who bled for Britain's colonial wealth. It has been estimated that British ships took almost 3.4 million enslaved people from Africa to the Caribbean and North America over a 245-year period between the first expeditions to the Americas and the abolition of the slave trade in 1807. These enslaved people provided Britain with the wealth, reach, and manpower to muscle their way to an empire which, at its peak, commanded nearly a quarter of the global population.

Slowly, accounts like Equiano's had begun to resonate with the British public, who, when faced with details of the true horror of the industry, could no longer indulge in sweet tea and slices of cake without tasting the bodies of the enslaved people who had suffered for that sugar. The inhumane conditions of sugar production didn't end with abolition, though. The sugar industry has been accused of complicity in forced labor in the U.S. as recently as 1989, and in the Caribbean in 2001, with the UN's International Labour Organization describing the treatment of Haitian sugar workers in the Dominican Republic as "one of the most widely documented instances of coercive labour contracting over the past two decades." A report by *Verité* found that workers in the Dominican Republic were often kept—through the prohibitive cost of transport compared to the meagerness of the wages, and thanks to their undocumented status—within workers' compounds of the plantations there, not given the liberty to move freely. Workers brought in illegally from Haiti were subjected to threats and kept in the dark about the kind of work they would be doing, what they would be paid, and what freedoms they'd have. What's more, these workers were found to be kept in a state of indebtedness to their employers, rendering them unable to leave. This exploitative and often unlawful transplanting of laborers is an example of what anthropologist Sidney Mintz was referring to when he wrote that "sugar . . . has been one of the massive demographic forces in world history . . . Sugar still moves people about the Caribbean today."

A Subtlety was dismantled in 2014, but in 2017 the sculpture's left hand made its way to the Deste Foundation Project Space on the Greek island of Hydra. In its new home, encrusted with yet more sugar, the hand was sweetened, not in spite of but because of displacement and dismemberment. This relic of a masterpiece was reborn as *Figa*. Fingers clamped in a now little-used expletive gesture—thumb clasped between index and middle finger—it was defiant. In pre-Renaissance Italy, this was *mano in fica*, or fig hand, both sweet and explicit, standing for the ripeness—and rudeness—of a cunt.

Walker is not the only black woman artist to eschew binaries and instead speak about life's necessary blending of sweetness and suffering. Walker's melding of opposites—blackness, whiteness, brutality, humor, industry, myth, blood, and sugar—is a resistance to and repurposing of the impossible demands society makes of black women: to be docile but also assertive, thick-skinned but still malleable, available but not free. From within this chaos, black women find a way to blend the sugar and the suffering.

Beyoncé is a vocal fan of Walker, calling her one of her favorite artists in a 2016 interview for *Garage* magazine. Like Walker, Beyoncé spins her own bittersweet narratives into art. "I'ma rain, I'ma rain on this bitter love/Tell the sweet I'm new," she sings on "Freedom."

As bell hooks writes of Beyoncé's *Lemonade* in her essay "Moving Beyond Pain," "to be truly free, we must choose beyond simply surviving adversity, we must dare to create lives of sustained optimal well-being and joy. In that world, the making and drinking of lemonade will be a fresh and zestful delight, a real life mixture of the bitter and the sweet, and not a measure of our capacity to endure pain, but rather a celebration of our moving beyond pain."

If Will Cotton's paintings—resplendent with pure, idealized fantasy—are the sweetness we lazily dream of, Walker's *A Subtlety* is the sweetness we actually live: rearing up through centuries of hurt and exploitation, planting its feet in the good and the bad, the pleasure and the pain. It crystallizes across the surfaces of our imperfect lives, and makes us shine.

MICHAEL W. TWITTY

I Had Never Eaten in Ghana Before. But My Ancestors Had.

FROM *Bon Appétit*

THE SIX OF us have given our undivided attention to Auntie Mabel, owner of the eponymous Mabel's Chop Bar in Ho, Ghana. Here the kitchen is an outdoor building, a complex of covered shelters where peeling, washing, and butchering happen. Large cast-iron pots sit atop fires built on three stones. The chop bar is a place where you eat whatever is made from day to day, and today Mabel's table is laden with ginger, garlic, *suya* spices (a West African version of garam masala), crushed Maggi cubes, tomatoes, and *shitor*, a hot pepper sauce made from bird's-eye chiles and powdered crayfish, tenderly simmered and stirred until it achieves the consistency of gravy-meets-preserves.

As she prepares stock for the meat (more on that in a moment), Auntie Mabel looks every bit the African American or Afro-Caribbean grandma we know from home, right down to tasting the resultant sauce off the back of her left hand. We are in the country of the Ewe people in eastern Ghana, and Mabel's courtyard is very still with the end-of-season dry heat, nearly 100 degrees. The covered space we sit in is a welcome shelter, and the whole scene, right down to the corrugated iron, reminds me of my first trips to the Deep South.

Auntie Mabel does not have time for our smartphone photos. She works with absolute disregard for our purpose, worrying instead about getting us fed before the afternoon rush. We are African American chefs who have come to Ghana to learn about the cooking of our ancestors. Our leader is fellow culinarian Ada

Anagho Brown, the president of Roots to Glory Tours, a group specifically charged with bringing African Americans linked by DNA to their ancestral homelands. Four of us have never set foot in Africa, and I have never been to Ghana. Of those who have tested to get a sense of our genetic roots, all of us trace back to this country. For me it's a staggering 32 percent of my DNA.

I am an African American, gay, Jewish culinary historian whose life has been shaped by a search for my roots and an exploration of the ways food shapes identity. Food has played a deep and active role in empowering my people to overcome oppression, and how we do so is our greatest form of cultural capital. For most African Americans, slavery forcibly cut our immediate ties to the motherland. Needing to know more about our roots has become one of the central issues in our identity. That's why we're here in Ghana. We need to know that this is really home.

Back at the chop bar, a bucket emerges from the refrigerated storage area. Power is precious in West Africa, and refrigeration in the countryside is a luxury, but Mabel is known for her dedication to cleanliness and order. She pulls off the top of the bucket and reveals the cut-up carcass of *Thryonomys gregorianus,* the lesser cane rat, known across English-speaking West Africa by its descriptive nickname, grasscutter. Pizza Rat has nothing on this 15-to-20-pound bad boy. Low in fat, high in protein, it is vegetarian and tender and said to be the number-one bushmeat, followed by antelope, porcupine, and certain types of snakes and lizards.

Kenyatta Ashford and Josmine Evans—fellow chefs on this journey—take turns picking up the grasscutters by the tail, snapping pictures, and admiring their heft. Both chefs have roots in Louisiana, where muskrats and nutria can be dinner. Perhaps that's the source of their fearlessness. I wince and laugh with Kezia Curtis, a caterer from Detroit, as earthy and open-minded as they come. Ada keeps saying *grah-hhs-kottah* the way the Ghanaians do, smiling and mimicking the animal's sharp front teeth. As a Jewish guy who loves his roast chicken and brisket, I am feeling mighty not in my roots at the moment. This rat is the *treif*-est thing I have ever been asked to eat.

My good friend Harold Caldwell, a historical interpreter at Colonial Williamsburg and a trained chef in the eighteenth-century tradition, is ready to engage with old *Thryonomys gregorianus.* Not far from the courtyard we walk through a back alley to the butchering yard, where a young man in his Sunday best is sweating over a fire. He places each grasscutter on the grate and quickly scrapes away the singed hair. Within seconds the carcass is white as snow. Harold, also in long sleeves and used to working in the searing heat, joins in and makes the young brother smile but stops after three scrapes, noting the singed hair on his own arms and hands. The grasscutters are gutted immediately and cut into pieces. While we watch this gruesome display, goats, cats, and chickens skulk around as if there is nothing to see, and a man arrives with freshly shot duiker, a dainty little antelope from the rainforest.

We retire to the back of the chop bar and take turns pounding *fufu,* a soft, gluey loaf of boiled yam. Immediately Harold and I think of possum cooked with yams, a treat mentioned often in collected oral histories from folks who were enslaved in the American South. Three women dipping pestles into water knock away at the yam in an ancient beat, making it look easier than it actually is. We stumble at the process, trying not to knock ourselves out and to keep the yam off the ground.

Harold and I start singing an old song passed down by our enslaved ancestors in America, changing the words "I'm gonna beat this corn" to "I'm gonna beat this yam, unh-huh!/I'm gonna beat it good/unh-huh/gonna beat this yam/gonna beat this yam and eat it 'til my belly full!" Within seconds the women whose muscles power the chop bar are clapping and call-and-response singing with us, absolutely delighted. When the *fufu* is ready, we retire to the courtyard. I eat chicken and stew while everybody else chows down on the grasscutter, admiring the perfect flavor of the stock and the juicy tenderness of the meat. Harold offers me a bite, but I shake my head no. As dedicated as I am to learning about the culinary heritage of a third of my ancestors, I'm not crossing this river today.

In the early 1770s my sixth great-grandfather was captured at war and exiled from his homeland in the Asante Kingdom, now the central heart of present-day Ghana. Within six months of his capture he found himself enslaved in the developing James River port of Richmond. By the time it was the new capital of Virginia, in 1780, he was under the lash of George Todd, a Scottish merchant whose surname would carry down through the centuries as our name while my African ancestors' name was lost. But what mattered most remains: our Asante origins, revealed to me some 240 years later by an elderly relative and later confirmed by DNA.

When oral history, genetic tests, historical context, and my informed imagination combined in a moment of revelation, my whole life danced before me. I was a teenager when I drifted into the Ghana embassy in Washington, D.C., as carelessly as you walk into a gas station. I interviewed everybody in that place, including a gentleman who became my Ghanaian cultural mentor. "The ancestors have sent me to make sure you become a proper Ghanaian man," he said.

In my mind I had been preparing for this trip for decades, nibbling at facts and words and recipes. Ghana, it seems, was calling me.

In Ghana it's clear I have inherited a remarkably rich culinary tradition, largely expressed through the chop bar. Yet everywhere we look are reminders of home. The white clay that people still eat as a sort of folk medicine in the American South is sold in the market in Kumasi. There is barbecued meat on every corner, roasted ears of corn and sweet potatoes, bits of fried chicken cooked fresh on the spot, and black-eyed-pea fritters. Deep-fried smelt and *akple* look like fish and grits.

Here are the gourds we used to scoop water out of wells, the profusion of fruit both wild and cultivated. Street vendors sell fried everything—river shrimp, cocoyam (taro) chips, plantains, mangrove oysters, and bananas. Hospitality is in every gesture. Our cousins love cooking with us; we help clean freshly caught anchovies and stir thick pots of molten corn mush destined to be *kenkey,* a popular fermented starch in southern Ghana. There is silver herring, orange-red palm oil, bright pink little rock lobsters, speckled guinea fowl, deep green *kontomire* (cocoyam leaves that look like collard greens), and basil grown by the front door just like our grandmothers did in the Deep South.

But this is not a food story that comes without cost. Hours after our arrival we visit the Nkrumah monument, a powerful symbol of African independence and the fight against colonialism. We learn about the welcome that Kwame Nkrumah, the man who spearheaded the movement that led to Ghana becoming the first independent nation in sub-Saharan Africa, in 1957, extended to Africans in the diaspora. He wanted us here, because this place is in part where we come from. To be here, though, is to recognize a painful truth: we left as enslaved people.

Coming back is reparative. We make our pilgrimage to Elmina, Anomabu, and Cape Coast Castle. "You are fulfilling your ancestors' dream to come back home," Ada tells us plainly. "They never thought they would come back. You are giving them peace." We step five feet into the pitch darkness of the men's dungeon at Cape Coast Castle, conspicuously placed under the chapel where the same men who violated women and children and subjugated formerly proud warriors prayed for their own souls' salvation. The sea roils and roars, but I hear nothing except silence down there. And then a weeping.

I turn around and my dear brother Harold, who had been bursting with joy at every new and familiar taste, is sobbing. Then we are all sobbing. This is a horrific space, where nail marks still mar the walls. Yet we are facing an inescapable gratitude. Every second endured in this hell, followed by the hell of the bottom of a boat in the Middle Passage, followed by the hell of slavery and sharecropping and Jim Crow and forty years of liberty(-ish), have led us back here, now finally with the freedom to return our genes and souls to the place where it all began, even humanity itself.

I cannot take my eyes off Josmine and Kezia. Their eyes are not their own but instead the lenses of defiant grandmothers, once young women themselves, from centuries past. The women's dungeon has a slot in one of the doors through which those who resisted violation were fed. These are the ones who kept the roots of soul going, from the village to the market to the memories in their own minds, from here to the Middle Passage to the plantation. This place, in all its horror, is indispensable.

We leave the dungeon sober and angry but still grateful. We tumble out the door of no return exhausted, watching the Fante fishermen and their children dutifully tending their nets as twilight sets in; drums and gongs signal the pulling in of the catch.

The door of no return has become the door of return. We re-enter the fort. A sign welcomes African Americans like ourselves —welcomes us home. We have the eyes of reclaimed orphans. Broken again, we are reset to heal in new ways. We pass around plates of jollof rice and *red-red* (plantains and beans cooked with red palm oil). Deep sighs turn to deep smiles and we offer up prayers of gratitude and hope, addressing one another in our new Ghanaian names—Dzifa and Sedzugi, Elikim, Yayra, Mawuli. Every step has increased knowledge of our past and set a path for the future. Aware that the ancestors' souls are inside us, we are hungrier than ever before. *Akpe na Mawu,* as they say in the Ewe language. Thanks be to the Creator.

BENJAMIN ALDES WURGAFT

On Reading Jonathan Gold

FROM *The Los Angeles Review of Books*

"PERHAPS YOU WOULD like to read a restaurant review this morning," Jonathan Gold often wrote, broadcasting his *Los Angeles Times* reviews on Twitter. I want to read an uncountable number of additional reviews by Gold, who died July 21 at the age of fifty-seven, just a few weeks after receiving a diagnosis of pancreatic cancer. To read one Gold review after another, which you can do in the collection *Counter Intelligence* (2000), is to enter a world in which flavors are vivid and the virtues and flaws of each eatery are picked out in fine detail. He covered food trucks, white-tablecloth restaurants, and 2-a.m.-hangover-recovery-noodle counters in Koreatown, and he described them all with a voice that was playful, literary, and just. July 28 would have been his fifty-eighth birthday, and several buildings in Los Angeles were illuminated with gold light in commemoration. He was, and remains, beloved, irreplaceable. Now Gold's trademark silhouette—a tongue-in-cheek imitation of Alfred Hitchcock—is drawn on the wall of a taqueria in the Arts District. One of his familiar mottos, "The taco honors the truck," is written next to it.

Gold offered weekly reviews of restaurants in the Los Angeles area, but he also represented Los Angeles both to the city's residents and to the world. His reviews and notes on food may bear the time stamp of workaday journalism, but they also transcend their time and geography. They constitute a full-fledged chapter of Los Angeles's literary history, and of the history of food writing. Encomia aside, I owe Gold a personal debt as a reader. His reviews taught me to love Los Angeles, shaking off cinematic and literary visions of the city that had taught me to mistrust the place. Needless to say, L.A. detraction is available for cheap. Mike Davis, in his well-known study *City of Quartz* (1990), surveys stereotypes of Los Angeles as a city where the mind in particular comes to ruin, a place that celebrates our appetites but not our intellects. Davis lists writers who seem to have been undone by L.A.:

> Fused into a single montage image are Fitzgerald reduced to a drunken hack, West rushing to his own apocalypse (thinking it a dinner party), Faulkner rewriting second-rate scripts, Brecht raging against the mutilation of his work, the Hollywood Ten on their way to prison, Didion on the verge of a nervous breakdown, and so on. Los Angeles (and its alter-ego, Hollywood) becomes the literalized Mahagonny: city of seduction and defeat, the antipode to critical intelligence.

The brain becomes the victim of the body's seduction, even as long episodes of sitting in traffic (perhaps en route to the next binge) wear down the body. Food, one old story went, was not so much appreciated in Los Angeles as consumed like gasoline. In 1971 the architectural historian Reyner Banham, an English celebrant of Los Angeles whose high estimation of the city Mike Davis would criticize, mused on the relationship between movement and food in a city built for the personal car:

> The purely functional hamburger, as delivered across the counter of say, the Gipsy Wagon on the UCLA campus, the Surf-boarder at Hermosa Beach or any McDonald's or Jack-in-the-Box outlet anywhere, is a pretty well-balanced meal that he who runs (surfs, drives, studies) can eat with one hand; not only the ground beef but all the sauce, cheese, shredded lettuce, and other garnishes are firmly gripped between the two halves of the bun.

Los Angeles still has its fast-food aficionados, but as I would learn, food as mere fuel for a city on the go has nothing whatsoever to do with Jonathan Gold's Los Angeles. The city is full of appreciative eaters for whom restaurants are more exciting destinations than beaches, or cinemas, or parties. L.A.'s chefs are eager to draw on a dizzying array of produce found at farmers' markets that put those of most other cities to shame. Los Angeles is full of people for whom three hours at a meal is not wasted time. Gold's affection for taco trucks had less to do with speed or restlessness than with the fact that the truck suits a city defined by its thoroughfares. The taco truck honors the city.

I moved to Los Angeles with my partner in the late spring of 2012. She had taken a new job, the kind that seems promising enough to move a person from the cooler (and for us happier) climatic conditions of Northern California to what struck me not as beautiful but rather interrogating sunshine. Each ray of light seemed to shout, "Why aren't you satisfied by your choices?" Unemployed, missing my bicycle rides through the Oakland hills, not to mention my security blanket made of fog, and knowing few people in our new city, I sat at our dining room table and tried to turn my three-year-old doctoral dissertation into a book. I noticed the restaurants, taco trucks, and produce markets (I have good instincts in this area of life, at least) and made the occasional foray, but I stubbornly refused to let their obvious quality change my opinion of our new home. Every once in a while I would pause in my work to hate Los Angeles in unhelpfully vocal ways.

I am not given to epiphanies, so I remember very clearly the day when my loathing for Los Angeles turned to love. I was in the middle of a long bus ride. It was my weekly routine to travel that way down Sunset, from our apartment in Echo Park down to the UCLA library. I was alternating (as is my distractible wont) between two different kinds of reading material, both of which I had picked up in an effort to get to know the city better: several of Gold's reviews, current to 2012, and Reyner Banham's classic work of urbanism from 1971, *Los Angeles: The Architecture of Four Ecologies,* the fruit of the years the Englishman spent visiting and studying Los Angeles. Although they were of different vintages, you might say the readings paired well. Gold's restaurants began to fit into Banham's map of the city as locations you could reach if you were just willing to see the highways as connections rather than barriers. The bus ride was not too jolt-filled. We had passed from the cold-molasses-like crawl that characterizes Sunset during rush hours to a somewhat smoother flow, as if the molasses had been brought up to room temperature. I had time to think clearly about what Gold's reviews and Banham's book share, namely a love for Los Angeles as a place, maintained in full knowledge of the city's flaws and shortcomings. They appreciate ramen and the Romanesque, respectively, as these elements crop up in places that seem entirely accidental or willful, apart from any considerations of planning.

From that point on I delighted in a minor form of Gold emulation. Not having a newspaper's budget to back my eating habits, I mostly ate tacos, ramen, and pho, avoiding $40-plus entrees and dishes of pork shoulder designed to feed six and priced accordingly. I found out-of-the-way markets and farm stands to support and inform my cooking. In my mid-thirties I followed a track Gold had laid in his twenties, learning to eat in Los Angeles by following Pico (and other streets) and eating every interesting thing I could reasonably afford. I continued to hate the traffic (and the heat), but as millions know in their guts, there is no incompatibility between traffic-hatred and love for Los Angeles.

At first blush, one thing was obvious: Gold's work recalls Calvin Trillin's *New Yorker* essays of the late sixties and seventies, in which Trillin described what he called "research" and what Trillin's wife, Alice, called "being a food crazy." I found this association comforting, having first read Trillin's essays as a high school student, finding them in collected volumes on my food-loving parents' shelves and coffee tables. Trillin was ultimately after stories of political or human interest, but he lavished attention on his own appetite for comic purpose, wandering New York and beyond in search of sausage rolls, steamed fish, maybe a pretzel. He devoted an essay to his fantasy of serving as a diplomatic tour guide to Chairman Mao, making sure that the chairman missed no important New York delicacy—all in the name of international relations, of course. Trillin's essays never betray the reader's pleasure by wasting time on, say, defining the Platonic form of a pastrami on rye or offering the correct definition of *béchamel*. Only later would I learn that Gold had read Trillin with devotion. If we were to trace out a family tree of North American food writers, one that would include James Beard, Helen Brown, M.F.K. Fisher, Craig Claiborne, Ruth Reichl, and so on, Gold would be Trillin's direct descendent, a generation younger but still animated by Trillin's revolt against the high-low culinary distinctions according to which French cooking had been enshrined for critics and the simple pleasures of seeking treats while wandering one's city never got their due. Gold loved the rebelliousness of punk music, and it's important to note that modern food writing contained a rebellious spirit of its own. Gold drew water from both wells.

Gold made his most famous statements about taco trucks relatively late in his career, which I feel should have been his midcareer; one of the features of a mortal creative life is that we never know whether or not our current style is in fact our "late style." Earlier, Gold specialized in discovering restaurants that the critics of an earlier generation might have abjured because of a prejudice against vernacular food, which rendered regional Mexican, Korean, and Chinese cuisines as simply ineligible for criticism per se. There is no single quintessential Gold food form, because his tastes were as broad as his knowledge was deep, but many fans know him as a connoisseur of the weird, who refused to turn up his nose at tripe, whose question about hagfish was not "How do I avoid eating this awful-looking creature whose stress response is to turn water to slime?" but rather "Does it taste good?"

If Gold was like Trillin insofar as he was on the side of the eaters, he was very unlike him in that he was also, and perhaps more unwaveringly, on the side of the cooks. The outpouring of grief from Los Angeles chefs after July 21 testifies to this. I do not know for sure, but I suspect Gold's affection for chefs was tied to his own identification with artists, as a writer. Addressing a 2013 UCLA graduating class, Gold told his audience that he came to them as an emissary from "the world of failure," in which artists (and critics) usually live. He went on: while he was now a "semi-successful writer, a chronicler of Los Angeles," he still thought of himself as his UCLA undergraduate persona, a recently failed cellist. This might have seemed like false modesty. Gold's youthful audience might have seen him as an avatar of literary success, bearing his 2007 Pulitzer, the first and still only such prize awarded for food criticism. But this address also hints at how Gold understood his own work. His creative process took time, like the work of any artist. He was famously late for dinner and his reviews infamously late to editors, but his sidetracks through books and films and other forms of living led to inspired observations. He was lucky that a combination of professional success and the patience of editors and loved ones gave him time to think and to write as he would, something few writers receive. But I think that we, his readers, were luckier still that Jonathan Gold took his time.

Gold was born in 1960, when, according to Mike Davis, Los Angeles was "the most WASPish of big cities." If that characterization was true in demographic or cultural terms, everything had changed by the time of Gold's maturity, and Gold would become a voice of that change, himself benefiting by it both gastronomically and professionally. Gold's tastes in music, art, and food were not always popular, and his interest in the cello and in classical music could be called downright anachronistic. And yet his career was defined by timeliness, by being on the scene for punk, gangsta rap, and grunge, by drawing connections between Los Angeles's struggles with diversity before, during, and after the L.A. riots, and by chronicling restaurants that would spring up and die off as waves of immigrant chefs tried to find their footing. Gold was born just five years before the Immigration and Naturalization Act of 1965, one of the most consequential legal turns for restaurant culture in the late-twentieth-century United States. The act eliminated a quota system that had favored western Europeans and enabled more skilled workers from other countries not only to immigrate but to bring their families too, creating favorable conditions for businesses like restaurants. The Chinese American population alone doubled within about ten years of the act's passage, bringing chefs from Hong Kong and Taiwan, along with their regional cuisines. Change came from other sources too. As Gold observed in his essay "The Year I Ate Pico Boulevard," when he was a young writer just out of college, many of the restaurants he encountered up and down Pico Boulevard were the happy result of an influx of immigrants who had fled political instability and war in Latin America. By the time Gold got his Pulitzer, it would have sounded ridiculous to call L.A. "WASPish."

Gold began his career as a music critic, writing first on the classical music that he had himself studied as a musician and then on rock and hip-hop, most notably covering the beginnings of gangsta rap and the recording sessions of Snoop Dogg and Dr. Dre. This was more than flexibility on Gold's part; it was a delight in exploding old ideas about the differences between high and popular genres of music. Gold did exactly the same thing in his writing on food, something I only started to understand when one of his reviews, just for a second, broke the skin of my culinary reverie, annoying me. This was his September 7, 2013, review of Echo Park restaurant Allumette (since closed), where the kitchen of chef Miles Thompson turned out dishes so carefully composed that they appeared to have been plated with tweezers, while bartender Serena Herrick transformed farmers' market produce into beautiful cocktails with punning names like Strega Genesis. Gold's mind seemed to drift from these delights to Ariza, the taco truck parked across the street, or to Chengdu Taste in Alhambra. "What about those potatoes!" I cried internally, thinking of the way a piping-hot plate of fried potatoes made *katsuobushi* shavings dance as they curled from the heat. "Focus, Gold!" I thought. I was only starting to realize that Gold was looking for joy, and he would go where it took him. He insisted on this freedom.

What makes restaurant criticism difficult is not the basic task of describing a meal or that of assessing the strengths and weaknesses of a restaurant, although these have their complexities and there is a vast difference between the way professionals and amateurs do them. What's hard is that mere description is boring. Much like coverage of a ball game, a description of a meal can run afoul of recursion: the report of a spectacular run to catch a ball exhausts its meaning (and some readers' patience) in the adjective *spectacular*, and in similar fashion food writers must say more about a dish than simply listing the qualities of its ingredients if they want us to keep reading week after week. This problem in food writing may explain what divides great criticism from a casual online customer review, and also why so much of the best food writing uses food as a jumping-off point from which to discuss family, heritage, personal identity, the complexity and fragility of our collective social life, and so forth. To read an essay by M.F.K. Fisher is to know that a segment of an orange both is and isn't the actual topic at hand, just as to read A. Bartlett Giamatti on baseball is to see the American immigrant experience traveling with the curve ball. Gold beat the problem of recursion by a different means. He simply learned so much about each dish, cuisine, or chefly community that there was always more for him to say.

I still want to live in Gold's reviews, which he wrote in a distinctive second-person style. For example, "You might follow a salad of ripe heirloom tomatoes and soft-cooked egg with a sliver of crisp-skinned *branzino* on a bed of chewy tapioca scented with shellfish stock," as Gold wrote in his review of Allumette. "You will wonder whether there is a point to an old-fashioned made with lamb-fat-washed bourbon or a pisco sour with pink peppercorns, and you will decide that there might be," as he wrote in one of his last reviews filed, of a new Middle Eastern restaurant called Bavel. Gold's *you* never seemed like an invitation for one, prompting me to choose my own culinary adventure, but a group invite, telling us that Los Angeles could be large in the sense of opportunities and small in the sense of neighborliness and access, of commensality. *Commensality* is one good word for what critics of L.A. think is impossible here. The word literally means "the quality of eating at the same table." It implies community.

Commensality is a special challenge in a city whose first language is movement; Banham said that he had learned how to drive in Los Angeles in order to "read Los Angeles in the original." Director Laura Gabbert, in her 2015 documentary film about Gold's life and work, *City of Gold,* established a clear parallel between Banham and the food critic: "I'm an L.A. guy, I drive. I am my truck, my truck is me," Gold says to the camera. The predominant urban form of a Jonathan Gold review is the mini-mall, a Chinese (or Filipino, or Persian, or Japanese) restaurant tucked in the corner, the car potentially driving up to the front door, depending on the neighborhood and how quickly Gold's readers have responded to his latest review. But cars are unavoidably separate and separating forms of travel. The highways often make L.A. into a city of origins and destinations without opportunities to connect with others en route. Gold seems to have understood full well that commensality in Los Angeles was both a goal and a challenge. In an elegiac piece written in response to the L.A. riots when he was a young critic, Gold celebrated neighborliness, meditating on the garlic pounded by his Korean landlords, whose son was tragically shot during the rioting. You could read so much of his later restaurant criticism as an extension of this essay's closing line, "I wish that they would invite me over to dinner."

"I want to make Los Angeles smaller," Gold once said. As his career progressed, Gold deepened everyone's knowledge of their neighbors, demonstrating that much of the most exciting cooking in Los Angeles took place within local enclaves where chefs cooked for audiences of their peers. But this is something less than ensuring that Angelenos eat together across the lines of geography, ethnicity, and culture. The irony of *City of Gold* is that it is a portrait not of an L.A. bound together by food across lines of identity but of distinct "food nations" that intermingle while remaining for the most part separate, and whose separateness is actually a great source of strength, in terms of the cooking itself. To produce an array of culinary microclimates—one way to think about L.A. and food—takes the relative isolation of cultures just as much as intermixing. Diversity doesn't necessarily mean togetherness. Gold's dream of commensality begins to seem like an ideal he held out for himself and for his readers rather than an observation of what was actually happening at street level in Los Angeles.

Just as Gold was the gastronomic beneficiary of post-1965 immigration to the United States, he also benefited from the fact that he came to prominence just as the restaurant took on a new centrality as a form of cultural expression in American life. People started to skip the movie and go directly to dinner, the restaurant experience supplying much of the sense of play and personality that we previously expected from light passing through celluloid. As restaurants rose, so did the trend to level value distinctions between different types of cuisines. Thus we enjoy the high-end taco, or a new restaurant in Koreatown that sells slightly polished versions of the stews already available down the block.

When Anthony Bourdain died, Gold wrote, "I cannot imagine how the food world is going to cope with this gaping Bourdain-shaped hole—not at its center but on its fringes, looking exactly like a man throwing rocks at the status quo." What was true of Bourdain's career was also true of Gold's, however: if you begin your writerly life "throwing rocks at the status quo" and find some success, don't be surprised if a new status quo that centers on rock-throwing emerges, with you canonized as a primal stone-tosser. Over the arc of Gold's career, "ethnic restaurants" and street food came to enjoy a visibility in Los Angeles dining they had not previously enjoyed, even as that term, *street food,* started to raise questions. What street? Do you mean carts? *Elote?* Tacos? What about the street is supposed to be delicious? Is this simply about middle-class (or upper-, or wealthy) diners longing for some magical form of culinary transformation imparted by that often-empty black box of a word *authenticity?* Unclear. When Gold's outline decorates the wall next to a booth at a very hip, very popular, post-truck L.A. taqueria, we are riding the line between deep appreciation and canonization. In honoring the critic and his legacy, we must be careful not to turn him into an image, part of a dearly loved status quo that must inevitably move on.

When Gold died, I felt a depth of sadness that I worried I had not earned. I had not known the man personally, after all. We had exchanged a few witticisms on Twitter, and Gold wrote me out of the blue once, to tell me he had read my work. I was floored. I had no reason to think my writing would have crossed Gold's desk. He was kind, and I was awkward, because Gold's work had inspired me, and I risked embarrassing him by telling him what his reviews meant to me: "Your work has made my life better." We then corresponded in the months right before he died. His range of reference was wonderful. We joked about the writing of Karl Ove Knausgaard and the sculptures of Joseph Beuys, and right after the passing of the philosopher Stanley Cavell we talked about the fact that Gold's daughter had just taken a seminar on Cavell; Gold seemed like a proud father and husband, and this is how I think of him now, open to learning from a world he had helped to create in Los Angeles but that he never pretended to control.

I left L.A. four years ago, but I continued to read Gold's restaurant reviews every week, it making no difference that I couldn't use them as dining advice. I will continue to reread them now. That taqueria in the Arts District I recently visited on a return trip to L.A. that felt a bit like a post-Gold pilgrimage? It belongs to Chef Wes Avila, and it is called Guerrilla Tacos, the same name as Avila's former truck, one of Gold's favorite places to eat tacos toward the end of his life, and one of my old favorites too. A framed photograph of Gold stands on a shelf above Avila's current kitchen, but when I think of Guerrilla and Gold, it is of a guy (I don't know his name) who used to turn up at the truck in the early evening with a bottle of wine and a few extra glasses. I wish I were there right now to toast the man who helped me love Los Angeles.

Contributors' Notes
Other Notable Food Writing
of 2018

Contributors' Notes

Sam Anderson is a staff writer for the *New York Times Magazine*. His writing has won a National Magazine Award as well as the National Book Critics Circle's Nona Balakian Citation for Excellence in Reviewing. He is the author of the book *Boom Town: The Fantastical Saga of Oklahoma City, Its Chaotic Founding, Its Apocalyptic Weather, Its Purloined Basketball Team, and the Dream of Becoming a World-Class Metropolis*.

Mark Arax is an author and journalist whose writings on California and the West have received numerous awards for literary nonfiction. His 2018 story "A Kingdom from Dust" was a finalist for the National Magazine Award in feature writing. His work has appeared in the *New York Times,* the *California Sunday Magazine,* and the *Los Angeles Times,* where he was a special projects writer. His previous books include a memoir of his father's murder, a collection of essays about the West, and the best-selling *The King of California,* which won a California Book Award and the William Saroyan Prize from Stanford University and was named a top book of 2004 by the *Los Angeles Times* and the *San Francisco Chronicle*. His newest book is titled *The Dreamt Land: Chasing Water and Dust Across California*. He lives in Fresno, California.

A Nigerian-born author, **Yemisi Aribisala** is best known for her thematic use of food to explore Nigerian stories. Her first book, *Longthroat Memoirs: Soups, Sex, and Nigerian Taste Buds,* uses Nigerian food as a literary substrate to think about Nigeria's culture and society. *Longthroat Memoirs* won a Gourmand World Cookbook Award, was shortlisted for the 2018 Art of

Eating Prize, and won the 2016 John Avery Prize at the André Simon Book Awards. Her second book, *Wait! I'm Bringing a Bird Out of My Pocket,* will be published by Chimurenga in Cape Town. She lives in London with her children. Her most recent articles on food and Nigeria can be read in *Popula: The Alt-Global Magazine of News and Culture.*

Burkhard Bilger has been a staff writer at *The New Yorker* since 2000. His book *Noodling for Flatheads* was a finalist for the PEN/Martha Albrand Award, and he is at work on a book about his grandfather's experiences during the Second World War. Bilger is a Branford Fellow at Yale University.

Mark Binelli is a contributing writer at the *New York Times Magazine* and the author of three books, including *Detroit City Is the Place to Be.*

Tim Carman is a James Beard Award–winning food writer and columnist for the *Washington Post.* His work has appeared in numerous editions of the *Best American Food Writing* collection as well as the sixth edition of *Cornbread Nation.* He has also written for *Imbibe Magazine, American Scholar, Food Network Magazine,* and other publications. Before joining the *Post* in 2010, he served as food editor and columnist for *Washington City Paper.* He lives in Hyattsville, MD, with his wife, the writer M. Carrie Allan, and their two naughty dogs, Lucinda and Hans Floofer.

Melissa Chadburn manages economic justice fellows at Community Change and teaches journalism at Loyola Marymount University. She will be attending USC's PhD in creative writing program in the fall of 2019. Her work has appeared in the *Los Angeles Times,* the *New York Times Book Review,* the *New York Review of Books, Longreads,* and dozens of other places. Her debut novel, *A Tiny Upward Shove,* is forthcoming.

Charlee Dyroff is a writer from Boulder, Colorado. Her work has appeared in *Guernica, Slate, Eater, Pacific Standard,* and elsewhere. She is currently pursuing an MFA in nonfiction at Columbia, where she also teaches undergraduate writing.

Priya Fielding-Singh is a sociologist and postdoctoral research fellow in cardiovascular disease prevention at the Stanford Prevention Research Center. Her research advances social-scientific theories of health and inequality while drawing methodological and empirical insights from public health. Her focus is on identifying mechanisms underlying the reproduction of health disparities across class, race, and gender. She holds a PhD in sociology from Stanford University, an MA in anthropology from the University of Bremen, Germany, and a BS in education and social policy from Northwestern University.

Ian Frazier is a staff writer at *The New Yorker* and the author of eleven books, including *Great Plains, Family, On the Rez, Travels in Siberia,* and *Hogs Wild.*

Hannah Goldfield is the food critic for *The New Yorker,* where she writes the weekly *Tables for Two* restaurant column in the Goings On About Town section of the magazine as well as food-related essays and reported stories for newyorker.com. Previously she was a fact-checker at *The New Yorker* and an editor at *T: The New York Times Style Magazine.* Her writing has appeared in the *Times, New York* magazine, and the *Wall Street Journal,* among other publications.

Living and working in France, **Kate Hill** is an American cook, teacher, mentor, and author with more than forty years' experience in the food world. She founded the Kitchen at Camont as a cooking school and retreat in 1991 after moving to the fruitful Gascon region of southwestern France on her barge. In 2016 and 2017 she traveled to Mexico to visit and work with Samantha Greiff, who, with indigenous Mayan Tsotsil women living in Puebla, created a women's literacy program, Yo'on Ixim, which means "Heart of Corn." Their first meeting with the group of twenty-seven families, working and learning together in both the city and their native mountain village in Chiapas, resulted in a small cookbook titled *The Cloud Forest Kitchen: A Heart of Corn.* Kate was honored to help the women provide their own recipes and share their lives as economic exiles from the poverty of the cloud forests of Chiapas. Her extreme love of tortillas and respect for the Yo'on Ixim families helped her understand and translate the basic recipes from the "women of the corn." Back at home she tells her own food stories from Gascony on her website, kitchen-at-camont.com.

Soleil Ho is the restaurant critic at the *San Francisco Chronicle.* Previously she worked in restaurant kitchens in New Orleans, Minneapolis, Portland, and Puerto Vallarta while writing for publications such as *TASTE, GQ, The New Yorker, Food & Wine,* and many more. In 2016 she and a friend started a podcast called *Racist Sandwich,* a show that poked at all the ways food could intersect with race, class, and gender.

Priya Krishna is a food writer who contributes to *Bon Appétit,* the *New York Times, The New Yorker,* and others. She previously worked at the food magazine *Lucky Peach.* Priya is the author of *Indian-ish,* a cookbook about the hybridized Indian food she grew up eating. Find her on Instagram and Twitter @pkgourmet.

Stephanie M. Lee is a science reporter at *BuzzFeed News* and lives in San Francisco. Visit her at stephaniemlee.com.

Shane Mitchell is the author of *Far Afield* and a longtime contributing editor at *Saveur Magazine.* Her essays for *The Bitter Southerner* and *Roads & Kingdoms* have received James Beard Foundation Awards, including the M.F.K. Fisher Distinguished Writing Award. Her work is included in *The Best American Food Writing 2018.* When not on the road for research, Shane resides in upstate New York with her husband and their dog, Dharma.

Marilyn Noble is an award-winning freelance food and agriculture journalist and cookbook author whose work has appeared in dozens of print and digital publications, including *The New Food Economy* and several *Edible* magazines. She's a member of the Association of Food Journalists and serves as the Arizona governor for Slow Food USA. You may follow her on twitter @mariwrites or reach her via her website, marilynnoble.com.

Tejal Rao is the California restaurant critic at the *New York Times* and a columnist for the *New York Times Magazine.* She lives in Los Angeles.

Helen Rosner is *The New Yorker*'s food correspondent. Her work as a writer and editor has won numerous James Beard and National Magazine Awards. Born and raised in Chicago, she now lives in Brooklyn, New York.

Kathryn Schulz is a staff writer for *The New Yorker* and the 2016 winner of the Pulitzer Prize for Feature Writing.

Mayukh Sen is an award-winning writer based in New York. His writing has appeared in the *New York Times,* newyorker.com, and the *Washington Post.* He won a James Beard Award in 2018 for his profile of missing soul-food restaurateur Princess Pamela, published in *Food52,* where he used to work as a staff writer. He is currently working on his first book of narrative nonfiction, on the immigrant women who have shaped food culture in America.

Khushbu Shah is a writer and editor who lives in Brooklyn and really hopes you will never spell her name incorrectly.

Ruby Tandoh is a food writer currently living in London. She is the author of two cookbooks and of *Eat Up: Food, Appetite and Eating What You Want.*

Michael W. Twitty is a culinary historian, living history interpreter, Judaic studies teacher, and food writer from the Washington DC area. He blogs at afroculinaria.com. He has appeared on *Bizarre Foods America* with Andrew Zimmern and *The African Americans: Many Rivers to Cross* with Dr. Henry Louis Gates, and has lectured to more than four hundred groups. He has served as a judge for the James Beard Awards, is a fellow with the Southern Foodways Alliance and TED, and was the first Revolutionary in Residence at the Colonial Williamsburg Foundation. Twitty's *The Cooking Gene* (2017) traces his ancestry through from Africa to America and from slavery to freedom and was a finalist for the Kirkus Prize and The Art of Eating Prize. *The Cooking Gene* won the 2018 James Beard Award for Best Food Writing as well as Book of the Year.

Benjamin Aldes Wurgaft is a writer and historian. His most recent book, *Meat Planet: Artificial Flesh and the Future of Food,* appears in fall 2019. His essays on food and other topics appear regularly in publications from *Gastronomica* to the *Los Angeles Review of Books* to the *Hedgehog Review.*

Other Notable Food Writing of 2018

DAYNA EVANS
>   Cooking Temperature: It's a Mercurial Thing. *Taste,* March 19.
>   Do You Even Bake, Bro? *Eater,* November 19.

J. J. GOODE
>   Dear Chefs, Will Eating This Kill Me? *Taste,* March 13.
>   Permission to Cook Normal Food. *Taste,* September 13.

JEFF GORDINIER
>   Land of the Stars. *Esquire,* April 24.
>   No One Lived Like Anthony Bourdain. But All Hope to Write Like Him.
>   *Esquire,* June 8.

JENN HALL
>   Writing the Clam's Next Chapter. *Edible Jersey,* September 5.

JAMES HAMBLIN
>   The Jordan Peterson All-Meat Diet. *The Atlantic,* August 28.

SHIRLEY HUEY
>   What "American Night" Meant to My Chinese American Family. *Catapult,*
>   March 29.

JAMIE LAUREN KEILES
>   This Oyster Farmer Ditched His Desk Job for Life on the Water. *Saveur,* July
>   11.

SAM KIM
>   NYC's K-Town Isn't What It Used to Be. *Eater,* July 31.

PRIYA KRISHNA
>   This Slice Shop Is Low-Key Milling Its Own Grains. *Bon Appétit,* May 22.
>   WhatsApp Is Changing the Way India Talks About Food. *New York Times,*
>   November 23.
>   H-E-B Forever. *Eater,* December 11.

EMMA LAPERRUQUE
>   I'm a Food Writer—with Some Food Issues. *Food52,* May 3.

FRANCES LEECH
>   Forgetting the Madeleine. *Longreads,* May 3.

JESSI LEWIS
>   False Morels. *Oxford American,* March 13.

DREW MAGARY
>   The Last Curious Man. *GQ,* December 4.

POOJA MAKHIJANI
>   The Path to an American Dream, Paved in Vienna Fingers. *New York Times,*
>   November 30.

REBECCA FLINT MARX
>   The Indomitable Jessica Largey. *Eater,* November 29.

BRYAN WASHINGTON
   The Year in Broth. *Hazlitt,* December 10.
WYATT WILLIAMS
   With Cultivation, Have Oysters Become Too Perfect? *T Magazine,* September
   20.

MICHELLE ZAUNER
   Crying in H Mart. *The New Yorker,* August 20.
JENNY G. ZHANG
   How the East Village Turned into NYC's Hippest Chinese Dining Destination.
   Eater, June 28.

   American Pie. *Eater,* August 27.

THE BEST AMERICAN SERIES®

FIRST, BEST, AND BEST-SELLING

The Best American Comics

The Best American Essays

The Best American Food Writing

The Best American Mystery Stories

The Best American Nonrequired Reading

The Best American Science and Nature Writing

The Best American Science Fiction and Fantasy

The Best American Short Stories

The Best American Sports Writing

The Best American Travel Writing

Available in print and e-book wherever books are sold.
Visit our website: hmhbooks.com/series/best-american